TRANSPORT POLICY:
LEARNING LESSONS FROM HISTORY

Transport Policy:
Learning Lessons from History

Edited by

COLIN DIVALL
University of York, UK

JULIAN HINE
University of Ulster, UK

COLIN POOLEY
Lancaster University, UK

Routledge
Taylor & Francis Group

LONDON AND NEW YORK

First published 2016 by Ashgate Publishing

2 Park Square, Milton Park, Abingdon, Oxfordshire OX14 4RN
52 Vanderbilt Avenue, New York, NY 10017

Routledge is an imprint of the Taylor & Francis Group, an informa business

First issued in paperback 2020

British Library Cataloguing in Publication Data
A catalogue record for this book is available from the British Library.

The Library of Congress has cataloged the printed edition as follows:
Names: Divall, Colin, author. | Hine, Julian, author. | Pooley, Colin G., author.
Title: Transport policy : learning lessons from history / by Colin Divall, Julian Hine and Colin Pooley.
Description: Burlington, VT : Ashgate Publishing Company, 2016. | Series: Transport and society | Includes bibliographical references and index.
Identifiers: LCCN 2015025163| ISBN 9781472460059 |
Subjects: LCSH: Transportation and state--History.
Classification: LCC HE151 .D59 2016 | DDC 388--dc23
LC record available at http://lccn.loc.gov/2015025163

ISBN 978-1-4724-6005-9 (hbk)
ISBN 978-0-367-66853-2 (pbk)

Contents

List of Tables   vii
Notes on Contributors   ix
Preface   xiii
List of Abbreviations   xv

Introduction: Why Does the Past Matter?   1
Colin Divall, Julian Hine and Colin Pooley

Using the Usable Past: Reflections and Practices in
the Netherlands   15
Bert Toussaint

PART I   MOBILITY AND SOCIAL JUSTICE

Structures of Disadvantage and Acts of Resistance: Remembering,
Skilling, History and Gender   31
Frances Hodgson

Balancing Social Justice and Environmental Justice: Mobility
Inequalities in Britain Since circa 1900   47
Colin Pooley

Mobility in Rural Ireland: A Study of Older People and the
Challenges They Face   65
Aoife Ahern and Julian Hine

Have Consumer Movements Enhanced Transport Justice?
Passenger Representation on Britain's Railways before 1947   77
Hiroki Shin

High Speed 2 Where? A Historical Perspective on the
'Strategic Case' for HS2   97
Colin Divall

'Interminably Delaying What Needs to Be Done': Drink-Driving
Control in Britain 1970–1985   115
Bill Luckin

PART II   MARKETING IM/MOBILITY

8   Marketing and Branding for Modal Shift in Urban Transport   1?
       Nicola Forsdike

9   Gaining Modal Share in Exogenously Driven Markets: Lessons
       from Urban Transport   1?
       Martin Higginson

10   Plane Crazy Brits: Aeromobility, Climate Change and the
       British Traveller   1?
       Peter Lyth

       Epilogue   1?
       Colin Divall, Julian Hine and Colin Pooley

*Appendix: Key Historical Resources for UK Transport Planners and
       Policy Makers*   1?
Index   1?

List of Tables

4.1   Composition of the focus groups   70

9.1   The development of urban transport, morphology and mobility   156
9.2   Phases of marketing after Tedlow and Jones (1993)   161

Notes on Contributors

Aoife Ahern completed a PhD in transportation at University College London in 2001, following a degree in civil engineering from Trinity College Dublin. She is currently a senior lecturer at the School of Civil, Structural and Environmental Engineering at University College Dublin and is a member of the Irish Transport Research Network Committee, of which she was chair from 2010 to 2013. She has also been the honorary secretary of the Institute of Highway and Transportation Engineers (Irish branch) and has participated in a number of European and Irish projects, including FP7 project Optimism, looking at national travel statistics and the role of ICT in encouraging more sustainable travel. Current research interests include the impact of the recent housing boom on transport infrastructure and travel needs, the interactions between residential self-selection and commuter travel, and equity issues relating to transport.

Colin Divall is a professor of railway studies at the University of York, UK, and was head of the Institute of Railway Studies and Transport History for 19 years from its founding jointly with the National Railway Museum in 1995. His recent projects have looked at the marketing of passenger travel by Britain's railways since the late nineteenth century, the shift from rail- to road-based distribution in the twentieth century, and the politics of railway closures in the Beeching era. He has published over 40 journal articles and book chapters and five books, the most recent being the edited collections: *Cultural Histories of Sociabilities, Spaces and Mobilities* (Pickering and Chatto 2015) and, with R. Roth, *From Rail to Road and Back Again? A Century of Transport Competition and Interdependency* (Ashgate 2015). As a member of the History and Policy network in 2014–15 he co-facilitated workshops on Framing Infrastructure Policy: The Lessons of British Railways 1955–75 for the UK's Civil Service Learning, Department for Transport and HM Treasury.

Nicola Forsdike is a Chartered Marketer and has some 28 years' experience in practising marketing, particularly within the area of transport. Joining British Rail in 1988 she worked in a variety of posts covering product management, the development of advertising campaigns, the delivery of market research and marketing planning. She was a member of the team that implemented the Regional Railways identity and led the development of the Northern Spirit brand. Since 2000 she has worked in consultancy, leading the development of business and marketing strategies for transport and infrastructure companies across three continents.

Martin Higginson, proprietor of Martin Higginson Transport Research & Consultancy, is a public transport economist whose career spans operational management, policy advice and academia. He was formerly London Transport senior lecturer at Birkbeck College, University of London; visiting fellow at the Transport Operations Research Group at Newcastle University; and an associate of the Institute of Railway Studies and Transport History, York. He is a member of the Transport Economics Commission of the International Public Transport Association (UITP). His historical publications include: as editor, *Tramway London: Background to the Abandonment of London's Trams, 1931–1952* (Birkbeck College with London Transport Museum 1993); *The Evolution of Municipal Trading* (Roads & Road Transport History Association 2006 Conference Papers, RRTHA, 2007); and, edited with C. Mulley, *Companion to Road Passenger Transport History* (RRTHA 2013).

Julian Hine is a professor of transport at the Built Environment Research Institute and School of the Built Environment at the University of Ulster. His research focuses on transport planning and policy, mobility and transport disadvantage, travel behaviour, and pedestrian behaviour and safety. He has published over 40 journal articles and book chapters and three books: with F. Mitchell, *Transport Disadvantage and Social Exclusion: Exclusionary Mechanisms in Transport in Urban Scotland* (Ashgate 2003); with F. Raje, M. Grieco and J. Preston, *Transport, Demand Management and Social Inclusion* (Ashgate 2004); and, edited with J. Preston, *Integrated Futures and Transport Choices: UK Transport Policy Beyond the 1998 White Paper* (Ashgate 2003).

Frances Hodgson currently provides leadership to research in mobilities at the Institute for Transport Studies, University of Leeds, UK. A sociologist by training, she has an MSc in transport planning and engineering and is a senior research fellow. She has 20 years of experience in researching travel and has specialist knowledge in the area of walking, skills, social networks, new information technology and social research methods. Her current research work focuses on Web 2.0 applications and transport exploring its potential for the travel of older people and its interaction with incentives for different communities and transport systems. Her work has been funded by a variety of national and international funders.

Bill Luckin is a research professor in urban history at the University of Bolton and associate at the Centre for the History of Science, Technology and Medicine at the University of Manchester. He is the author and editor of several books and numerous articles on the histories of disease, technology and environment. In recent years his research has focused on accidents, and particularly road traffic accidents, in twentieth-century Britain and Europe before and during the dramatic movement to mass motorisation. Bill Luckin's selected essays, written over the last 40 years, *Death and Survival in Urban Britain: Disease, Pollution and Environment, 1850–1950*, was published by I.B. Tauris in 2014.

eter Lyth is a transport and tourism historian, and was a teaching fellow at ottingham University Business School, UK, until 2014. He is a past editor f the *Journal of Transport History* and has research interests across a range of ubjects from the history of air transport to the growth of heritage tourism. He is ne author of: with Hans-Liudger Dienel, *Flying the Flag: European Commercial ir Transport since 1945* (Macmillan 1998); with Philip Bagwell, *Transport i Britain, 1750–2000: From Canal Lock to Gridlock* (Continuum 2002); with ichard Coopey, *Business in Britain in the Twentieth Century* (Oxford University ress 2009); 'Fast Forward: Speed, Streamlining and National Pride, 1912–1952' i Ralf Roth and Karl Schlögel (eds), *Neue Wege in ein neues Europa: Geschichte nd Verkehr im 20. Jahrhundert* (Campus Verlag 2009); and 'Carry On Up the ile: The Tourist Gaze and the British Experience of Egypt, 1818–1932' in lartin Farr and Xavier Guegan (eds), *The British Abroad: Travellers and Tourists* 'algrave 2013).

olin Pooley is emeritus professor of social and historical geography at the ancaster Environment Centre, Lancaster University, UK. His research focuses n the social geography of Britain and continental Europe since circa 1800, with ecent projects focused on residential migration, travel to work and other aspects f everyday mobility, including walking and cycling. He has published over 100 efereed journal articles and book chapters and 13 books, including: *Migration nd Mobility in Britain since the Eighteenth Century* (UCL Press 1998); *A Mobile entury? Changes in Everyday Mobility in Britain in the Twentieth Century* Ashgate 2005); and *Promoting Walking and Cycling: New Perspectives on ustainable Travel* (Policy Press 2013).

liroki Shin is a researcher in history at Birkbeck College, University of London. e was previously a postdoctoral research associate in the AHRC-funded project he Commercial Cultures of Britain's Railways, 1872–1977, led by Professor Colin ivall and conducted at the Institute of Railway Studies and Transport History, niversity of York / National Railway Museum. His publications include: with olin Divall, 'Cultures of Speed and Conservative Modernity: Representation of peed in Britain's Railway Marketing' in B. Fraser and S. Spalding (eds), *Trains, ulture, and Mobility* (Lexington Books 2011), pp. 3–26; 'The Art of Advertising ailways: Organisation and Coordination in Britain's Railway Marketing, 860–1910', *Business History* 56(2), 2014, pp. 187–213; and, with Frank rentmann and Rebecca Wright, *From World Power Conference to World Energy ouncil: 90 Years of Energy Cooperation, 1923–2013* (World Energy Council 2013).

ert Toussaint is senior historian at the Rijkswaterstaat agency, Dutch Ministry f Infrastructure and the Environment. His current research focuses on Dutch and nternational water management history, technocracy in interwar Netherlands, the istory of the Rijkswaterstaat and the concept of learning history. He has published bout 45 book chapters and articles and three books, including: edited with Louis van Gasteren et al., *In een Japanse stroomversnelling* (Walburg Pers 2000 'History as a Powerful Learning Instrument in the Search for Innovation' M. Veenswijk (ed.), *Organizing Innovation. New Approaches to Cultural Chang and Intervention in Public Sector Organisations* (IOS Press 2005); and, edited wi H.S. Danner et al., *Polder Pioneers: The Influence of Dutch Engineers on Wat Management in Europe, 1600–2000* (Koninklijk Nederlands Aardrijkskund Genootschap 2005).

Preface

Like many edited collections this volume has been long – too long – in the making. Ironically, given our emphasis on the urgent need for transport policy to address climate change, its origins lie partly in a meeting in 2008 between two of us at a conference held far outside the UK, in Ottawa: that the conference theme was mobility and the environment only redoubles the irony. That meeting sparked a series of conversations between us all that culminated in an Arts and Humanities Research Council grant (AH/I001212/1) to fund the international research network Mobility Cultures: Making a Usable Past for Transport Policy. Three two-day workshops followed, at the National Railway Museum, York (November 2010), the University of Ulster, Jordanstown (May 2011), and Lancaster University (September 2011); a final workshop was held a year later in York thanks to additional funding from the Transport Research Institute at Edinburgh Napier University and the National Railway Museum. We are also pleased to acknowledge financial and other support from the Institute of Railway Studies and Transport History, York; the Department of History and the Centre for Evolution of Global Business and Institutions, both at the University of York; and the Centre for Mobilities Research (CeMoRe) at Lancaster University. For administrative and other practical assistance that ensured the smooth running of these workshops, we thank: Martyn Halman, Alex Medcalf, Hiroki Shin and Matt Thompson (York), Sadie Magee and Liz McKeown (Ulster) and Pennie Drinkall (Lancaster).

Although this collection contains only a small proportion of the papers presented at the workshops, they have all benefited from the lively discussions that often continued well beyond the confines of the formal timetable. Participants were drawn from an eclectic mix of backgrounds: as well as academics from transport studies, history, geography, politics and sociology, colleagues from print and broadcast media, local politics and (in either a personal or official capacity) several transport industries, consultancies, consumer bodies and authorities enlivened and enriched the conversations. In addition to the authors represented here we should therefore like to thank: Rachel Aldred, Jon Barry, Mark Beecroft, Mark Casson, Roy Edwards, Terry Gourvish, Ian Gray, Margaret Grieco, Michael Heller, Dave Horton, Juliet Jain, Katrina Jungnickel, Teresa da Silva Lopes, Daryl Martin, Aodhan O'Donnell, Philip O'Neill, Nicholas Oddy, Alex Medcalf, Chris Nash, Mike Parker, Gordon Pirie, Gina Porter, Tom Reid, George Revill, Griet Scheldeman, Barbara Schmucki, Bruce Seely, Jim Steer, Matt Thompson, Jonathan Tyler, Margaret Walsh, Alan Whitehouse, James Wickham and Christian Wolmar.

Colin Divall, Julian Hine and Colin Pooley, May 2015

List of Abbreviations

AA	Automobile Association
ANWB	Algemene Nederlandse Wielrijders Bond (National Dutch Touring Club)
BAAS	British Association for the Advancement of Science
BAC	blood alcohol concentration
BCR	benefit–cost ratio
BEA	British European Airways
BMJ	*British Medical Journal*
BoT	Board of Trade
BR	British Rail(ways)
BRB	British Railways Board
CBA	cost–benefit analysis
CBI	Confederation of British Industry
CIM	Chartered Institute of Marketing
CTC	Cyclists' Touring Club
CTCC	Central Transport Consultative Committee
DfT	Department for Transport
DoE	Department of the Environment
DoT	Department of Transport
FoE	Friends of the Earth
GDP	gross domestic product
GER	Great Eastern Railway
GHG	greenhouse gas
GWR	Great Western Railway
HMSO	Her Majesty's Stationery Office
HO	Home Office
HS1	High Speed 1
HS2	High Speed 2
HS3	High Speed 3
HSR	high-speed rail
ICAO	International Civil Aviation Organisation
IPCC	Intergovernmental Panel on Climate Change
LBSCR	London, Brighton and South Coast Railway
LCA	low-cost airline
LMS	London, Scottish and Midland Railway
LNER	London and North Eastern Railway
LSWR	London and South Western Railway

MCTramD	Manchester Corporation Tramways Department
MCTranspD	Manchester Corporation Transport Department
MoT	Ministry of Transport
MTP	mega transport project
NARP	National Association of Rail Passengers
NART	National Association of Railway Travellers
NER	North Eastern Railway
NIMBY	not in my backyard
NSE	Network SouthEast
ODRPA	Orpington and District Rail Passengers Association
ONS	Office for National Statistics
PA	Pedestrians' Association
PR	public relations
PTA/E	Passenger Transport Authority/Executive
QM	Quality Management
RCA	Railway Companies Association
RCH	Railway Clearing House
ROI	return on investment
RoSPA	Royal Society for the Prevention of Accidents
RRTHA	Roads and Road Transport History Association
SR	Southern Railway
TfL	Transport for London
TNA	The National Archives
TOC	train operating company
TUC	Trades Union Congress
TUCC	Transport Users' Consultative Committee
UITP	International Public Transport Association
UKCTA	United Kingdom Commercial Travellers Association
UNFCCC	United Nations Framework Convention in Climate Change
WYPTE	West Yorkshire Passenger Transport Executive

Introduction

Why Does the Past Matter?

Colin Divall, Julian Hine and Colin Pooley

In our everyday lives we are all constantly learning from past experiences. Although we may not consciously recognise the fact, many everyday actions that we take and behaviours that we exhibit are shaped by previous experiences. This is true for the most significant aspects of most people's lives, for instance in personal relationships or at work, but also for the apparently more mundane aspects such as the choice of route or transport mode used for a journey. If one choice proves problematic we are likely to make adjustments and choose, where possible, to adjust travel plans. Where no alternatives are available, we are likely to become frustrated at the lack of choice available and by our inability to turn those things we have learned from previous experiences into practice in our everyday lives. Given that at this level learning from the past is so ubiquitous it is perhaps surprising that an understanding of past processes and experiences do not more fully inform present-day policy making at either national or local levels. This is certainly the case for most transport policy (the focus of this volume), where, as in most other areas of policy making, decisions tend to be taken on the basis of short-term political or practical (usually financial) expediency. We are not arguing that history repeats itself, or that every contemporary transport dilemma has an historical counterpart, but we are suggesting that in many contexts of transport planning a better understanding of the context and consequences of past decisions and processes could lead to more effective policy decisions. This requires not only that those who make these decisions are aware of, and learn from, past events; but also that historians analyse and present the past in a way that is useful for the present. The chapters in this volume collectively explore and demonstrate these points across a wide range of transport modes and contexts.

There are a number of reasons why an understanding of the past is particularly relevant to the development of contemporary transport policy. First, the transport technologies that we use today have been remarkably persistent. All have been available for more than a century and despite massive technological refinements and improvements they have remained fundamentally the same. Thus a modern train or car would be instantly recognisable to a traveller from a century ago as essentially the same form of transport, providing a similar service and placing similar demands on the environment. Certainly most forms of transport have become more widely available, and volume of use has increased massively for the more expensive and environmentally damaging forms of transport (most notably for motor vehicles and air travel), while less environmentally demanding modes such as walking and cycling have declined in importance; but in essence we sti have much the same transport options as we did a century ago (Dyos and Aldcro 1969; Freeman and Aldcroft 1988; Knowles et al. 2008; Shaw and Docherty 2014.

Second, the role of transport and travel in our everyday lives has also change little over the past century and more. Although the availability, affordabili and speed of much modern transport has broadened horizons and enabled mo people to travel further, faster and more often, the fundamental importance mobility to people's lives has not in essence changed. The need to travel f work, education, shopping, socialisation, pleasure and leisure was as central everyday life a century ago as it is today. Journeys may have been slower ar in some cases shorter, though even in the twenty-first century most everyde travel is over relatively short distances and in urban areas travel speeds are n necessarily significantly faster, but the rhythms of daily life for most people, ar the significance of transport and travel to those routines, has remained large unchanged (Pooley et al. 2005, 2006).

Third, the impact of past transport infrastructure continues to have a maj impact on how we travel and on our everyday travel experiences. Most of th rail routes that exist today were originally constructed at least a century and half ago; and, especially in urban areas, long-standing road patterns continue exert a major influence over present-day planning decisions. For instance, th problems of managing modern traffic in any urban area such as York, Chest or Ludlow with a mediaeval street plan and many historic buildings are all t obvious (Larkham 2002). Even with air transport a decision in 1930 to build airfield on the present site of Heathrow continues to influence debates about ho the demand for air transport in southern England should be managed (Heathro Airport website). Physical presences from the past continue to influence ar shape many aspects of travel and transport today.

Fourth, and related to the above point, transport is to a large degree subje to considerable inertia or 'path dependency' (Arthur 1994). Because of hig infrastructure costs, the power of large companies that provide fuel and transpo and the persistent travelling habits of the population, the ways in which we trav have been remarkably slow to change. Once the car was perceived and establishe as the most desirable form of personal private transport in the early years of th twentieth century in Britain (and long before most households had access to car), the dominance of the internal combustion engine was secured. The marketir strategies and political power of major motor manufacturers and petroleu companies helped to create an environment in which the position of the car in th transport system was not seriously challenged with, for instance, the reshapir of cities to suit cars and to the detriment of other forms of transport. In this w; systems of automobility became firmly established as a path-dependent proce (Sheller and Urry 2000; Urry 2004; Featherstone et al. 2005; Conley 2009).

Counterfactual history is not especially fashionable or well-regarded by mar historians (Hawthorne 1991; Ferguson 2003; Bunzl 2004; Evans 2014), but the can sometimes be merit in considering how things might have been different h;

an alternative path been taken. From such analysis it might be possible to learn lessons for the future. For instance what role would rail transport have played in the British transport system today if the line closures recommended by the Beeching Report (1963) had not taken place (McKie 2013), and how might everyday travel be different in the twenty-first century had the development of the automobile been restricted in Britain in the early twentieth century (Pooley 2010)? In one sense, what are being considered in such scenarios are simple opportunity costs: all too often in transport planning and development one path is followed (usually for political or financial reasons) without due consideration being given to other possibilities. Potentially a similar situation is occurring today with the development of the HS2 rail link from London to Birmingham and, eventually, to northern England. As Divall shows in Chapter 6, more effective and more socially equitable improvements in transport in Britain could probably be achieved if the money committed to HS2 was spent differently. We believe that there is a powerful argument for planners and policy makers to be at least aware of relevant transport history when proposing new schemes: and for historians to strive to make an understanding of the past available and accessible to planners and policy makers. The chapters in this volume seek to provide such understanding across a range of transport modes and time periods, chiefly in relation to the United Kingdom.

Where Are We Now?

Arguing that the past can provide important information relevant to the present is, of course, not new although it has been rarely applied in the field of transport policy. The well-known phrase that the past is the key to the present is usually attributed to Kenneth M. Stampp, writing about US slavery in 1956, but it can clearly be applied much more widely and most probably has older antecedents. Since the early 2000s a group of academic historians has sought to promote an understanding of relevant issues from the past to policy makers and planners via the History and Policy network. Its on-line forum freely publishes historical research that is relevant to policy makers, journalists and others concerned with a range of contemporary issues, and historians lead workshops and seminars within Whitehall with the goal of enhancing civil servants' appreciation of the relevance of the past (Thane 2009; History and Policy (a)). These services have received considerable praise from users but, so far, there is limited coverage of transport issues with one policy paper by Duncan Needham (2014) on the history of the debate about London's third airport, and a short opinion piece by Colin Divall (2010) on expansion of the rail network the most prominent items. Interestingly transport does not currently appear as a separate theme in the site's listing of research papers, despite its obvious centrality to British economy and society and the controversial nature of many transport-related policy decisions. Divall has also argued elsewhere for an historical perspective to transport policy (Divall 2011, 2012, 2015; Merriman et al. 2013), and in 2014–15 he co-facilitated several workshops within Whitehall on behalf of History and Policy. But for the most part transport historians and transport policy makers have trod separate paths. The focus of the recent Research Excellence Framework 2014 (REF) on the 'impact' that research by British academics has had may serve to focus more research in this direction (REF website), but in transport studies there remains a long way to go.

Policy makers and politicians are certainly not totally unaware of the significance of a historical perspective: as the British Labour Party MP Frank Field states on the History and Policy website, 'History has a huge amount to teach us about how we got to where we are and how we might move forward' (History and Policy (b)). Some recent academic research has also achieved substantial publicity and has generated real debate among politicians and policy makers. Examples include Thomas Piketty's (2014) long-run economic analysis and critique of global capitalism and inequality, and Richard Wilkinson's and Kate Pickett's (2009) analysis of why more equal societies do better on almost all measures of social and economic health. Furthermore, Jo Guldi and David Armitage have recently published their *History Manifesto* (2014) which arose from discussion (mainly in the US) about the future of history and the role of academics in public culture. However, while William Hague (himself a published historian) employed full-time historians at the British Government's Foreign and Commonwealth Office to provide a long-term perspective on international issues during his term in office as secretary of state for foreign and commonwealth affairs (2010–14) (Armitage 2014), there is little evidence of this practice being more widely adopted by British government ministers. Those who can reflect on their own past experiences, and bring them to bear on present-day issues, often have more regard for the value of the past. For instance Jonathan Powell, Downing Street chief of staff under Prime Minister Tony Blair from 1995 to 2007, and also the chief British negotiator on Northern Ireland during the peace talks that led to the Good Friday Agreement (1998), has brought these experiences of conflict resolution to his more recent writings on dealing with the threat of terrorism, and to his role as CEO of the charity Inter-Mediate, that works on the resolution of armed conflicts. Based on his experiences in Northern Ireland, he argues strongly that military solutions to terrorist threats are not possible, and that only negotiations can lead to successful resolutions (Powell 2014a, 2014b).

Some countries do appear to have more regard for the power of historical understanding in transport policy making, as shown in Chapter 1, where Bert Toussaint examines the role that historians play within the Dutch ministry of infrastructure and environment. Although the individual case studies that follow are all concerned with the British Isles, this international theme is important for the future health of the relationship between history and policy in the UK: we argue strongly that it is incumbent on both historians and policy makers to learn from experiences elsewhere. In the policy area of transport and mobility the stakes are high. High levels of mobility are central to the success of all economies and societies, but this mobility has severe costs in terms of resource use, pollution (both local and global), congestion and human health (Banister 2005, 2007). Given that societies have been grappling with problems of transport and mobility for centuries, and that the basic parameters and components of everyday travel have changed relatively little over more than a century, it seems obvious that there is potential to learn lessons from the past in the development of present-day transport policy.

The Scope and Aims of the Volume

It is first necessary to define the terminology used in this volume (and in the title) and to delimit the scope of the book. By transport we are not referring only to the physical infrastructure of roads, rails, airports and so on, along with the motor vehicles, trains and planes that use these structures, but also to the wider concept of mobility: the ability of people to move freely and easily in ways that enable them to undertake their daily life of work, education, leisure and pleasure. Most everyday travel in Britain is over short distances: in 2013, 18 per cent of all trips were under one mile and 67 per cent under five miles in distance. Only 5 per cent were more than 25 miles (DfT 2014). For most people, most of the time, what is important to them is how the transport system works and enables their mobility within a relatively circumscribed locality. We argue that this has changed little over time (Pooley et al. 2005). Moreover despite the obvious increase in car use over the twentieth century, a significant proportion of all journeys are still undertaken on foot. Walking accounted for 22 per cent of all trips undertaken in 2013, second only to travel by car as a driver or passenger (64 per cent), and substantially greater than travel by bus (7 per cent) and train (3 per cent). And 78 per cent of all trips less than one mile were on foot (DfT 2014). A century ago, walking was the dominant form of transport, and although it has declined it remains a crucial element of most people's everyday travel experience, despite being barely recognised as a mode of transport in many policy documents and receiving less investment even than cycling (which accounts for fewer than 2 per cent of all trips), let alone road and rail infrastructure. Chapters in this volume range across almost the whole spectrum of transport and travel experiences in Britain. Of course transport is important not only for personal mobility but also for the movement of freight from one location to another. Increasing consumer demand for an ever wider range of goods places significant demands on both the road and rail networks that are used for distribution (Roth and Divall 2015). While recognising the importance of freight transport the chapters in this volume focus principally on passenger transport and the mobility of people. Likewise, we do not deal explicitly with the important and increasing role of the internet and social media in enabling virtual mobility, focusing instead on physical movement from place to place.

We should also define what we mean by policy. Our understanding is a broad one encompassing both national and local policy making. We recognise that although there may be a national policy framework (for instance DfT/DoH 2010;

DfT 2011), the decisions that most affect people's lives and the ways in which they travel are taken at the local level. It is important to consider how national guidelines are interpreted and implemented, and to recognise that not every ministerial policy statement is translated into action. There can often be a large gap between what is in a policy document and what actually occurs on the ground (Vigar 2002). It should also be recognised that many of the forces influencing the delivery and development of transport are not directly related to transport policies at all. For instance economic policies adopted by a national government may have a significant effect in, say, limiting funds during periods of financial austerity and thus frustrating attempts by local government to provide or improve transport. Furthermore, while some such effects can be predicted, central government policies may sometimes have unintended consequences that can influence transport provision and everyday mobility. It is also important to recognise that individuals also develop their own views, or policies, on how they should travel. Although influenced to some extent by government (national or local) statements on policy, and by media coverage of such statements, in practice most everyday travel decisions are based on a personal evaluation of what will work, and can be afforded, by an individual or family. In this sense policy making interacts with individual decision making and, arguably, through the ballot box individual choices and preferences can feed back to shape local and national government policies. For instance the dominance of car use for everyday transport makes policy makers very reluctant to restrict, or financially penalise, drivers, even though such policies may follow logically from national statements about the need to develop more sustainable transport systems.

Learning lessons from history (the subtitle of this volume) is a bold statement and also requires some further explanation. None of the chapters in this volume argues that history repeats itself, or that conditions today are identical to those decades ago. However we are collectively suggesting that it is foolish to completely ignore what has gone before. While the recent past may appear at first sight to be most relevant, as stated above most forms of transport used today as well as the types of mobility that are most important on an everyday basis have been present for a century or more, and thus a longer time perspective can also be valuable. Part of the lesson to be learned may be to recognise the ways in which past practices can be adapted to suit contemporary society and transport needs. One difficulty of producing and presenting transport and mobility history in a form that is useful to planners and policy makers lies in the sources that are available. Statistics are rarely constant over time (for instance even definitions used in the National Travel Survey have changed, making direct comparisons difficult) and other sources can be much more problematic. All policy statements must be read within the context of the political climate and complexion of the time; and it is hard to gather reliable accounts of individual travel experiences beyond the recent past. Although oral testimonies gathered today may go back to the mid-twentieth century they inevitably become less robust the more distant they are from the present. Sources used by each author are discussed in individual chapters and an appendix to the volume also attempts to provide some guidance on key sources relevant to transport history and policy.

The Individual Chapters

As already mentioned, following this introduction, further context is provided by Bert Toussaint, who draws on his experience in the Rijkswaterstaat, the ministerial agency for water management and infrastructure in the Netherlands, to discuss the development and use of history-learning concepts and tools as applied to transport projects. He distinguishes two aspects of history learning: contextual learning and behavioural learning. Contextual learning focuses on gaining insight into broader temporal processes of policy making; behavioural learning aims at changing professional attitudes by applying historical knowledge and insights in policy-making trajectories and implementation projects. Contextual learning sessions in transport-history projects have included workshops, where research results were discussed with policy makers, strategic advisors and project managers; behavioural learning is still in its infancy, but a transport-policy decision-simulation project is being developed and tested. It is argued that the Dutch experience demonstrates the value of both developing clear conceptual tools for the use of historical knowledge in transport planning, and of applying these history-learning concepts to specific transport projects.

The remainder of the volume is divided into two parts. The first, Mobility and Social Justice, contains six chapters focussing on different aspects of travel from the perspective of social justice and mobility identities. By examining a wide range of different travel modes these chapters discuss the ways in which some travellers can become marginalised within the transport system, with restricted mobility that fundamentally affects the quality of their everyday lives. The second part, Marketing Im/Mobility, contains three chapters examining the ways in which transport and mobility are marketed, and the role of marketing strategies in shaping the ways in which we travel.

Frances Hodgson's focus, in Chapter 2, is on gender and walking in the urban environment. She carefully develops an understanding of the patterns of disadvantage and social justice that particularly affect female pedestrians through historical gendered analysis of women's walking and women's resistances. It is argued that the historical patterns of statutory underinvestment in walking provision, and neglect of gender in transport policy, result in gendered patterns of temporal and spatial exclusion. The analysis presented draws on two separate community studies conducted in 1984 and 2007 from one inner-city neighbourhood, together with archived visual evidence, to build a layered account of walking strategies and resistances to exclusion. Analysis of women's own accounts of walking provides evidence of women using competencies and strategies to stay safe, and evidence of women's individual and collective resistance to disadvantage through history. In remembering, documenting and archiving social practice of women in this neglected area this chapter contributes to a usable social history for transport planning and for women skilling, individually and collectively to resist spatial and temporal patterns of exclusion. This focus on gender and walking is particularly salient as women are still less likely than men to have regular access

to car transport, and are more likely than men to be pedestrians for some of the
journeys (Pooley et al. 2013). In Chapter 3 Colin Pooley examines the tensions tha
arise between principles of social justice and environmental justice in transpo
and mobility and, especially, the contention that principles of social justice an
environmental justice are often incompatible when applied to contemporar
transport and mobility. For instance, restrictions on car use that would mee
principles of environmental sustainability may unduly penalise some of the mo
disadvantaged members of society. Drawing on a range of recent research by th
author, and focusing especially on trams and bicycles as key forms of everyda
transport, the chapter demonstrates that at certain periods in the past social an
environmental justice in transport were more closely aligned than they are toda
and that better understanding of past mobility may help to achieve more social
and environmentally equitable transport systems in the future.

Everyday travel in rural areas can be especially problematic, especially fc
those without access to a car. In Chapter 4 Aoife Ahern and Julian Hine examin
this problem by focusing on the travel experiences of older people in rural are
across Ireland. The aim of the study was to discover what challenges, if any, fac
older people when trying to travel in rural areas and to examine if older peop
have unmet transport needs as a result of living in rural areas. They argue tha
older people in rural areas do have unmet transport needs, generally arising du
to poor provision of alternatives to the car. Trips are difficult to make without
car and both social/recreational and health trips are among the most problemat
for older people. The chapter focuses particularly on the difficulties faced by th
generation of older people in adjusting to life without a car in rural areas. Usin
focus groups it was shown that this generation of older people, who are the fir
Irish generation to have experienced widespread car ownership and car use, a
very car dependent, and find the adjustment from a motorised life to a car-les
life very difficult. While the focus of the original study was not the interaction c
history and transport policy, the findings are of relevance for policy makers. Th
older generation represent a watershed moment: they are the first generation t
grow up with expectations of car ownership, and so recording their experience
of travel as they approach an age when car use becomes more difficult, or in som
situations impossible, is important. In addition, future generations will be eve
more car dependent, so understanding and recording the challenges faced by olde
people in rural areas today will help in creating a better transport policy for ou
ageing, car-dependent society.

Chapters 5 and 6 both focus on different aspects of rail travel. Arguably, th
is one of the most fruitful areas for making links between the past and the prese
as the British railway network has been well-established for more than a centur
and a half, and the number of people travelling by rail has increased significant
in recent years. Hiroki Shin provides an historical overview of Britain's railwa
passenger representation up to 1947. He explores the emergence of passenger
collective interests in the late nineteenth century, and examines how the subseque
development of the situation surrounding passenger issues in the early twentie

century consolidated a specific configuration of passenger representation, without paying much attention to the travelling public. The historical configuration of passenger interests affected the ways in which transport users' consultative bodies were formed in post-war Britain. By viewing voluntary passenger movements as a legitimate part of passenger transport, the chapter sheds light on the potentially significant role that a passenger- representation policy could play in balancing transport justice and the passenger business. In contrast, Colin Divall focuses on one of the most recent developments in British rail transport (HS2), and shows how the project to develop a high-speed rail link from London to Birmingham and then to northern England might be repeating mistakes of the past. In the nineteenth century, and to the detriment of rail travellers, politicians failed to insist on a strategic plan for the development of the country's railway network: much the same situation exists today. The arguments in favour of HS2, based upon the promise of economic growth and regional development, are grounded partly on a combination of apparently wilful ignorance or on the selective reading of the now half-century experience of high-speed railways across the globe. Furthermore, history warns that the kinds of long-term projections of the need for future capacity on Britain's trunk railways being used to justify HS2 are likely to be subject to much greater levels of uncertainty than is being assumed. In sum the project bears all the hallmarks of the kinds of prestigious infrastructure projects that Bent Flyvbjerg et al. (2003) argue rich countries can afford to build, but that do not contribute much to the sum of economic well-being let alone social equity or ecological sustainability.

The final chapter in this part focuses on the human cost of our love affair with the car and, especially, on the halting history of attempts to develop effective control of drink driving in the UK. Bill Luckin carefully traces developments between two key moments in the history of drink-driving control in Britain, Barbara Castle's Road Safety Act in 1967 and Norman Fowler's lesser known Transport Act in 1981. The 1960s witnessed cumulative legislative activity, culminating in the introduction of the breathalyser test. This was followed by a period of confusion and inertia. In 1976 the Blennerhassett Report confirmed that Castle's measure had lost its cutting-edge and that further reform would be urgently needed. The chapter explains why successive governments stalled, compromised and succumbed to electoral and pro-motorist libertarian pressure. A concluding part suggests that a usable past in this area will only come more fully into focus when greater scholarly attention has been devoted to a crucial and still marginalised aspect of twentieth-century social, political, cultural and mobility history: death and serious injury on the road. Although road casualties in Britain have fallen and are now among the lowest in any developed country, it can be argued that in almost any other arena the number of deaths and serious injuries linked to car use would have led to much more draconian intervention. The fact that death and injury on the roads goes largely unnoticed and unreported, apart from a few major incidents, emphasises the degree to which motoring has attained a dominant and almost unchallenged position within the British transport system.

In the twenty-first century many of our everyday decisions are affected by the marketing and advertising with which we are bombarded by a wide range of different media. This is just as true of how we travel as it is of what brand of coffee we choose to buy. The three chapters in the second part all explore the role of marketing in shaping the mobility choices and decisions of the British travelling public. In Chapter 8, Nicola Forsdike explores how history is relevant to contemporary transport and marketing practitioners. In particular, she considers whether and how knowledge from the past is applied in day-to-day practice. Issues are explored from the practitioner's standpoint with particular reference to how marketing and branding theories can and have been used to deliver modal shift in urban transport. The theoretical context – how contemporary business marketing and branding theory can be applied to a transport context to deliver modal shift – is first examined. Case studies are then brought in to demonstrate whether historical evidence can show if and how theory has worked in practice. This theme is further developed in Chapter 9 by Martin Higginson, who explores approaches to influencing modal share in markets where overall growth is not the providers' primary concern, such as 'captive' commuter markets. It considers the challenges faced by transport professionals, policy makers, academics and historians seeking to understand the past; and asks what historical processes might be relevant to the present. Demand is shown to result from a combination of commercial efforts by providers and governments to expand markets, and external influences such as changes in populations, demographics and economic geography: phenomena that are at the heart of the debate on 'predict and provide' versus demand management in transport investment. Specific regard is paid to individual modes of transport and to markets in which a particular mode is under threat from competition, such as where established modes are being overtaken by new arrivals in the market place. The history of how marketing and branding shape and respond to public opinion is examined to help explain why demand for personal mobility has reached today's levels and forms. Finally in this part Peter Lyth focuses on air travel. Although for most people travel by plane still cannot be considered everyday transport, air travel is one of the fastest growing transport sectors with significant environmental and infrastructural implications. The chapter looks at the state of British civil aviation in the second decade of the twenty-first century, in an age of serious concern about climate change, and asks the question: why do we fly so much? It considers the marketing of leisure flying – tourism – in the short-haul market of low-cost, 'no-frills' airlines like Ryanair and EasyJet, and asks to what extent that marketing effort has created a brand out of 'aeromobility', itself a marker of a troubled prosperity and uncertain identity in a postmodern consumer society. It can be argued that the role of marketing practitioners in shaping travel behaviour often goes unnoticed, and these three chapters focus attention on one of the more hidden forces influencing mobility in the UK.

The issues raised by the chapters suggest that future research should attempt to place transport and mobility in Britain within a wider European and global context. We suggest that there are distinctive and deeply embedded characteristics of the history of mobility in Britain that inhibit the development of more environmentally sustainable forms of everyday travel, but that better understanding of these path-dependent historical processes could usefully inform current transport policies. As shown in Chapter 1 some countries and institutions do take the past more seriously than is common in Britain, and we suggest that there is definitely scope to learn from experiences elsewhere. The chapters in this volume are, necessarily, selective in their approach and there are many other areas of transport and mobility where insightful links could be made between the past and the present. Of course, the past is not directly relevant to all present-day policy, but we argue that in many cases it is. Our hope in producing this set of chapters is that policy makers will begin to pay greater attention to the lessons of history, and that historians will seek to present their data and analyses in forms that policy makers can engage with, thus going some way towards producing a more usable past.

References

Armitage, D. (2014). Why Politicians Need Historians. *The Guardian*, 7 October. http://www.theguardian.com/education/2014/oct/07/why-politicians-need-historians (accessed 10 May 2015).

Arthur, W. (1994). *Increasing Returns and Path Dependence in the Economy*. Ann Arbor, MI: University of Michigan Press.

Banister, D. (2005). *Unsustainable Transport: City Transport in the New Century*. London: Routledge.

——— (2007). The Sustainable Mobility Paradigm. *Transport Policy* 15, pp. 73–80.

Beeching, R. (1963). *The Reshaping of British Railways*. 2 vols. London: HMSO.

Bunzl, M. (2004). Forum Essay – Counterfactual History: A User's Guide. *The American Historical Review* 109, pp. 845–58.

Conley, J., ed. (2009). *Car Troubles: Critical Studies of Automobility and Automobility*. Aldershot: Ashgate.

Department for Transport (DfT) (2011). *Creating Growth, Cutting Carbon. Making Sustainable Local Transport Happen*. London: HMSO.

——— (DfT) (2014). National Travel Survey 2013. London: DfT. https://www.gov.uk/government/statistics/national-travel-survey-2013 (accessed 10 May 2015).

Department for Transport (DfT) and Department of Health (DoH) (2010). *Active Travel Strategy*. London: HMSO.

Divall, C. (2010). A return to Victorian levels of railway building? http://www.historyandpolicy.org/opinion-articles/category/colin-divall (accessed 10 May 2015).

——— (2011). Transport History, the Usable Past and the Future of Mobility. In *Mobilities: New Perspectives on Transport and Society*, ed. M. Grieco and J. Urry. Farnham: Ashgate, pp. 305–19.

———— (2012). Business History, Global Networks and the Future of Mobility. *Business History* 54, pp. 542–55.

———— (2015). Introduction: Cultural Histories of Sociabilities, Spaces and Mobilities. In *Cultural Histories of Sociabilities, Spaces and Mobilities*, ed. C. Divall. London: Pickering and Chatto, pp. 3–16.

Dyos, H.J. and Aldcroft, D. (1969). *British Transport: An Economic Survey from the Seventeenth Century to the Twentieth*. Leicester: Leicester University Press.

Evans, R. (2014). *Altered Pasts: Counterfactuals in History*. London: Little Brown.

Featherstone, M., Thrift, N. and Urry, J. (2005). *Automobilities*. London: Sage.

Ferguson, N., ed. (2003). *Virtual History: Alternatives and Counterfactuals*. London: Basic Books.

Flyvbjerg, B., Bruzelius, N. and Rothengatter, W. (2003). *Megaprojects and Risk: An Anatomy of Ambition*. Cambridge: Cambridge University Press.

Freeman, M. and Aldcroft, D., eds (1988). *Transport in Victorian Britain*. Manchester: Manchester University Press.

Guldi, J. and Armitage, D. (2014). *The History Manifesto*. Cambridge: Cambridge University Press.

Hawthorne, G. (1991). *Plausible Worlds: Possibility and Understanding in History and the Social Sciences*. Cambridge: Cambridge University Press.

Knowles, R., Shaw, J. and Docherty, I. (2008) *Transport Geographies: Mobilities, Flows and Spaces*. Oxford: Blackwell.

Larkham, P. (2002). *Conservation and the City*. London: Routledge.

McKie, R. (2013). How Britain Got It Wrong About Britain's Railways. *The Guardian*, 2 March. http://www.theguardian.com/uk/2013/mar/02/beeching-wrong-about-britains-railways (accessed 10 May 2015).

Merriman, P., Jones, R., Cresswell, T., Divall, C., Mom, G., Sheller, M. and Urry. J. (2013). Mobility: Geographies, Histories, Sociologies. *Transfers* 3, pp. 147–65.

Needham, D. (2014) Maplin: The Treasury and London's Third Airport in the 1970s. History and Policy website. http://www.historyandpolicy.org/policy-papers/papers/maplin-the-treasury-and-londons-third-airport-in-the-1970s (accessed 10 May 2015).

Piketty, T. (2014). *Capital in the Twenty-First Century*, trans. A. Goldhammer. Cambridge, MA: Belknap Press.

Pooley C. (2010). Landscapes without the Car: A Counterfactual Historical Geography of Twentieth-Century Britain. *Journal of Historical Geography* 36, pp. 266–75.

Pooley, C. with Jones, T., Tight, M., Horton, D., Scheldeman, G., Mullen, C., Jopson, A. and Strano, E. (2013). *Promoting Walking and Cycling: New Perspectives on Sustainable Travel*. Bristol: Policy Press.

Pooley, C., Turnbull, J. and Adams, M. (2005). *A Mobile Century? Changes in Everyday Mobility in Britain in the Twentieth Century*. Aldershot: Ashgate.

———— (2006). The Impact of New Transport Technologies on Intra-Urban Mobility: A View from the Past. *Environment and Planning A* 38, pp. 253–7.

owell, J. (2014a). How to talk to terrorists. *The Guardian*, 7 October. http://www.theguardian.com/world/2014/oct/07/-sp-how-to-talk-to-terrorists-isis-al-qaida (accessed 10 May 2015).

——— (2014b). *Talking to Terrorists: How to End Armed Conflicts*. London: Bodley Head.

oth, R. and Divall, C., eds (2015). *From Road to Rail and Back Again: A Century of Transport Competition and Interdependency*. Farnham: Ashgate.

haw, J. and Docherty, I. (2014). *The Transport Debate*. Bristol: Policy Press.

heller, M. and Urry, J. (2000). The City and the Car. *International Journal of Urban and Regional Research* 24, pp. 737–57.

tampp, K. (1956). *The Peculiar Institution: Slavery in the Ante-Bellum South*. New York: Vintage Books.

hane, P. (2009). History and Policy. *History Workshop Journal* 67, pp. 140–45.

Jrry, J. (2004). The 'System' of Automobility. *Theory, Culture and Society* 21(4/5), pp. 25–39.

'igar, G. (2002). *The Politics of Mobility: Transport, the Environment and Public Policy*. London: Spon Press.

Vilkinson, R. and Pickett, K. (2009). *The Spirit Level: Why More Equal Societies Always Do Better*. London: Allen Lane.

Websites

Ieathrow Airport. Heathrow's History. http://www.heathrowairport.com/about-us/company-news-and-information/company-information/our-history.

Iistory and Policy (a). http://www.historyandpolicy.org/.

Iistory and Policy (b). Statement by Frank Field MP. http://www.historyandpolicy.org/about-us/what-we-do.

JK Research Excellence Framework (REF) website. http://www.ref.ac.uk/.

All accessed 10 May 2015)

Chapter 1

Using the Usable Past: Reflections and Practices in the Netherlands

Bert Toussaint

The Rijkswaterstaat is the agency for infrastructure management and water management in the Dutch Ministry of Infrastructure and the Environment. Its core tasks are national flood safety, the provision of clean and sufficient fresh water and the facilitation of quick and safe traffic flows. With nearly 8,400 staff (in 2015) the Rijkswaterstaat is one of the largest central public agencies in the Netherlands. As the organisation focuses on building and maintaining national engineering structures, it is not at all obvious why it should have a lasting commitment to history. Moreover, a systematic interest in the past is not generally a feature of public agencies in the Netherlands, with the exception of the Ministry of Foreign Affairs and the Ministry of Defence; the latter has a large history staff, fitting into a strong network of military history research and higher education (Hoogerwerf 1989: 63–74). Although the Rijkswaterstaat cannot boast about spending similar amounts on corporate history, it has been funding a small history unit since 1981. The Rijkswaterstaat's history programme has developed continuously since then, and over the last decade learning from history has been a conspicuous strand within it.

As history does not seem to be a natural ally of an engineering organisation, how can we explain the Rijkswaterstaat's commitment to a programme of historical research and education over the last three decades? Secondly, how does the development of history learning fit into this programme? In this chapter I shall first set out briefly the development of the Rijkswaterstaat's history programme and then detail the emergence within it of history learning, unravelling a few key concepts. Subsequently, I shall point out the relevance of history-learning concepts and tools for transport and mobility policy. Finally, I shall briefly assess the policy problem-solving potential of history learning in today's society.

Why History in the Rijkswaterstaat?

When in 1981 the Rijkswaterstaat set up a history unit, the organisation was approaching its second centennial. Established in 1798, the service has always performed more or less the same set of core tasks: protection against flooding, building and maintaining a national infrastructure and facilitating mobility. In the

1970s another essential task was added, monitoring water quality: but this green flavour has mainly enriched the Rijkswaterstaat's identity as the national engineering service that has played and still plays an important role in the development and management of the national infrastructure and water management.

The Rijkswaterstaat's engineering history is tangible: its engineering products like harbours, bridges, sluices, weirs, roads and polders can be observed; they play an undisputed role in Dutch society. As such these structures with their image of dynamic modernism are attractive and alluring. Corporate history promises to give insights into these accomplishments, even if this involves identifying drawbacks and occasional failures in the interrelated processes of policy formation and building. Besides, new projects often draw on existing structures: new road schemes, for instance, cannot be designed from scratch but have to take into account existing road networks, including historical building techniques and technical specifications.

The Rijkswaterstaat's impact on shaping the Dutch infrastructure and landscape has contributed substantially to its image as one of the most powerful public organisations in the country. Obviously this image fuelled a sense of pride within the organisation, concomitant with a strong and widespread sense of a distinct organisational identity, fostered by the top management. In 1981 the impending 190th birthday led to the establishment of a small historical unit. A programme of historical research was developed, encompassing a broad spectrum of subjects concerning the Rijkswaterstaat's organisational past and its core tasks. Books and reports were issued, exhibitions organised and documentation compiled. These activities reached a climax in the 1998 jubilee, as the bicentennial was celebrated with a range of activities and the publication of a corporate history, *Twee eeuwen Rijkswaterstaat* (Two Centuries of the Rijkswaterstaat) (Bosch and van der Ham 1998). During the 1998 festivities, communication with the public about water management and transport history was greatly intensified. That was a conspicuous difference from the other corporate-history programmes developed by a handful of Dutch private companies from the 1990s. For example, the electronics firm Philips commissioned a multi-volume corporate history but apparently had no ambitions to use this in its external communication strategy. Similarly, in 2007 another (Anglo-) Dutch industrial giant, Shell, published a corporate history (Heerding 1986; Blanken 1999; van Zanden, Howard and Jonker 2007). But this publication also stood out as a separate event, primarily underscoring Shell's status as a big global company and not integrated into a broader vision of how corporate history might be used for learning or communicative aims.

Rijkswaterstaat's Evolution into a Learning Organisation

In the first decade of this century the Rijkswaterstaat strongly intensified its commitment to organisational learning. This process did not happen overnight, and it has been substantially influenced by the need to adjust to growing criticism from politicians and the public of governmental organisations, labelled by neoliberal rhetoric as slow, sluggish, not innovative and not transparent. Even the Rijkswaterstaat felt the urgency to improve its problem-solving capabilities by permanently investing in training courses and other learning activities, such as coaching. Moreover, the organisation underwent a metamorphosis as it began, in response to political criticism of its staff size, to outsource its engineering design tasks. Simultaneously, it formulated an ambition to improve communication with the public. To achieve all this the majority of staff members had to acquire new skills. Learning became a key to successful performance.

Training courses, competence development, knowledge management and learning on the job are all tools meant to improve the Rijkswaterstaat's managerial, financial, communicative and public-satisfaction performance. The Rijkswaterstaat's learning ambitions have also an international dimension. History learning apparently fitted into this widening scope for organisational learning. Using history had, it was felt, the potential to add specific aspects to the organisation's learning climate. The first history-learning tool was developed in the late 1990s, making use of the classical technique of storytelling. Telling stories about the organisational past has been used as a communicative tool to illustrate and convey core corporate cultural values and thus give a sharper insight into the Rijkswaterstaat's strengths and weaknesses, aiming to improve young staff members' and junior managers' corporate consciousness and understanding.

Since the 1990s storytelling has been increasingly used in private enterprises in the US and other countries. Deep-set organisational values tend to change very slowly and are fundamentally shaped by the corporate past. Stories about the evolution of these deeply embedded cultural mechanisms may thus reveal organisational continuity and change over long periods (Neuhauser 1993: 51–5). This emphasis on organisational culture has been influenced by the influential insights offered by E.R. Schein. Schein makes a distinction between deep and more superficial layers of cultural repertoires and symbols. The deepest layer of an organisational culture form a set of shared basic assumptions that are usually taken for granted, rarely made explicit, and yet are so embedded that they are internalised as the correct way to perceive, think and feel in relation to an organisation's problems (Schein 1992). Telling and sharing stories about the organisational past can reveal these mechanisms, and may suggest which cultural phenomena might be influenced by learning programmes and which are resistant to change.

A variant of storytelling is the elaboration of a learning history in teams or departments. The writing of learning history was developed in the 1990s as a structured method by A. Kleiner and G. Roth (Kleiner and Roth 1997: 172–7). A learning history is a written narrative of a company's or team's critical event or process, where relevant episodes are described by all those who were involved. Trained experts identify recurring themes and interview participants by posing questions intended to raise critical issues. This results in a rich collective story of the shared past that subsequently forms the basis of group discussions, which may in turn help cope with future organisational change and generate a focus on innovation. A growing number of Dutch for- and not-for-profit organisations and public agencies have developed learning histories in order to bolster their corporate learning capabilities (M en O 2006). The Rijkswaterstaat has initiated a few small-scale projects with teams that have experienced profound changes, holding interviews with participants and compiling documents drawing upon and quoting these interviews to generate collective stories.

Learning from History: Some Conceptual Considerations

History-learning projects in the Rijkswaterstaat were developed with the aid of a conceptual perspectives. We mentioned a few of them above. Other important conceptual insights are offered in the pioneering work by R. Neustadt and E.R. May, *Thinking in Time: The Uses of History for Decision-Makers* (Neustadt and May 1986). In this book Neustadt and May develop a 'mini-method' for policy makers that enables the systematic use of history in decision-making processes. Case studies in past political decision making that are sufficiently similar to present-day policy problems are identified. Assuming a suitable case can be found, the history of the policy problem, the relevant actors, their attitudes and motives, the policy options and decision methods are reconstructed and compared to the present policy process. Policy decision making may thus profit from past experience.

Neustadt and May's approach has promising elements as well as disadvantages. The use of a historical case to reconstruct a policy-making process through a focus on unravelling key actors' attitudes, motives and interests can be very fruitful. Psychological mechanisms tend to be repeated, and can thus be described as repertoires that are stable over time. However, it is not easy to identify a case from the past that is sufficiently similar to a present-day policy challenge, as usually the broader context has changed. Even if the actors are identical, other factors – the economic climate, the involved public, media responses – are likely to be different. An identical context will rarely, if ever, return (Hirsh 2011: 6).

Historical cases, however, can also be used in simulation games. In these games participants are asked to identify with an actor from the selected case, and they are then provided with sufficient contextual information relating to that actor to allow them to role play. The participants are then invited to jointly prepare an informed decision as if they had been present in the past. A decade ago the 1986 Sandoz disaster (an explosion in a Swiss pharmaceutical firm that caused high poisonous effluents in the Rhine) was simulated in a workshop with the participation of high-ranking managers from the Ministry in order to analyse their decision-making capacity in a crisis. Serious gaming is currently developing into a powerful learning instrument in profit and non-profit organisations, notably for managers, and historical situations, actors and problems may well be used to construct a credible case (Abt 1970; Michael and Chen 2006).

A Dutch public-administration researcher, Jos Raadschelders, has developed another history-learning perspective. Raadschelders argues that by revealing geographical and historical contexts, historical studies show how an administrative body's organisational development is entwined with the external environment. He further emphasises the continuity of policy processes. Present-day policy problems are often rooted in the past and are partly the result of decisions taken then. By analysing the history of decision-making processes, the options either adopted or rejected, a reservoir of solutions will be disclosed that might be very helpful in formulating solutions for present problems (Raadschelders 1994: 117–29). This argument has also been put forward recently by Richard Hirsh, drawing on the views developed by Julian Zelizer (Hirsh 2011: 12–13; Zelizer 2000: 369–94). I often use the metaphor of history as a treasure room: historians have to use the proper key and select the pearls for the policy makers.

From these conceptual perspectives, I derive two aspects that can be applied in a learning setting: *contextual learning* and *behavioural learning*. By contextual learning I mean gaining insight into the temporal dimension of a policy process: the actors and their expertise to articulate specific solutions in order to address the problems of a past era. Histories of river management or infrastructure policy, for instance, enable a policy maker or expert to understand more fully past decision-making processes, the repertoires of policy options, the cultural background and the views of the actors. Thus, best or worst practices can be distilled, and if a history covers more than a brief episode, the trends or structures that characterise a policy field can be identified, all of which contributes to a better insight into the present policy context.

Behavioural learning goes one step further. To be effective behavioural learning requires not only a sensitivity to contextual learning but also the mental flexibility to modify professional attitudes. Project leaders who can be motivated to read not only engineering manuals but also historical accounts, to analyse views and options that were articulated in the past and to use these in a present project, enlarge their frame of reference and stimulate their conceptual flexibility. Thus they may be able to broaden their repertoire of solutions for use in the strategic management of processes and stakeholders. As Hirsh has pointed out, history analyses may clarify the functions, interests and motives of stakeholders and institutions (Hirsh 2011: 8). This socio-cultural dimension has often been neglected in infrastructural policy making and policy implementation.

Historical contextual-learning has been used in various Dutch policy contexts. First, historical policy analyses have informed a few policy documents; for example, a Rijkswaterstaat scenario study (2007), sketching strategic forecasts for 2020, and the latest Rijkswaterstaat water policy strategy (2009). Historical analyses provided a broader and richer context by describing long-term societal trends and their impact on the Rijkswaterstaat organisation (Toussaint 2008; Rijkswaterstaat 2009: 8–9). These texts also identified a few key factors and trends in the Rijkswaterstaat's development over the last decades that otherwise would have been ignored. Secondly, in workshops and group discussions with managers, retired managers and senior policy advisors, the key conclusions of history books and reports were critiqued and their learning potential assessed. Thirdly, introduction courses for new staff members now ask participants to compose a corporate history time line, by putting together historical sources. By comparison, the Dutch Ministry of Social Affairs and Labour offers new personnel a more elaborate version of this concept, displaying a multimedia time line of the development of the Dutch social-security system.

Behavioural history learning is still in its initial phase. The Rijkswaterstaat learning programme, which primarily aims at developing competences and changing attitudes, now includes a few modules on historical topics. A module on the assessment of the heritage value of older engineering structures (sluices, weirs bridges and so on), is being developed. The training of young, fast-track civil servants invites participants to write an essay on the ministry's corporate culture drawing on a few historical sources. These modules aim at integrating historical knowledge into the repertoire of professional attitudes.

Factors in Gaining Corporate Support for History Projects

During the last decade a number of projects have been initiated in the Rijkswaterstaat with the intention of stimulating learning from history. Three factors seem to be relevant to the crucial support given to these projects. The Rijkswaterstaat's top management had a genuine interest in corporate history as it was convinced that history shapes today's organisation. It thus showed commitment either by commissioning projects or by giving them explicit support and approval. Furthermore these history projects were linked to some of the organisation's priority projects and programmes; as pointed out previously, there is a widespread interest in corporate history among the staff, stimulating further interest in these projects.

The primary goal of these research projects is to produce history books or reports that meet academic standards of critical analysis, combined with a clear style of writing. But something has been added to this: not 'lessons' in the strict sense, least of all prescriptions, but stimuli to discussion and reflection. These points of discussion focus not only on problematic situations, failures or conflicts, but also on successes, brilliant concepts and best practices. Or the present dilemmas, which give an insight in the difficult choices policy makers had to make in the past. Current historical research has been discussed regularly in workshops or presentations, where its learning potential was explored. Readers or participants in workshops can be more readily motivated to reflect if they read or hear colourful stories rather than a dull, routine survey. Form and style matter: a vivid recreation of the past might allure policy makers or experts above all when they read about bold, innovative engineering achievements made possible by ideas, motivations and actions of experts, who, after all, might well be their predecessors.

Occasionally, history projects aimed at the public have been developed. The 75th anniversary of the inauguration of the Dutch highway network was celebrated in April 2012, and a small exhibition on its evolution was opened by the minister of transport along the Netherlands' oldest route. An extended version of this exhibition was offered on a website, and there was national and regional media coverage. The national mobility-user organisation ANWB – cherishing its own corporate history – participated in this event, and set up an exhibition on infrastructure history. Jubilees are not only attractive to organisations but also to the media, offering ample opportunities for telling stories about history and policy and even linking a few highlights from the past to recent policy developments: although the learning effects are, obviously, transient.

History can also play a distinct role in internal communication. This can be illustrated by the Rijkswaterstaat's keen interest in corporate heritage objects, encompassing valuable documents, audiovisual sources and artefacts from the corporate past. Making such artefacts accessible with an organisation may inculcate collective experiences of core cultural values. Stimuli of the senses are often more appealing, or at any rate more immediate, than intellectual challenges. Corporate history exhibitions and multimedia objects include representations of past transport schemes and projects. These events and objects not only alert the Rijkswaterstaat's staff to continuities between the corporate past and present but also illustrate the links between past and present transport policies and project trajectories.

Learning from Transport History

A few major Rijkswaterstaat research projects cover transport history. The first of these projects was the production of the first academic overview on the development of the Dutch transport system since 1800, covering rail transport, coach transport, navigation, road infrastructure, truck transport and car mobility. In 2008 a two-volume handbook *Van transport naar mobiliteit* (From Transport to Mobility) was published (Filarski and Mom 2008). The book launch in the National Railway Museum in Utrecht was accompanied by a panel discussion on current transport-policy issues and the relevance of the past in addressing these.

This handbook had a follow-up in an international project: a comparative study of the development of railway networks, tramways, car mobility, the rise of truck transport and modal coordination policies in the UK, Germany, France, Switzerland, the Netherlands, Belgium and the United States. This project connected more than forty historians and social scientists from Europe and the US, who wrote essays that were then discussed in three workshops. The intensive debates between these scholars and invited Dutch transport policy makers produced large quantities of rich policy-learning material. The first topic included the role, on the one hand, of politics and state-administrative bodies and, on the other, of market-orientated institutions in the development of transport systems; notably the railways in the nineteenth century, tramways around 1900 and infrastructure for cars and trucks in the twentieth century. The use and efficiency of regulatory mechanisms by public authorities to control market bodies in order to obtain adequate levels of performance (punctuality, service, price arrangements, safety levels) was a second, much-debated issue. A third topic focused on interwar coordination policies and their relevance to present transport-system problems. A selection of these essays has been published (Filarski 2011; Weber 2011; Thompson 2011; Ryckewaert 2012; Moraglio 2012; Merriman 2012).

In a fourth workshop, managers, policy advisers and experts from the Ministry of Infrastructure and the Environment (into which the Rijkswaterstaat had been incorporated) and from the academic world were brought together to discuss the learning potential to be distilled from this international transport-history project, attempting to identify lessons for current transport policy in the Netherlands. These four transport-history workshops can be regarded as learning niches: platforms of free discussion, where cross-fertilisation between scholars and policy makers are likely to materialise. However, whether the learning effects will last depends on the Rijkswaterstaat's structural commitment to behavioural learning, as pointed out above.

In addition, a book developing a systematic comparative perspective was published in 2011. In *Shaping Transport Policy*, Ruud Filarski (Filarski and Mom 2011), the main author, offers a lot of fascinating, if sometimes controversial, learning material. In his chapter on railway systems, he concludes that when railways companies in the nineteenth century were granted concessions to build railway tracks, strong governmental regulation was needed to ensure adequate performance across a range of measures. By the end of the nineteenth century, Belgium had the best functioning railway system because of the state's strong role, which developed railways as a coherent network rather than a patchwork of lines and which maintained strict regulation of prices and safety levels. Railway construction in the US was much cheaper than in Europe, due to scale advantages, and freight tariffs were low. On the other hand, lack of administrative regulation in Switzerland and the UK resulted in incoherent, suboptimal networks and high fares. Numerous interesting observations can also be made about car mobility. Tax regimes had a clear impact on trends in car design: high taxes on fuel excise, cylinder capacity and expensive cars resulted in small and compact European cars, low fuel excise taxes in the US stimulated the mass production of over-sized Chevrolets and other big car types, epitomising American car culture of the 1950s (Filarski 2011: 30–43, 107–8).

Relevance of Transport History to Policy Makers

Contextual learning has a great potential to open eyes – this type of narrative refers to a world with which intended readers are familiar, and yet, while reading, they discover forgotten and unnoticed facets. These tales offer a blend of the known and the unknown. As such, they may provide a policy maker or expert with a broader frame of reference that enables him or her to sharpen strategic insights into important policy issues, like the evolution of transport systems and mobility shifts.

Historians are able to sketch the rise and decline of transport modes and to describe with accuracy and vital colour the underlying driving forces. Trends in mobility patterns and shifts can be traced in studies covering longer periods, not just by producing facts and figures, but also – even predominantly – by presenting the important psychological and socio-economic factors behind them. Thus, for instance, in 2004 Filarski wrote a booklet on the rise and decline of certain Dutch transport systems. He concluded that in the Netherlands the adoption of new modes of transport were influenced by just a few factors. Early adopters used three criteria to assess a new mode of transport: social status, adventure and speed. The second and larger group of users switched to a new means of transport if they had a favourable opinion on speed, status, convenience and the possibility of independent travel. Price levels and other factors played a lesser role (Filarski 2004: 93). These enduring motives will likely have a similar impact on today's preferences of innovative transport concepts in Europe or even beyond. As Divall has pointed out, an analysis of people's mobility choices may reveal the underlying assumptions about the temporal evolution of technologies (Divall 2010b: 938–60).

Since the late 1960s most transport planning projects in Western Europe have been subjected to prolonged public discussion; some have been highly controversial. Since then, planning authorities in most of these countries have been adjusting to dealing with a broadening range of stakeholders. The policy process associated with complex transport schemes has developed from being an exercise in top-down bureaucratic decision making into something more like an arena in which multiple and often conflicting voices are heard and – eventually and for the most part – reconciled. Historical case studies can analyse the cultural factors that play a crucial role in these projects: understanding the views of decision makers, the cultural background of stakeholders, and the dominant motives found among the more engaged parts of the general public. Unravelling the communicative processes used by stakeholders – power plays, prejudices, negotiation strategies, the use of trade-offs, feel-good factors, and the use of persuasive language – reveals a hidden historical reality that lingers on and thus has much relevance to present (and even future) transport policies. In this sense, historians can demonstrate the force of continuity, as well as the creative and disruptive impact of innovations and shifts. In this vein Divall has pleaded for a techno-cultural history of mobilities (Divall 2010b: 949).

Historians have unravelled numerous innovative processes that were successful precisely because they had an enduring impact on travellers' attitudes and preferences. The current attempts to persuade travellers to use sustainable transport systems may benefit from these success stories from the past. The history of bicycle use is a good example. German policy experts, for instance, studied Dutch bicycle policy practices and its impact on popular use, which has been deeply entrenched in Dutch culture, and are now successfully developing a bicycle infrastructure in the Land of Nordrhein-Westfalen (Ministerium für Bauen, Wohnen, Stadtentwicklung und Verkehr des Landes Nordrhein-Westfalen 2013). Recent research indicates that if bicycle facilities are integrated into the public-transport networks (bike parking, bike racks on buses and tramways, bike lanes), bicycling as well the use of public transport is boosted. Bicycle facilities have been introduced in at least six major American cities since 1995. To improve these facilities further, Dutch and Danish bicycle cultures have been studied by American experts (Pucher, Buehler 2009: 79–104). Thus while Marshall McLuhan's statement, 'Mass transportation is doomed to failure in North America because a person's car is the only place where he can be alone and think', was an appropriate description of American mobility practices in the 1960s, 40 years later a window of opportunity has been opened to public transport in a number of American cities. Using best practices from history may help open this window elsewhere, and keep it open.

Thus historians have a lot to offer to policy makers. However, strategic policy makers, and senior civil servants in general, do not have the opportunity to read books or extensive reports on history. The message will more likely be heard if it has been adapted and tailor-made for their consumption. Brief texts, short narratives, supplemented by hard-boiled facts, figures and diagrams will appeal more to the decision-maker's mind than detailed voluminous accounts. History has to be addressed to a focus group – to use a marketing concept – that scans rather than reads texts. Hence simulation games are potentially very attractive, as these provide decision-makers with realistic problems and dilemmas and challenge their management competences. Thus a new Rijkswaterstaat transport-history project (launched in 2012) on the development and entanglement of Dutch and Belgian transport and land-use planning policies since 1910 will offer a simulation game designed for policy makers in the Dutch ministry, produced in cooperation with Eindhoven University.

Conclusion

For a decade the Rijkswaterstaat has been exploring the potential for history learning, adding a new aspect to its commitment to the corporate past. Learning from the policy past has been applied to policy documents, by presenting historical analyses and long-term trends. Learning points have been shared in workshops with researchers and representatives from the Ministry. History modules have been adopted in training courses. So far support for the idea that learning from history in policy making (and in policy implementation) is sensible is increasing, but it is still not a common practice. Yet the concept of learning from history is gathering growing interest, not only in (strategic) niches of the administration but also in scholarly circles.

For about a decade the Groningen University's history department has been setting up postgraduate student seminars and projects in writing learning histories. An excellent example of their method is the learning-history project on Philips' major reorganisation and rationalisation, launched in 1990; the so-called Operation Centurion. The researchers looked at the role of the top and middle management of Philips during this major and turbulent change, focusing on the role the history of the organisation played in it. They analysed historical records and conducted interviews with former Philips top managers. The Groningen researchers conclude that many radical changes had been set in motion within the company, yet in the course of this process deeply embedded management concepts like Quality Management (QM) were rejuvenated. Indeed, precisely by making deliberate use of this historical element of Philips' corporate culture – the still widely accepted ideas and practices of QM, along with its concomitant bottom-up approach – top management had enabled fundamental organisational change (Karsten et al. 2009: 73–92).

The growing interest in 'applied' or 'usable' history is probably not a coincidence. It mirrors a widespread feeling of uncertainty in an era of unsettling globalisation, international financial crises and multicultural unrest. Not surprisingly, Dutch public confidence in economic modelling, which was unshaken until a decade ago, has been in sharp decline. History has no claims to general truths or shining mathematical models. Instead, it offers more modest tools: accurate and lucid accounts of complex processes and events that nevertheless provide fuller pictures of human behaviour than economic analyses, where the *homo economicus* and allegedly rational choices still dominate. An excellent example of economic-history learning has been provided by the Dutch Ministry of Finance, which in its 2010 budget outlook devoted two sections to financial crises in the 1930s and 1990s, drawing lessons from the similarities with and contrasts to the situation in 2008 (Ministry of Finance 2010: 3.2, 3.3). Unlike economists, historians are used to addressing uncertainty, whimsical aspects of reality and complex behavioural patterns, recognising irrationality and emotions as credible driving forces in explaining historical processes. Learning from history requires historians to use their scholarly skills to address today's urgent questions. When carving out pieces of the narrated past, historians may well provide fuller insights to policy makers, the media and the public, also germinating, hopefully, better solutions.

References

Abt, C. (1970). *Serious Games*. New York: The Viking Press.

Albert de la Bruhèze, A.A. and Veraart, F.C.A. (1999). *Fietsverkeer in praktijk en beleid in de twintigste eeuw*. Eindhoven: Stichting Historie der Techniek.

Blanken, I.J. (1999). *The Development of N.V. Philips' Gloeilampenfabrieken into a Major Electrical Group*. Zaltbommel: European Library.

Bosch, A. and van der Ham, W. (1998). *Twee eeuwen Rijkswaterstaat, 1798–199*
Zaltbommel: Europese Bibliotheek.

Divall, C. (2010a). Briefing note. Inaugural Workshop: Marketing and Branding In mobility UK Transport and Policy Network, National Railway Museum, York.

———— (2010b). Mobilizing the History of Technology. *Technology and Cultur* 51(4), pp. 938–60.

Filarski, R. (2004). *The Rise and Decline of Transport Systems*. Rotterdam Rijkswaterstaat.

———— (2011). The Emergence of the Bus Industry: Dutch Transport Polic during the Interwar Years. *Transfers* 1 (2), pp. 61–82.

Filarski, R. and Mom, G. (2008). *Van transport naar mobiliteit*. Zutphen: Walbur Pers.

———— (2011). *Shaping Transport Policy. Two Ages of Struggle between Publ and Private – A Comparative Perspective*. The Hague: SDU Uitgevers.

Heerding, A. (1986). *The History of N.V. Philips' Gloeilampenfabrieke* Cambridge: Cambridge University Press.

Hirsh, R.F. (2011). Historians of Technology in the Real World. Reflections on th Pursuit of Policy-Oriented History. *Technology and Cuture* 52(1), pp. 6–20.

Hoogerwerf, A. (1989). Het gebruik van geschiedenis in het beleidsproces. I *Geschiedenis buiten de perken, De waarde van de geschiedwetenschap vo andere wetenschappen, politiek en beleid en cultuur*, ed. J.W. ter Avest et a Leiden: Stichting Leidschrift, pp. 63–74.

Karsten, L., Keulen, S.J., Kroeze, D.B.R. and Peters, R.G.P. (2009). Leadershi Style and Entrepreneurial Change: The Centurion Operation at Philir Electronics. *Journal of Organisational Change Management* 22(1), pp. 73–9.

Kleiner, A. and Roth, G. (1997). How to Make Experience Your Company's Be Teacher. *Harvard Business Review* 75(5), pp. 172–7.

M en O (2006). Learning histories in leer- en veranderingstrajecten. *M en O* (3/4 pp. 85–97.

McKee, R. and Frywer, B. (2003). Storytelling That Moves People. *Harvar Business Review* 81(6), pp. 51–5.

Merriman, P. (2012). Britain and 'the Motorway Club': The Effect of Europea and North American Motorway Construction on Attitudes in Britain, 1930 1960. *Transfers* 2(1), pp. 106–33.

Michael, D.R. and Chen, S.L. (2006). *Serious Games: Games that Educate, Trai and Inform*. Boston: Thomson Course Technology PTR.

Ministerium für Bauen, Wohnen, Stadtentwicklung und Verkehr des Land Nordrhein-Westfalen. *Radverkehrsnetz NRW*. http://www.radverkehrsnet nrw.de. (accessed 4 May 2015).

Ministry of Finance (2010). *Miljoenennota*. The Hague: SDU Uitgevers.

Moraglio, M. (2012). European Models, Domestic Hesitance: The Renewal of th Italian Road Network in the 1920s. *Transfers* 2(1), pp. 87–105.

Neuhauser, P.C. (1993). *Corporate Legends and Lore, the Power of Storytelling a Management Tool*. New York: McGraw-Hill.

Neustadt, R.E. and May, E.R. (1986). *Thinking in Time: The Uses of History for Decision-Makers*. New York: Free Press / London: Collier Macmillan.

Pucher, J. and Buehler, R. (2009). Integrating Bicycling and Public Transport in North America. *Journal of Public Transportation* 12(3), pp. 79–104.

Raadschelders, J.C.N. (1994). Administrative History: Contents, Meaning and Usefulness. *International Review of Administrative Sciences* 60, pp. 117–29.

Rijkswaterstaat (2009). *Beheer- en Ontwikkelplan voor de Rijkswateren 2010–2015*. The Hague: Rijkswaterstaat.

Roth, G. and Art Kleiner, A. (1996). *Field Manual for the Learning Historian*. Boston: MIT Press.

Ryckewaert, M. (2012). Building a Hybrid Highway System: Road Infrastructure as an Instrument of Economic Urbanization in Belgium. *Transfers* 2(1), pp. 59–86.

Schein, E. (1992). *Organisational Culture and Leadership: A Dynamic View*. San Francisco: Jossey-Bass.

Thompson, G.L. (2011). Public Policy or Popular Demand? Why Californians Shifted from Trains to Autos (and Not Buses), 1910–1941. *Transfers* 1(2), pp. 105–29.

Toussaint, H.C. (2005). History as a Powerful Learning Instrument in the Search for Innovation. In *Organizing Innovation. New Approaches to Cultural Change and Intervention in Public Sector Organisations*, ed. M. Veenswijk. Amsterdam/Washington, DC: IOS Press, pp. 92–103.

———— (2008). *Scenariostudie RWS 2020: Historische achtergronden Ondernemingsplan 2004–2008*. The Hague: Rijkswaterstaat.

Weber, D. (2011). Road against Rail: The Debate on Transport Policy in Belgium, 1920–1940. *Transfers* 1(2), pp. 83–104.

van Zanden, J.L. Howarth, S. and Jonker, J. (2007). *Geschiedenis van Koninklijke Shell*. Amsterdam: Boom.

PART I
Mobility and Social Justice

Chapter 2

Structures of Disadvantage and Acts of Resistance: Remembering, Skilling, History and Gender

Frances Hodgson

The starting point for this analysis of walking, social networks and social interaction is similar to that of Willis (1977), in that there is a presumption that those participating in the study are skilled and knowledgeable both discursively and tacitly about their social activities, in this case, social interaction and walking. It is also informed by theories of the construction of gender and the importance of the public and the private' and embodiment in understanding that construction. Gendered space involves processes of exclusion and studies have shown women to be extremely skilled in the negotiation of space and articulate in expressing those processes (for example, Hanmer and Saunders 1984; Koskela 1997; Vesely and Gaarder 2004). This has led to the adoption of mobile methods in this research, and a focus on the skills, competencies and practices talked about and exhibited by both men and women while on walking interviews (and while encountering others). Willis (1977), in his work on schooling and the reproduction of patterns of inequality, shows the importance of co-presence for skilling together. One of the central practices in subverting the authority of the school is 'having a laff' and it is clear from Willis's account that 'having a laff' requires co-presence and a dexterous handling of a complex set of communication skills, social synchronicity skills, nuanced understanding of authority and the subverting of routines. 'Having a laff' in all its nuances can only be learnt from others; it is not formally taught in lessons. It is this understanding of an informal collective learning processes and the necessity of being co-present, to learn the roles together, to swap roles, to experience the rhythms of the humour; these all informed the prominence given to skilling and competence in this analysis. Grieco (1996) highlights the importance of collective skilling in her analysis of social networks and migration of hop-picking families from London to Kent and Hampshire in the early twentieth century. It is argued that:

> The key argument emerging from our investigation of hopping and the social organisation which surrounded it is that any discussion of skill training must engage with the issue of *natural training relationships*. Skill is more readily and reliably transmitted in a context where there are dense social networks.

> Dense social networks permit the repeated transmission of both the direct and background information necessary for the transmission of skill. The acquisition of skill inside the context of dense social networks enables training to take place with least disruption of performance. (Grieco 1996: 217, original emphasis)

In this context, practices of the use of public space and perceived entitlements to belong vary across different social communities. As Bauman argues in exploring time and space, 'the principal dimensions of the current evolution of urban life are a definition of community that features the creation of defensible enclaves restricted entry and access to public areas, the patrolling of borders and surveillance and a 'separation in lieu of the negotiation of life in common, rounded up by the criminalization of residual difference'. He argues that the greatest danger to public culture is the construction of public space as something to be fearful of 'The blood-curdling and nerve-breaking spectre of "unsafe streets" keeps people away from public spaces and turns them away from seeking the art and the skill needed to share public life' (Bauman 2000: 94). This chapter will argue that this can be illustrated if we consider the practices to build community, used in walking by both men and women. Understanding of the social construction of gender gives prominence to the appreciation of the constructions of 'public' and 'private' domains and the appropriate times and places for women in public space. Gendered space involves processes of exclusion. Studies in the UK (Hanmer and Saunders 1984; DfT 2009; Hodgson 2011), Finland (Koskela 1997) and the US (Duneier 1999; Wesely and Gaarder 2004) have shown women in particular to be extremely skilled in the negotiation of time-space.

The historical patterns of statutory underinvestment in walking provision and neglect of gender result in gendered patterns of temporal and spatial exclusion. Walking has held a place in the policy climate as a worthy aspect of transport policy, but not a particularly glamorous one. More recently walking particularly as part of the concept of 'active travel', has been promoted as part of the solution to reduce congestion; reduce environmental pollutants emitted by engines; improve the health of communities; and improve the social inclusion of various communities (DfT 2000, 2004; Middleton 2009). Policy practitioners are expected to reinforce the hierarchy of road users in which low-environmental impact modes are supposed to be actively promoted. Despite its acknowledged important policy position walking is underfunded compared to its position in the UK government's transport-planning hierarchy of road users. Despite travel behaviour being a traditional concern of transport research, the issue of gendered access to social resource in journeys, particularly when walking, and the issue of social networks and patterns of encounters upon journeys, has rarely been addressed. One implication of this is the under-problematising of social capital and resource in understanding travel; and within transport studies and policy making there is an over-reliance on the monetisation of travel benefits and disbenefits and a concomitant lack of knowledge about the social resources involved in travel and the positive aspects of travel (Mokhtarian, Salomon and Redmond 2001

Jain and Lyons 2008; Lyons and Urry 2005). Transport provision – the policies, implementations and management, singularly and in interaction with other sectors such as land use planning – impacts on an individual's, on social groups', and on a community's sense of belonging, identity and strategies for inclusion and access.

Method

The analysis presented here draws on two separate community studies conducted across a period of 26 years in 1981 and 2007 from one inner-city neighbourhood, and archived visual evidence to build a layered account of walking strategies and resistances to exclusion over almost a quarter of a century. The first community study was that of Hanmer and Saunders, the results of which were published in 1984. This community study interviewed women about their understandings of safety within a context of the 'Yorkshire Ripper'. The second study, part of a research project on methods,[1] interviewed 23 people, both men and women, whilst they were travelling around their neighbourhood. The neighbourhood areas involved in both studies overlap. Taking the accounts of walking provides evidence of competencies and strategies that men and women use to stay safe, and in particular evidence of women's individual and collective resistance to disadvantage through history. In remembering, documenting and archiving the social practices of women in this neglected area, this chapter contributes to a usable social history for transport planning and for women skilling, individually and collectively, to resist spatial and temporal patterns of exclusion.

Community Studies

Memory and Remembering: Collective Skill and Travel Competence

Remembering practices, events, people and paths and sharing experiences and ideas with others forms a collective skill. Memory and skills are not simply the properties of an individual or of the brain, they can be collectively held within a social network (Grieco 1996; Dijck 2004). Collective skill is a process and a product of memory, knowledge and performance interdependencies in a social group; it is a network process. Experiencing together is also skilling together and can result in new skills being taught, and when experiencing something similar again can result in the use of different skills, the adoption of different roles, the performance of different actions and even the swapping of roles within a social group or network. For example, consider the group of parents teaching the child to cross the road. The patient building of the skills and sharing of knowledge and communicating how to negotiate the traffic to the youngsters and swapping

---

1   Generated as part of the ESRC Connected Lives project, interviewer Andrew Clark.

of skills and strategies among the adult carers provides the framework for the learning of travel competences. This is the creation of a behavioural path enacted in a learnable environment and an example of collective memory. Skill development requires rehearsal, trust, and a relationship to the passage of time. The building up of skills together collectively as an informal practice necessarily requires synchronisation and the synchronisation of practice frameworks is an outcome of iterative opportunity and the property of proximity and duration. Through language and shared experience, including non-verbal communication, the rehearsal of appropriate practice can be achieved. Interdependencies of knowledge, quality of communication structures and processes of synchronisation are elements of skilling. However, the practice of sharing a memory is a renewal; a sharing and something that can be done both through the synchronisation of practice and as an asynchronous exchange.

In our qualitative study of community (2007), one participant, a male student, in response to being asked if there was anywhere he would avoid, gives details of how practices of 'being safe' and having locally relevant travelling competencies are passed on from one to another:

Interviewer:	Is it dangerous up there?
Participant:	Apparently, so I've heard. People getting mugged, raped and allsorts in XXXX.
Interviewer:	Do they?
Participant:	Yeah, apparently.
Interviewer:	Who told you this?
Participant:	I don't know, just the students, word of mouth around the student area. People seem to hear it and things like that. Yeah. That's where from really, just other students, present students.

(Participant #1, 2007)

The collective skilling and acts of remembering are passed on from student to student as a resource, and are articulated as a resource, that is, advice when passed on from students who have studied at the university longer than the newcomers is particularly a practice passed from the experienced student to the 'freshers'. It can also be seen as a process of asynchronous skilling. Student communities in England are characterised by moving into an unfamiliar area, an area or city they have not previously lived in. For this community, the ability to receive and to pass on strategies, practices and competencies that enable them to move around and engage with the area facilitate the quality of the time spent living there. As time living in an area for this community is usually restricted to 40 or 45 weeks of the year, depending on the remit of the housing tenancy agreement, one can surmise that collective skilling – a community of skills – can be an asset rather than having to learn all of the competencies oneself.

Remembering, Archiving and Distributed Practice

The development of the internet provides opportunities to archive as a social practice. Not simply as a way of 'keeping' things but with new social media it is possible to 'remember together'. One such example is the archive kept as part of Leeds City Libraries services, the Leodis photograph archive (Leeds City Council website), which allows people to upload and share photographic images of Leeds. It not only allows people to save and share images but also to remember collectively as they are able to comment on the photographs. A recent conversation thread about photographs of a local school has attracted a lot of comments whereby people have been recalling the names of children attending, discussions about the correct name of school teachers and the recollection of past notorious events. As well as the City Council's photographic archive, Leeds is the location for the Feminist Archive North, an ambitious project to attract women to curate and archive their own artefacts and recollections from the feminist movement. The principal characteristic of this archive is that this is the opportunity for people to curate their own recollections to build their own oral and written history with contemporaneous artefacts. Reclaim the Night, an international organisation active in London and many other British cities (Reclaim the Night website), is also a form of distributed memories as women offer their own recollections and photographs of participation in Reclaim the Night protests. These are constantly being added to and developed. Other less 'mediated' practices are those of Flickr and GoogleEarth in which the software packages offer the opportunity for people to geotag and geocache their experiences, images, photographs and videos.

'Vigilances': Reading Structures of Encounterability

'Vigilance' skills include those skills of spotting others and 'reading' the environment, and the danger-reduction skills of choosing paths that avoid pursuit, or of entering shops or pretending to be visiting a house and using the threshold as safe ground. Mobile phones have added to the strategies that can be used by allowing people who are not co-present to act as witness or as an escort while we are travelling. People are now able to call others when travelling to 'pull' them through areas where they feel unsafe or to send a signal that someone, albeit on the end of a phone, is acting as witness. There is need for more attention to be paid, particularly in the transport-policy environment, to the gendered nature of these strategies and skills, how they change according to age and with different experiences, and how they may alter with the development of internet, mobile communication technology and Web 2.0 (that is, user-generated content) technologies and applications. One relevant piece of research conducted in Leeds in 1981 (and reported in 1984) is the community violence study of Hanmer and Saunders (1984). Using qualitative interviews they concluded that:

Each woman works out, possibly only semi-consciously, the places, times and means governing her use of public space. For example, a woman may not feel able to use the local public open space, even during the day (except to walk across), unless someone is with her, who can be a child as well as another adult. (Hanmer and Saunders 1984: 65)

At the time of the survey, and particularly in Leeds, public violence and the fear of public stranger violence was prominent for women because the so-called 'Yorkshire Ripper', Peter Sutcliffe, was being sought for the successive murders of 13 women, due to the surrounding publicity, and not least because the police advice was for women to stay indoors at night. Hanmer and Saunders reported that:

The vast majority of women we interviewed were scared and were more frightened than usual of going out at night. Most said they had not always been frightened to do so. Over the previous year the majority of women had restricted their movements in a variety of ways. The most frequent was never walk alone, followed by changing their mode of transport. Women acquired bikes, cars, used public transport, including taxis, for the first time or more frequently, and women students used the university minibus service provided by the students union (this worked like a taxi service). When not going out alone if possible is combined with never doing so, 83 per cent of the women interviewed were restricted in this way. The 'Ripper' scare did not change behaviour for a substantial minority (18 per cent), however, as they were already not going out alone, or not at all, at night. (Hanmer and Saunders 1984: 45)

Women interviewed 26 years later reported similar experiences and strategies, particularly around skills of 'vigilances', and entitlements and expectations around night-time and day-time and spatial areas of exclusion. In 1981 a participant talking about her neighbourhood said:

I have been approached and followed by vagrants. You get a lot around here and they ask for money. I don't carry much on me so it's often true that I have none. But I put a pace on then. It happens quite frequently. If it were the other end of the day after they have been drinking I just would not go near somebody like that, but it's usually in the mornings around 8am. (Hanmer and Saunders 1984, Participant #37)

In 2007 a female participant in a discussion about feeling safe and routes to walk at night-time and day-time responded by detailing her diurnal and seasonal patterns of places she felt unsafe in and excluded from, and how she kept herself safe from unwelcome encounters by vigilances and avoidance:

Interviewer: Where else would you not go at night?
Participant: The tennis courts er – canal.
Interviewer: Right, why not?

Participant:	Er, a lot of people drink down there at night.
Interviewer:	Right.
Participant:	Er, and it just – it isn't a particularly nice area so –
Interviewer:	Yeah.
Participant:	I'll run home along the canal in summer.
Interviewer:	Yeah.
Participant:	And up till about October.
Interviewer:	Yeah.
Participant:	But then not really again at night time after work until March.
Interviewer:	Okay. Yeah.
Participant:	Er, because you'll see – and it's actually as soon as you get past the XXXX Gym.
Interviewer:	Yeah. The –
Participant:	There's like a little dark bit that's frequented by – I don't know, alkis, winos and kids that are always looking for fights. There's been a couple of ac- incidents down there when I have been started on.
Interviewer:	Right.
Participant:	So it's not really – although that was during the day [laughs].

(Participant #2, 2007)

In 2007 one of the female participants gave details of her vigilances competencies: 'Like before when you can go out down the street and you'd see a big group of kids where you'd have to, you'd, you'd turn and do another turn cos you scared of are you gonna get robbed, or …' (Participant #3, 2007).

Both participants detailed their strategies using speed and direction change to avoid pursuit. Travelling with others to scan less well known environments or environments which are regarded as more dangerous only appears in traditional transport studies in the more minimal form of an attention to the presence of 'escorts' on a journey, but the group organisation of journeys to improve personal security has been subject to less consideration and implementation development. For example, the use of a stretch limousine to transport young female drinkers between 'clubs' and home is a practice that is well known and well remarked upon in popular culture, but has little register in the world of transport studies where the travel and transport properties of the night-time economy have had less consideration.

The interview surveys undertaken in 1981 and 2007, and briefly reported here, highlight some of the skills women have used to ensure 'safe movement', and yet it is also clear that little is known about the household negotiation and inter-household coordination to provide escorts. In the course of the analysis of the 2007 dataset, Google Earth was used and it was discovered that on one map the site of the killing of a woman by Peter Sutcliffe has been archived. That one small icon on a map immediately reminded the author of a time of severe immobility. For those women and teenage girls (and this author is one of them),

living in Leeds at the time, there is a specific memory and legacy. These ar
memories of constrained mobility – a confinement to the house after dark an
a restricting of hitherto taken-for-granted freedoms of movement. There is
memory of developing different practices of escorting. If one visited a friend an
needed to go home then one would be watched over as one ran between house
across the back street, but as soon as the path took one out of the line of sight the
one would have to be escorted. This involved social synchronisation – escortin
each other or meeting with another so two could walk back together – or th
often socially embarrassing accompanied walk with a friend's father back hom
Telephones and mobile phones were not prevalent and could not be used a
checks of having arrived safely or as safety monitors during the short walks, an
physical co-presence had to be arranged between groups to ensure the level o
safety that was felt necessary. Of course there is also a story from the perspectiv
of the lone adult male walking the streets back from such an escorting journe
and the suspicion with which they are viewed.

Another memory or legacy was extraordinary acts of resistance, as individua
women argued that they should not be constrained, and enacted their resistance i
walking out alone, as Koskela argued:

> The fact that some women are bold and confident shows that women are not only
> passively experiencing space but actively take part in producing it. They reclaim
> space for themselves, not only through single occasions such as 'take back the
> night' marches, but through everyday practices and routinised uses of space.
> Their everyday spatial practices can be seen as practices of resistance. By daring
> to go out – by their very presence in urban sphere – women produce space that is
> more available for other women. Spatial confidence is a manifestation of power.
> Walking in the street can be seen as a political act: women 'write themselves
> onto the street'. (Koskela 1997: 316)

Women developed tactics and vigilances to stay safe: walking down the middle o
back street roads; walking against the flow of traffic making it harder for cars t
stop behind you; triangulating between groups of strangers to use them to 'watc
over' each other and bear witness; choosing paths with others; crossing over
another walker behind you; entering shops or knocking on doors if another wa
on the path behind you; avoiding dark spots and mouths of junctions, alleyway
and doors; keeping distance from garden walls and fences. There were also grou
acts as women banded together and marched demanding the right to walk i
the street. 'Vigilances' and collective skilling are somewhat interlinked. As ca
be seen from the discussion, vigilances can be practices of lone individuals o
collectives. The development of internet, mobile communication technology an
Web 2.0 technologies and the cultures of use around such technologies, offer th
potential to archive social practices. This potential allows us to become skilled b
developing new asynchronous practice frameworks.

Resistances

Women, argues Koskela (1997), engage in individual acts of resistance in their everyday activities as they continually make and re-make the spatial and temporal boundaries to their movements. Bold walking, she argues, is not anything spectacular or glamorous but simply women consciously or unconsciously, deliberately or unintentionally by their presence, pushing at the social mores of spatial and temporal boundaries that restrict women's movements. As well as individual practices, there are collective protests of resistance: in walking, one of the most persistent protests is the Reclaim the Night marches. The first of these in the UK was held in Leeds in 1977 and Al Garthwaite gives her personal account of organising this event with Sandra McNeil and others (Reclaimthenightleeds blog). This author was one of those who also marched on those first Reclaim the Night marches. It is thought the very first march was held in Germany in 1976. In Leeds the march had a particular significance as this was a period of around thirty six months during which Peter Sutcliffe murdered and attacked over 20 women. During this time (as mentioned above) a high-profile manhunt took place and the police advice to women was to remain indoors and only to travel outside if they were accompanied. Many women felt this was an unfair restriction on women and served to place the blame on the victims and women generally. To bring this up to date, a recently started protest in Canada, spreading throughout North America, is that of 'sluts walking' (Slutwalk Toronto website).

This has been a student-initiated march, and again is a resistance of the social mores surrounding women's walking and presence in the environment. The movement was initiated as a response to comments made to students at York University (Toronto, Canada) by a policeman from the Toronto police force in January 2011, when he said that women could help themselves avoid being assaulted by not dressing like sluts, thereby unintentionally echoing the advice given out to women by policemen in Leeds 35 years earlier.

Messages from Environment: Barriers, Boundaries and Bereft Spaces

We 'read' the environment, its form, its fabric, its history, the way it is being used to make decisions about the paths we want to make. Traffic can deter people from walking. Social isolation is one of the most commonly cited reasons why particular spaces are avoided. People prefer to walk with other people (Kelly et al. 2011; Hamilton et al. 2005; Crime Concern 2004). Where people are sparse they want to walk among the 'right' kind of other people, and where people are plentiful and of varied backgrounds, although not crowding, people are more secure. In this excerpt a female respondent tells us about entitlement to walk in a park.

Participant: ... I wouldn't actually come up here at night just because I'm
                 not familiar with it.
Interviewer: What do you mean you're not familiar?
Participant: I'm not familiar enough to know whether or not it is safe.

                                                              (Participant #2, 2007)

These messages from the environment vary according to daylight and dark. Some of the least unattractive spaces are those that are dark, for example, parks, alleys, doorways, bus shelters, the mouths of side streets, gaps between buildings, hedgerows and undergrowth alongside footpaths. We found that dark affected both women and men, as this (male) participant says: 'It's dark, no light. The lighting is the key thing' (Participant #1, 2007).

A (female) participant explains how the seasonal patterns affect her movement:

Participant: I'll run home along the canal in summer.
Interviewer: Yeah.
Participant: And up till about October.
Interviewer: Yeah.
Participant: But then not really again at night time after work until March.
Interviewer: Anywhere else where you wouldn't go?
Participant: Er, I wouldn't necessarily walk home from town late at night
                 after about nine, or half nine but up till then I would.

                                                              (Participant #2, 2007)

*Social Expectations on the Journey and Journeying: The Entitlement to
Communication on Journeys*

As well as competencies of 'facework', as described by Goffman (1959) and the social synchronicity of the body in encounters, there are skills associated with negotiating 'the entitlement to talk'. There are strategies and competencies associated with the initiating and concluding of a discussion and an encounter, and these can vary according to different types of encounters. The creation of the opportunity to talk and to be acknowledged, and the skill of being able to repeat that opportunity using different daily rhythms and spaces, are key strategies. The repetition of the exchange is important for changing strangers into familiar faces and changing oneself into a familiar face to others, for creating a history. It is important for understanding the processes of 'belonging', of developing 'community', of developing social networks around your residence and of developing identity.

The opening or closing of the encounter; the prolonging and sustaining of the encounter to become something more; a more significant relationship that might make you feel good; or a relationship that makes you feel like you belong; that you have a history in the neighbourhood or that you have some influence or a part to play; or a relationship that you can turn to in an emergency are all significant elements in the practice of travelling and creating social networks. To turn strangers into familiar faces, members of the community, and to turn oneself into a member of the community are important travel competencies and strategies. During the walking interviews one of the female participants negotiated an encounter. This is a routine encounter, one that she negotiates frequently and its reproduction here gives us an opportunity to see the skills and competencies involved in negotiating the entitlement to talk:

Participant:	That's my sweetie run a homeless man looking at me [Participant laughs and waves at a man over the road]
Interviewer:	Why are you waving at that man?
Participant:	Because he's the local alcoholic. [laughs] It's the guy that buys white wine and sits outside and chats to everyone
Interviewer:	Where does he sit?
Participant:	It's on that wall.
Interviewer:	What's his name?
Participant:	I've no idea.
Interviewer:	Okay.
Participant:	He's waving but sometimes; he waved at me first actually but he sometimes follows you up the way.
Interviewer:	Right, and does that worry you?
Participant:	[laughs] No, he is harmless enough. No, he is absolutely harmless.
Interviewer:	Right, but do you always wave at him?
Participant:	If he waves first, you do or say hello.
Interviewer:	If he waves first.
Participant:	Yeah.
Interviewer:	Why won't you wave first?
Participant:	Because then you will get followed up the road er –
Interviewer:	Whereas if he waves first he won't
Participant:	No, you're walking past. If you wave first he'll come across and say what do you want?
Interviewer:	Oh will he?
Participant:	Not in a bad way.

(Participant #2, 2007)

This exchange illustrates some of the skills and practices of negotiating encounters necessary to ensure a safe journey. This was a female participant who articulated and demonstrated her own understanding and clear rules of exchange and entitlement during this mobile interview. She has developed a set of practices to manage the encounter and ensure that the relationship is not developed further and that she can continue to use that service and that walking route. This is something also found in a study of a sidewalk area in Greenwich Village by Duneier (1999) in which he detailed how encounters can be abused by men transcending social norms of exchanges forcing women into being rude (ignoring them) or uncivil (responding negatively).

Another female participant, a long-standing resident of the area, articulated the importance of familiarity, and the social mores the participant has about contact, encounters and speaking with others in response to a question about why there is community: 'I can't say that with everybody. But if I come out my house and I see you more than once I go hiya, you alright?' (Participant #6, 2007). This participant goes on to describe what community means to her:

> And like I say, I just, type of person probably I've been, if I was to come down here now and see a group of lads, some little fight going on, I'd be opening my big gob and saying, oi, what you doing? Come on, don't be like that, so, I, I involve myself in trying to erm, make community. But that isn't just me, there's lots of other people like that in the area.
>
> And to articulate the sense of entitlement they feel about making community: Just say hi to everybody. And I think that's the way it should be. And when I talk to people, and we say, same thing, it costs nothing. It's a God given gift that we've got, a free gift, and why should you not feel able to say hello to somebody? (Participant #6, 2007)

Another participant, a male student, was asked if there is much community around his house: 'Erm, yeah I think so but, we don' experience much of it' (Participant #1, 2007). The participant then elaborated and in doing so pointed to the importance of the iterative opportunities to be seen and to see others, as well as the importance of being able to negotiate the encounter to make community or friends or fewer strangers:

> I think in the summer there might be because people are out and about then. Well, I say summer, I'm usually here til the end of June, start of July. That's when I'm thinking, when all the exams are on. I came here before we moved in, just to have a look. I guess to see what the community looked like, before we moved in. and there were people barbequing on their front walls, here, like that. And I thought that was quite nice. (Participant #1, 2007)

The participant goes on to say: 'and I'd like to do that and I think that'd be a chance for us to get to know more people on the road probably' (Participant #1, 2007); and in response to being asked why he would like to know more people on the road, he says: 'I feel a bit. I don't know. When I walk out of the house and there are people across the road, you know, getting into their cars or coming out of the house as well. I sometimes feel as if I should say hello to them because I live opposite'. In response to further prompting the participant described how he negotiates the encounter and the entitlement to initiate contact:

Participant: Sometimes I look to, you know, I look to give them a smile or
                 something. Just to acknowledge them, because they've seen me

come out of the house. And I think maybe they might do the same thing, you know.

Interviewer: And do they smile back?

Participant: Sometimes, occasionally, yeah. And sometimes they do what they are doing and (inaudible) and sometimes I don't if they're purposefully don't look back. Sometimes I don't look if I'm not in the mood.

(Participant #1, 2007)

The respondent then goes on to elaborate the strategies he and housemates use to create geographies of opportunity to be seen and encounter others. They sit out on chairs, choosing the front of the house even though it has only a small garden rather than at the back of the house.

Interviewer: You prefer to sit out the front?

Participant: Yeah, I prefer to sit out here because of the sun. I guess it's the social thing as well; there are a lot of people walking up and down. Like I said earlier you give people like a nod or a smile as they walk past.

Interviewer: And you like that?

Participant: Yeah, I do. You should be friendly to people and get a response.

(Participant #1, 2007)

Another female participant articulated the development of a relationship between strangers living in the same street that turned into a resource. In response to questions about her neighbours she started by saying it has taken her six months to get to know her neighbours, and then she articulated how encounters built to a relationship.

Interviewer: How come it's taken six months?

Participant: Well we did, it sort of starts off with hello and then it's more of a talk every, each time we see each other it builds up (oh okay) into a chat I'd say that's why and now.

Interviewer: And now you are at chatting stage?

Participant: Well now because I came back the other night and I was locked out, I knocked on the door like oh! And asked if I could erm come in for a bit while I was waiting for my boyfriend Tom to get back (yes) and they said yes and then we chatted and they gave me some tea and so they're kind of …

(Participant #7, 2007)

These excerpts illustrate the importance of strategies of 'being seen' in creating social networks and a sense of community focused around a specific area of residence. They also illustrate strategies that people adopt to create geographies and temporal opportunities to create encounters and develop relational resources. Participant #1, who was a student, showed how the academic year and the expectation of leaving a residence in the summer can alter the character of the geography of opportunity, and Participant #7, in particular, illustrated the length of time, from their experience, that it takes to develop the relationship. This participant also went on to argue that there was a link between a feeling of belonging and permanence. They argued that they wanted to buy their own home to be able to signal to others and to self that they were permanently based in an area. They saw temporary residency as a barrier to belonging and community in the neighbourhood.

There are also other elements to the geographies of opportunity offered by the provision of services in an area, places to meet and encounter others such as pubs, paths, parks, shops and bus stops. Some of the women interviewed (this was not articulated by the men interviewed) said they did not feel entitled to enter some public spaces, particularly pubs. This echoes similar findings and analyses of the gendered nature of public space, and the views expressed earlier in this article on strategies of vigilance. One of the student participants articulated a vulnerability and a worry that some people did not like students, and this affected how they would enter public spaces that they perceived were not part of the 'student areas'. This analysis has focused on the data generated as part of the walking interview undertaken some eight years ago, and in those interviews electronic adjacency and skills, strategies and competencies associated with the internet and Web 2. applications did not really arise.

Conclusion

Resistance to spatial and temporal exclusions is shown in the skills and competencies of walking evidenced in the analysis of individuals on walking trips, in the collective protest of the Reclaim the Night marches, and in the more recent 'slutwalking' marches of North America. The chapter has used evidence from both men and women about the skills they use to walk and to stay safe. Web 2.0-based technological developments offer opportunities to develop new archiving practices and for those social groups that experience inequality they offer the opportunity to engage and remember collectively, and to use those memories to challenge and change inequalities in walking practices. User-generated content archives such as the Feminist Archive North, archiving social practice, offer evidence of material challenges and resistances to the injustice of spatial and temporal exclusion in walking as experienced by women. In remembering, documenting and archiving social practice of walking, and particularly highlighting women's practices of walking, this chapter contributes to a usable social history for transport planning and for women skilling, individually and collectively, to resist spatial and temporal patterns of exclusion. This chapter offers an understanding of connectivity through a focus on sociality and time-spaces. It develops an analysis of social practices competencies and the social capital inherent in walking to highlight processes of social reproduction and change that recognise an individual's agency and power. This has implications for transport as a policy activity, and underlines the necessity of recognising that there is an interaction between who walks, who has opportunity to (or not to) walk, and public provision and investment in walking. The organisation of time-space has different contours for different communities but persistent patterns over time. Finally, the interaction of user-generated content and the practices of remembering collectively offered by archiving and Web 2.0 applications have implications for civic participation, governance and provision. It presents the opportunity for groups to act together to overcome and resist historic policy inequalities and engage in the act of provision of safe transport infrastructure.

References

Bauman, Z. (2000). *Liquid Modernity*. Cambridge: Polity.

Crime Concern (2004). *People's Perceptions of Personal Security and Their Concerns about Crime on Public Transport*. London: Department for Transport. Available at: webarchive.nationalarchives.gov.uk/20121107103953/http://www.dft.gov.uk/pgr/crime/ps/perceptions/researchfindings (accessed 14 May 2015).

DfT (Department for Transport) (2000). *Encouraging Walking: Advice to Local Authorities*. London: The Stationery Office.

——— (2004). *Walking and Cycling: An Action Plan*. London: The Stationery Office.

Dijck, J. van (2004). Memory Matters in the Digital Age. *Configurations* 12(3), pp. 349–73.

DoT (Department of Transport) (2009). *Passengers' Perceptions of Personal Security on Public Transport – Qualitative Research Report*. Report for the Department of Transport, London. Available at: http://webarchive.nationalarchives.gov.uk/20110130095432/http://dft.gov.uk/pgr/crime/personalsecurity/passengerperceptionssecurity/ (accessed 14 May 2015).

Duneier, M. (1999). *Sidewalk*. New York: Farrar, Strauss and Giroux.

Goffman, E. (1959). *The Presentation of Self in Everyday Life*. Garden City, NY: Doubleday.

Grieco, M. (1996). *Workers' Dilemmas: Recruitment, Reliability and Repeated Exchange – Analysis of Urban Social Networks and Labour Circulation*. London: Routledge: London.

Hamilton, K., Jenkins, L., Hodgson, F. and Turner, J. (2005). *Promoting Gender Equality in Transport, Working Paper 34*. London: Equal Opportunities Commission. Available at: http://www.ssatp.org/sites/ssatp/files/publications/HTML/Gender-RG/Source%20%20documents/Technical%20Reports/Gender%20and%20Transport/TEGT2%20Promoting%20gender%20equality%20in%20transport%20UK%202005.pdf (accessed 14 May 2015).

Hanmer, J. and Saunders, S. (1984). *Well Founded Fear: A Community Study of Violence to Women.* London: Hutchinson in association with The Explorations in Feminism Collective.

Hannam, K., Sheller, M. and Urry, J. (2006). Mobilities, Immobilities and Moorings. *Mobilities* 1(1), pp. 1–22.

Hodgson, F.C. (2011). Structures of Encounterability: Space, Place, Paths and Identities. In *Mobilities: New Perspectives on Transport and Society*, ed. M. Grieco and J. Urry. Farnham: Ashgate, pp. 41–64.

Jain, J. and Lyons, G. (2008). The Gift of Travel Time. *Journal of Transport Geography* 16, pp. 81–9.

Kelly, C., Tight, M., Hodgson, F. and Page, M. (2011). A Comparison of Three Methods for Assessing the Walkability of the Pedestrian Environment. *Journal of Transport Geography* 19, pp. 1500–508.

Koskela, H. (1997). Bold Walk and Breakings: Women's Spatial Confidence Versus Fear of Violence. *Gender, Place and Culture* 4(3), pp. 301–20.

Lyons, G. and Urry, J. (2005). Travel Time Use in the Information Age. *Transportation Research Part A* 39, pp. 257–76.

Middleton, J. (2009). 'Stepping in Time': Walking, Time, and Space in the City. *Environment and Planning A* 41, pp. 1943–61.

Mokhtarian, P., Salomon, I. and Redmond, L. (2001). Understanding the Demand for Travel: It's Not Purely 'Derived'. *Innovation* 14(4), pp. 355–80.

Turner, J., Holmes, L. and Hodgson, F. (2000). Intelligent Urban Development: An Introduction to a Participatory Approach. *Urban Studies* 37(10), pp. 1723–34.

Urry, J. (2008). *Mobilities.* Cambridge: Polity.

Wesely, J. and Gaarder, E. (2004). The Gendered 'Nature' of the Urban Outdoors: Women Negotiating Fear of Violence. *Gender and Society* 18(5), pp. 645–63.

Willis, P. (1977). *Learning to Labour.* Aldershot: Gower.

Websites

Leeds City Council. www.leeds.gov.uk.

Reclaim the Night. http://www.reclaimthenight.co.uk/why.html.

Reclaimthenightleeds blog. https://reclaimthenightleeds.wordpress.com/rtn-leeds-history/.

Slutwalk Toronto. http://www.slutwalktoronto.com/.

(All accessed 14 May 2015)

Chapter 3

Balancing Social Justice and Environmental Justice: Mobility Inequalities in Britain Since circa 1900

Colin Pooley

The production of societies and economies that embody principles of both social and environmental justice is an almost un-contestable aspiration, but agreement on how such goals might be met is often illusory. Achieving both social and environmental justice in transport and mobility seems particularly difficult as, in some respects at least, the two concepts conflict with each other. Thus while much of the literature on social exclusion in transport focuses on the need to improve access for all to the dominant transport modes, issues of environmental justice might argue for restrictions on personal mobility to reduce vehicle emissions. Clearly, any restrictions that operate through a price mechanism run the risk of increasing rather than decreasing mobility-related social exclusion and thus of contravening principles of social justice (Hine 2003, 2012; Lucas 2006, 2012; Preston and Raje 2007; Preston 2009). This chapter, first, explores the concepts of mobility-related environmental and social justice in more detail, focusing especially on the ways in which these concepts may be applied to short trips in urban areas over approximately the last century, and, second, develops an argument that at various points in the twentieth century there were opportunities to produce a transport infrastructure that delivered more socially and environmentally just patterns of everyday mobility, but that such opportunities were lost as subsequent decisions reinforced existing mobility inequalities. This chapter focuses on two specific forms of urban transport: trams and bicycles. In each case it examines the paradoxes that concepts of social and environmental justice present, assesses the historical context in which each has developed, and argues that alternative paths that would have delivered greater social and environmental justice were possible. In conclusion, the chapter outlines a policy framework that might avoid such opportunities being missed in the future, thus ensuring that present-day planning learns from past experience.

Mobility-Related Environmental and Social Justice

Environmental justice is not straightforward to define and has evolved significantly since it developed as a concept in the US in the 1980s. The origins of the concept of environmental justice, and its theoretical and empirical underpinnings, are explored in a number of extensive reviews (Agyeman and Evans 2004; Walker and Bulkeley 2006; Walker 2009). Agyeman and Evans (2004: 156) cite the Commonwealth of Massachusetts definition of environmental justice:

> Environmental justice is based on the principle that all people have a right to be protected and to live in and enjoy a clean and healthful environment. Environmental justice is the equal protection and meaningful involvement of all people with respect to the development, implementation and enforcement of environmental laws, regulations and policies and the equitable distribution of environmental benefit.

They argue that this has the advantage of combining 'procedural' and 'substantive' aspects while also stressing the need for equitable distribution of resources. In a more recent paper, Walker (2009) focuses especially on the spatial aspects of environmental justice, arguing for a pluralistic approach to both the definition of and theoretical underpinnings for the analysis of environmental justice.

Relatively few papers focus explicitly on the environmental justice implications of transport and mobility (though many more include transport-related issues briefly or implicitly), but the topic is explored most fully in the context of the unequal distribution of vehicle-related emissions (Mitchell and Dorling 2003; Buzzelli et al. 2004; Pearce et al. 2006; Harvard et al. 2009). All studies demonstrate clearly that the environmental impacts of vehicle exhaust emissions are unequally distributed with strong socio-economic gradients, and with those who produce the least pollution themselves often suffering the worst consequences of pollution produced by others. In turn, this is displayed in differential mortality and morbidity rates across urban populations. At the city level there are many other negative consequences of vehicle use that are felt disproportionately in particular locations and, most usually, by the poorest and most vulnerable in society. This is the case not only with regard to road traffic accidents (Azetsop 2010) where children are particularly vulnerable (Hillman et al. 1990), but also with respect to noise pollution and the negative impacts that traffic congestion has on the urban environment and the health of urban residents (Davies et al. 2009; Barregard et al. 2009; Selander et al. 2009). Environmental justice implications of motor vehicle use also have global ramifications. Some 25 per cent of the UK's greenhouse-gas emissions come from the transport sector with road transport accounting for 70 per cent of transport-related emissions (European Commission, 2009). While other forms of transport (air, rail, ships) all contribute towards greenhouse-gas emissions, motor vehicles (located overwhelming in the richest countries of the world) thus make a significant

contribution to global climate change with the consequences felt most severely
in some of the poorest nations (Parry et al. 2007). Application of environmental
justice principles at both the global and local scales would lead to the restriction
of motor vehicle use and/or the reduction of harmful emissions from vehicles.

There is an extensive literature on the social justice implications of mobility
and everyday travel, mostly focusing on concepts of social exclusion. One widely
used definition is that:

> Social exclusion is a complex and multi-dimensional process. It involves the
> lack or denial of resources, rights, goods and services, and the inability to
> participate in the normal relationships and activities, available to the majority
> of people in a society, whether in economic, social, cultural or political arenas.
> It affects both the quality of life of individuals and the equity and cohesion of
> society as a whole. (Levitas et al. 2007: 9)

In the context of everyday transport it is interpreted primarily as those people
who are unable to travel freely (due to poverty, disability and/or poor access to
public transport) to such an extent that it impairs their ability to participate fully
in the economic, social and political life of their community. It may restrict access
to work and education, reduce interaction with friends and family, and lead to
limited choice of food sources, thus impacting upon diet and health (Hine and
Mitchel 2003; Lucas 2004, 2012; Preston and Raje 2007; Lucas and Stanley 2009;
Cerin et al. 2009). It includes the concept of 'forced car use' where due to (often
rural) inaccessibility those on low incomes are forced to own a car to carry out
everyday tasks when they can ill-afford to do so, thus impacting on their ability to
allocate money to other activities (Currie and Sensberg 2007; Currie et al. 2009;
Johnson et al. 2010; Shergold and Parkhurst 2012). Policy responses to such issues
in developed countries are usually framed in terms of both providing improved
public transport and ensuring that all those who need to do so are able to access the
dominant mode of everyday travel: the motor car. Thus Lucas (2006: 808) argues
that pricing policies to reduce car use are 'undesirable within a society that aims
to promote social progress for all sectors of society' and that they could 'force
people into inactivity and disengagement from society'. The extent to which car
use is deemed essential for most people in twenty-first-century Britain has also
been underlined by the recent Joseph Rowntree Foundation report on minimum
acceptable income levels, which, for the first time, considered car ownership to
be an essential requirement for families outside London (Davis et al. 2012). In
this sense policies to counter transport-related social exclusion could be seen to
be incompatible with those used to promote both global and local environmental
justice, though Kenyon et al. (2002) counter this to some degree in their exploration
of virtual mobility solutions to social exclusion, and Stanley and Vella-Brodrick
(2009) argue that current conceptions of social exclusion as applied to transport
are too narrowly focused.

Such issues have rarely been directly tackled in an historical context; though there has been some research on the health and (by implication) environmenta justice implications of factors such as urban air quality and road traffic accidents For instance, in a US context the dominant role of the automobile in America culture and urban structure has received extensive attention (Frost 2001 Schrag 2004; Blanke 2007; Ladd 2009), and in the UK Luckin has provided detailed examination of a range of accidents and other problems within an urba context, including the impact of road traffic accidents in the interwar years and th response of urban authorities (Luckin 1993; Cooter and Luckin 1997; Luckin an Sheen 2009). The role of sound in the urban environment, including problems c noise pollution, has also received limited attention (Garroch 2003; Payer 2007) while Ishaque and Noland (2005) review the historical development of pedestria facilities in Britain, emphasising their marginalisation within urban road space However, most such papers focus mainly on the institutional and regulatory issue raised in the context of urban areas, and rarely explicitly link pollution or nois caused by traffic (or other sources) to social and environmental justice. Thi chapter examines the twin issues of environmental and social justice in the contex of key moments of change in urban transport policy in the mid-twentieth century and suggests implications for twenty-first-century policy formation. I argue tha better understanding of past processes can usefully inform current practices i transport policy.

Sources of Evidence

Evidence discussed in this chapter is drawn from three research projects o different aspects of everyday mobility in the past and the present.[1] For fu details see Pooley et al. (2005), Pooley and Turnbull (2000, 2005) and Poole et al. (2013). This section provides a very brief overview of methods and dat sources. Full details are provided in the relevant publications. Data on trave to and from work in the twentieth century were collected in two ways. Firs existing contacts with family historians and genealogists were used to collec data on 12,439 individual journeys to work reconstructed from life histories c people living in all parts of Britain and who began work after 1890. Secon more detailed information was collected through 90 in-depth interviews wit respondents living in three cities (London, Manchester and Glasgow) and wh (mostly) began work in the period 1930–50. These data were used to construc both quantitative and qualitative profiles of changes in the journey to work ove the twentieth century. A follow-on project focused specifically on the everyda travel of children in the second half of the twentieth century. Data were collecte

---

1   'The Journey to Work in Twentieth-Century Britain', funded by The Leverhulm Trust, 1996–99; 'Changing Patterns of Everyday Mobility', funded by the ESRC, 2000–0 and 'Understanding Walking and Cycling', funded by EPSRC, 2008–11.

from in-depth life-history interviews with four cohorts of respondents: those born 1932–41, 1962–71, 1983–84 and 1990–91. In each case respondents were asked to reconstruct their everyday mobility at ages 11, 17/18, mid-30s and mid-60s as appropriate. In total 156 interviews were conducted with respondents in Manchester and Lancaster. Using these data it was possible to examine changes in the everyday mobility of children from the 1940s to the present. The third project used a multi-method approach to examine the ways in which household decisions about everyday travel for short trips in urban areas are made in the twenty-first century. Attention was focused especially on the practices of walking and cycling with respondents drawn from four case study towns: Leeds, Leicester, Worcester and Lancaster. Data were collected through a large-scale questionnaire survey, spatial analysis of land use and of the permeability of the urban areas and, especially, via in-depth interviews whilst walking and cycling, household interviews and ethnographies. This rich data set has revealed the complexities and contingencies involved in decision making for everyday travel, and it has allowed the formulation of policy recommendations to promote more sustainable travel in urban areas. In this chapter data generated from these projects (and focusing particularly on the city of Manchester, UK) are drawn on selectively to provide evidence to support the core argument about persistent inequalities in the provision of transport infrastructure in Britain over the twentieth century.

The Tram: A Ubiquitous and Accessible Form of Public Transport

> Well, there was only one way in those days and that was by tram which was excellent, ... there was one along every ten minutes into the city centre. A very good service. (R04, Manchester, male, 1930s)

> I mean the trams were very very frequent, all from Altrincham through to Manchester. I mean it was a tremendous tram service. There was one every two to three minutes. (R14, Manchester, male, 1930s)

In the first half of the twentieth century the tram provided a relatively cheap and convenient form of mass public transport in many British towns and cities. In this chapter it is argued that large-scale provision of urban public transport by tram came nearer to meeting the needs of both social and environmental justice in transport provision than most other forms of urban public transport. The tram was convenient, in that many cities had a dense network of lines that linked residential areas to workplaces; it was affordable by all but the very poor; it was used by both men and women and by people of all ages; and twentieth-century electric trams were relatively environmentally friendly, producing minimum pollution in the urban environment, though there were, of course, emissions from electricity generating stations together with noise pollution from the trams themselves.

Evidence from a case study of Manchester is used to briefly substantiate some of these points. Manchester Corporation ran one of the densest networks of tramlines in any British city in the early twentieth century, with by 1926 some 258 miles of track on which ran 892 tram cars and carrying 318 million passenger journeys in 1926 (Manchester Corporation Tramways Department 1902–28). The Manchester trams were well integrated with the network in the neighbouring authority of Salford so that travellers could move easily around the whole conurbation, and there was a particularly extensive network of suburban lines linking the city centre to suburban industrial and residential areas (Simon 1938; Gray 1967; Frangopulo 1977). Thus, in the early twentieth century, the development of the tram transformed Manchester (and many other cities) from an environment in which all but the wealthy walked to most destinations to one in which mass public transport was available to the majority of the population. If principles of both environmental and social justice had been applied to public transport provision in Manchester in the 1930s then the tram network would have been maintained and extended. Instead, annual passenger journeys fell from their 1926 peak of 318 million to 201 million a decade later and just 89 million in 1946, and trams ceased running in Manchester in 1949 until the reintroduction of a (limited) modern light-rail network in 1992 (Manchester Transport Department Annual Reports (MCTranspD) 1928–46; Knowles 1996). Why was this opportunity to continue to provide relatively equitable transport around the city missed?

As in many other British cities, from the 1930s the Manchester trams were increasingly marginalised by road transport in the form of both the motor bus and the private car. As early as 1929 Manchester Corporation began to replace some tram routes with motor buses (prior to that although the corporation had run some motor buses they had been seen as secondary to the tram network), and in the year 1930–31 some 39 miles of tram route were converted to motor bus operation. By 1941 64.6 per cent of passengers on Manchester Corporation's public transport system travelled by motor bus with just 23.9 per cent travelling by tram and a further 11.5 per cent on the newly-introduced trolley buses (MCTranspD 1931–41). There were multiple motivations for this change. First, although private car ownership was still low, motorised transport (whether private or public) was increasingly seen as the future. It was appropriate for a modern city whereas trams were seen as old fashioned and contrary to the spirit of change that existed in the 1930s. Second, trams were seen as causing traffic congestion because they travelled on fixed routes and thus obstructed motorised vehicles, thus slowing traffic flow. Private motorists objected to trams on these grounds and Manchester Corporation viewed the motor bus as more flexible and better able to provide services to new suburban estates. This was expressed especially forcefully in the Manchester press by the chairman of Manchester's traffic congestion committee following the failure of a new traffic management scheme: 'If there was any failure in the scheme today it seems that it was due to tram cars. We should all like to rid ourselves of tram cars, but it will take time' (Manchester Evening News 1938). Third, from the perspective of Manchester Corporation, motor buses were cheaper, both because they did not require the infrastructure of a fixed route (particularly important with the provision of new suburban routes where motor buses could run on existing roads), and because the Corporation felt it could legitimately charge higher fares for motor buses than for trams (which had traditionally been subsidised) because they offered a more modern form of transport (Clay and Brady 1937/38; Bruton 1927; MCTranspD 1935, Simon and Inman 1935; Eyre 1971; MCTranspD 1931–41).

Although most respondents in Manchester spoke enthusiastically about the tram service in the 1930s (as evidenced by the quotes at the start of this section), there were some people for whom the tram was inconvenient because they lived far from a route, and one respondent compared trams unfavourably to trolley buses because of their noise: 'The trams were always a bit rattly, ... they had trolley buses after the ... trams, and they were much quieter' (R24, Manchester, male, 1940s). Most travellers also transferred their journeys from the tram to motor buses relatively easily so that by 1950 the Manchester bus network was carrying 417 million passenger journeys, some 30 per cent more than the trams carried in 1926. Thus there is little evidence that the switch from trams to motor buses as the main means of mass public transport in Manchester excluded large numbers of people, though fares did increase, but the significance of the change lies more in the associated social and cultural assumptions that motor vehicles were superior to the tram, thus reinforcing the growing path-dependent movement towards a society dominated by the automobile. In other words, the move from tram to motor bus was one of a number of factors that privileged motor vehicles and thus, it can be argued, also encouraged increased use of the private car. These changes to public transport in Manchester can therefore be seen as part of a wider process that marginalised non-car users, increased inequalities in access to transport, and produced significant negative environmental effects in urban areas. Despite the introduction of a light-rail system to Manchester in 1992, and recent extensions which enable up to 90,000 passenger journeys daily on the network (Transport for Greater Manchester, Metrolink, website), the modern tram network by no means replaces that which existed in Manchester in the 1920s.

Cycling as Mass Urban Transport

Well it [cycling] was really the only way. Cause there was such a tremendous detour using public transport and walking that, well the time factor ... (R14, Manchester, male, 1930s)

Used the cycle. For leisure as well, but it was very handy going into town when the/ well money was short for a start ... so going by bike was very much cheaper. Save all the bus fares. ... Yes, you've got freedom on a bike. You can go when you want and the speed you want. Admitted it was a bit difficult when it was pouring down with rain, but I had a cape and sou'wester. (R24, Manchester, male, 1930s/40s)

In terms of environmental justice cycling is an almost perfect means of transport: it produces no pollution at the point of use (though a full life-cycle analysis should incorporate the environmental costs of manufacture and disposal of bicycles), and compared to other forms of transport it produces few negative externalities (though conflicts with pedestrians in shared space are not negligible). Cycle enthusiast might also claim that cycling meets principles of social justice, and the CTC (the UK's national cyclists' organisation) states its aim as: 'Making cycling enjoyable, safe and welcoming for all' (CTC website). Although entry costs are certainly lower than for driving (though by no means negligible), and cycling saves on bus or tram fares, cycling does required both a level of physical fitness that not all people have, together with the confidence to cycle on busy urban roads. In this sense, it can be argued that cycling provides a less inclusive means of travel than cheap and frequent public transport such as the tram system of the 1920s. Certainly, levels of cycling in Britain today indicate that travelling by bike is not perceived by most people as a viable option as nationally only 2 per cent of trips are undertaken in this way (National Travel Survey 2013). However, in much of continental Europe (especially the Netherlands, Belgium, Germany and Scandinavia) bicycle use in urban areas is very much higher (Pucher and Buehler 2008), and in Britain in the 1930s and 1940s levels of cycling, amongst men, at least, reached a level where it could be argued that the bike provided a form a mass transport that met at least some of the principles of environmental and social justice. Using a range of examples the experience of cycling in the mid-twentieth century is now explored with a view to identifying opportunities for developing cycling as a an environmentally and socially just form of mass travel in twenty-first-century Britain.

Nationally over 20 per cent of all journeys to work undertaken by men in the 1930s and 40s were by bike, and during these decades cycling was the single most important means of travelling to work for men. Women were less likely to cycle than men but even so approximately 10 per cent of journeys to work by women were by bicycle in this period. Overall, in Manchester 16.3 per cent of all journeys to work (by men and women) were by bike in the period 1920–39, and 18.6 per cent in the period 1940–59 (Pooley and Turnbull 2000; Pooley et al. 2005). This volume of cyclists in Britain's roads was not seen as unproblematic by all, and there was considerable debate in the national press in the 1930s about the regulation of cyclists, the excessive number of road accidents involving cyclists, and the provision of dedicated road space for those travelling by bicycle. These issues came to a head in December 1934 when the first dedicated cycle lane in Britain was opened by the minister of transport, Hore-Belisha. This was a 2.5 mile stretch of 8 ft 6 in wide concrete cycle path alongside a section of Western Avenue in Middlesex (now the A40), provided for the 'greater convenience and safety of cyclists' (The Times 15 December 1934: 9). The Minister called the road a 'perfect example of arterial road construction' in which 'the two cycling tracks which had been provided gave effect for the first time to the principle that classes of traffic should be segregated in accordance with the speed at which they travel.

Such segregation assured the comfort and enhanced the safety of vehicles of every class' (The Times 15 December 1934: 9). Other similar schemes were also under consideration at this time – for instance on the new Coventry by-pass (The Times 12 December 1934: 11) and also in initial plans for a new north–south route through Lancashire, although the road was never completed in this form (The Times 5 December 1934: 11; Pooley 2010). However, cycling organisations saw the provision of segregated routes as an assault on the rights of cyclists to use the road and the National Cyclists' Union in particular objected strongly to the cycle paths. Their fear was that the use of cycle paths would be made compulsory for cyclists and they expressed the view that 'The only way to deal with road problems ... was to remove the cause of the danger, namely excessive speed, having regard to prevailing conditions and inefficient driving, and not by depriving any class of road users of its rightful use of the highway' (The Times 15 December 1934: 9). The minister responded that 'He did not know why it should be considered less reasonable to provide cycle paths for cyclists than to make pavements for pedestrians' (The Times 15 December 1934: 9).

The safety of cyclists, and their potential conflict with motorists also arose in other ways, including concern about cyclists in the new Mersey Tunnel (opened 1934) where they were accused of poor lane discipline and of slowing the flow of traffic (The Times 24 December 1934: 6) and with regard to their use of rear lights rather than reflectors). There were regular press reports on road traffic accidents involving cyclists; with cyclists accounting for 18.4 per cent of fatalities in 1933 1,324 deaths). Although at the time this was viewed as excessive (The Times 5 December 1934: 9), it is almost exactly the same percentage as the number of trips made by bicycle (reported above). For comparison, in 2011 there were 107 cyclists killed in road traffic accidents on British roads, representing 5.6 per cent of all road fatalities (Department for Transport 2012). Given that only about 2 per cent of trips are made by bicycle today it could be argued that the 1930s were relatively safer for cyclists than twenty-first-century roads. It can also be argued that one reason for this relative safety was the greater volume and visibility of cyclists as road users. These issues were debated throughout the 1930s, and in 1938 the National Committee on Cycling in a memorandum on the Report of the Transport Advisory Council on Accidents to Cyclists stated that:

> It does not feel that any practicable scheme for segregating cycle traffic can materially affect the safety of cyclists. It is pointed out that almost half of the accidents to cyclists take place at cross-roads where cycle paths are impracticable, and that cycle paths are only possible where cycle traffic is comparatively light. All new and reconstructed roads of sufficient width, it is suggested, should have lanes marked off primarily for cycle traffic. Where a cycle path already exists, an experiment might be made of throwing the path into the present highway, while marking off a suitable strip as primarily for cycle traffic. (The Times 21 November 1938: 9)

Thus in this period the merits of separating (either completely or partially) cyclist from motor vehicles were hotly debated with the main cyclists' organisation resolutely against segregation. For the most part this has continued to be the case until a combination of research (including that cited in this chapter) and media focus on cycling safety has led to a more widespread acceptance that whereve practicable separated cycle lanes should be provided on busy urban roads. Thi is slowly beginning to happen in parts of London, but in most towns and citie progress remains slow.[2]

Evidence from oral histories of everyday travel in the mid-twentieth centur gives two contrasting views of cycling. For some respondents (mainly men cycling was a fast, convenient and cheap form of everyday travel which gav independence and avoided crowded trams and buses, but for others (mainl but not exclusively women) cycling was unattractive due to the physical effor required (especially where there were hills), exposure to the elements and concer about bicycle theft. However, few respondents in the 1930s and 1940s expresse concerns about road safety which suggests that the views of politicians of th time were not necessarily representative of the general public. In addition to th two quotes at the start of this section a range of such views from respondents i Manchester and London are given in Box 3.1.

It was only in the 1980s that respondents began to cite road safety as a ke factor that inhibited utility cycling (though not off-road leisure cycling), as state by this respondent: 'I have always thought it [cycling] was really dangerou and it kind of terrified me a bit' (RJ97, small town, female, 1980s/90s). Thi coincided with the most rapid growth in car ownership and traffic in town creating road conditions that were unattractive to most cyclists. Althoug travelling to work by car was the single most important mode by the 1960 with approximately one third of the modal share, it was the 1990s before ove half of all journeys to work were by car (Pooley et al. 2005). Such views hav been strongly reinforced by current research on everyday travel in the twenty first century. Interviews and household ethnographies demonstrate that, with th exception of a small number of committed cyclists, most people are unwillin to cycle on busy urban roads. By far the most common response when aske about cycling was for respondents to request more investment in fully separate cycle lanes. A selection of responses from participants from four English town is given in Box 3.2.

From the above discussion it can be argued that cycling both in the past an the present has a contested relationship with concepts of social and environmenta justice. Even in the 1940s, when cycling was relatively common, it appealed onl to certain segments of the population (mainly men who viewed the bicycle a giving them more freedom and independence). It was never a fully democrati

---

2   For instance, *The Times* cycling safety campaign (see Cities Fit for Cycling websit *The Times*); the Cycling Embassy of Great Britain website; and the vision for cycling i London produced by the mayor of London and TfL (2013).

Box 3.1   Views on cycling, 1930s–1950s

I'm afraid I never liked travelling on trams. ... they were never very comfortable and if you went on the top deck it was very uncomfortable because there was smoking on the upper deck. I would sooner ride a bike. (RJ32, Manchester, male, 1930s)

If I'd got to look particularly smart for some reason to see somebody, and you've got to keep yourself spick and span. Can't always do it on bicycle, it depends on the weather, so any things like that would have changed the routine. (RJ41, London, male, 1940s)

No, I couldn't [cycle], my mother couldn't have afforded one in the first place and I never thought about a bicycle at all. ... no use up here at all because it's so hilly. (R19, Manchester, female, 1930s)

I didn't use a bicycle to go to town. I don't think really there was anywhere to put it you know. (R32, Manchester, male, 1930s)

No, I didn't. Well I cycled a lot for pleasure but never cycled to work, no. ... I don't no why I didn't. I just never. (R20, Manchester, female, 1940s)

Shift work, yes. ... Those times were so that you didn't clash with the manual workers when they were changing shifts. You changed shifts different times to them and of course/and the bike it was so good it gave you that freedom of not having to wait for buses. It would have been easier to use public transport if you had worked normal hours. (R06, Manchester, male, 1950s)

Well I had ridden a bicycle to school and it was just slightly easier. I didn't have the long walk to the bus stop. ... I didn't have to change buses, it was just easier to go on the bike. (RJ03, London, female, 1950s)

Box 3.2   Present-day views on separated cycle lanes

I think my main issue for not cycling would be because I don't want to go on the roads. (P130, Leicester, male)

If there were cycle lanes ... I certainly would cycle more. (P79, Worcester, male)

The cycle lanes are very haphazard, they start then stop, people park in them. (P177, Leeds, female)

I love going round these cycle ways, I feel safe, I feel it is safe. Not keen on the road, particularly when lorries are coming past. (P86 Worcester, female)

Cycle paths are a joke as most cyclists know cycle paths I think in some ways increase rather than decrease the danger to cyclists by giving the appearance of safety so yeah designated cycle routes, that are separate to pedestrian paths as well because pedestrians and cyclists don't get on very well. (P176, Leeds, male) form of everyday transport. While concerns about the safety of cycling were current (especially in political circles) in the 1930s, these crystallised much more strongly among the general population by the 1980s, so that on-road cycling rapidly became associated with unacceptable levels of risk.

Paradoxically, national cycle organisations – largely representing committed and confident cyclists – have since the 1930s often adopted a stance that can be seen as elitist and exclusionary. Their (understandable) position that cyclists have a right to use the road and that roads should be made safe for cyclists was at odds with the views of many politicians and transport planners in the 1930s, and also conflicts with the views of many occasional or potential cyclists today. It can be argued that to make cycling truly socially inclusive there is need to create an environment where all actual and potential cyclists feel safe and that, in recognition of the current road and traffic conditions in Britain, the only way to do this at least on busy arterial roads is to construct dedicated cycle lanes that are separated from pedestrians and traffic. Current conditions for cycling inevitably lead many cyclists to utilise pavements to avoid traffic but this leads to conflict with pedestrians. It can be argued that, in doing this, cyclists are also contravening principles of environmental justice in that they are significantly reducing the quality of the urban environment for pedestrians.

Policy Issues: Lessons from History

The dominance of the automobile in the late twentieth century, and the associated concept of automobility, is well documented (Sheller and Urry 2000; Urry 2004). I have argued elsewhere that there could have been alternative pathways, with restrictions on car use from the early twentieth century enabling public transport to remain dominant and requiring cities to be planned for people rather than for cars. Furthermore, I have argued that such a scenario would not necessarily have reduced the ability of people to travel, although it would have required changes both to people's expectations of everyday movement and to the structure of cities, with more facilities provided close to residential areas (Pooley 2010). This chapter has focused explicitly on issues of social and environmental justice and has argued that two key periods of change in urban transport – the removal of trams as a form of mass public transport and the decline of cycling for everyday journeys – represent periods in which, if the course of history had been different, it would have been possible to create systems of everyday urban transport that more closely met the needs of both social and environmental justice. Motor buses were less accessible to all than trams and, crucially, the switch to motorised public transport also privileged the private car in urban planning; failure to develop fully separated cycle lanes has since the mid-twentieth century contributed to a decline in cycling in the face of increasingly busy (and dangerous) main roads.

Taking into account lessons from the past century – especially with regard to the rise of motor vehicles and the decline of both cheap and attractive public transport and of cycling – together with contemporary research on everyday travel, what policy implications can be suggested for the twenty-first century? It is clear from historical and contemporary analyses that most people choose to travel around towns and cities in a way that they (and they hope others) will perceive as normal. In the 1920s travel by tram was routine. As one respondent quoted above said, 'there was only one way in those days and that was by tram', and for many men at least cycling was also seen as the obvious choice in the 1930s and 1940s. As also quoted above, one respondent used almost identical words with regard to cycling: 'Well it [cycling] was really the only way'. By the late twentieth century travel by car had become normal ('the only way') for most people; or as one respondent from as early as the 1960s stated: 'There might have been the odd days [I cycled] but in the main once you got the car you know. It was far more convenient' (RJ31, London, male, 1960s). The degree to which car use is today viewed as normal and expected was summed up neatly by one contemporary female respondent from Leeds: 'People still assume that there's something wrong with you if you don't drive' (P121). The problem is that although in twenty-first-century Britain most households can aspire to car use, some individuals (especially those on restricted incomes, children, the elderly and anyone who does not to drive) are excluded; while motor vehicles contribute significantly to the unequal burdens of environmental pollution at both the local and global scales. In other words, what is 'normal' is also socially and environmentally unjust. One message from both past and present data is thus that if we wish to create a system of everyday travel in urban areas that meets principles of both social and environmental justice, we must first create conditions in which such travel options appear to be normal and rational: again, to quote the two respondents from the 1930s, 'the only way'.

It is recognised that such aspirations would require very significant changes to the principles and assumptions that underpin contemporary urban and transport planning in Britain at both the national and local level; and it is also accepted that current conditions do vary in different parts of the UK, and thus that solutions may need to be adapted to local circumstances. However, it is suggested that a three stage approach could begin to shift both public and policy attitudes towards transport patterns that are both accessible to all and that create minimal environmental harm (Pooley et al. 2013). First, it is argued, there needs to be substantial investment in infrastructure: fast, frequent, accessible and attractive public transport in urban areas (the modern equivalent of the tram network that existed in many British cities in the 1920s), together with attractive and fully-segregated spaces for pedestrians and, at least on busy roads, for cyclists. Second, there needs to be significant and enforceable restrictions on car use in urban areas including such measures as 20 mph zones in residential areas (and especially on residential streets where segregated cycle lanes are not possible), together with congestion charging and/or road pricing schemes appropriate to the locality. Third, and most difficult, it is argued that there need to be changes in society that can only be partially introduced and enforced by legislation. Such attitudinal change includes giving respect to the most vulnerable road users (pedestrians and cyclists), and creating working and living conditions (and the associated expectations of everyday life) that enable people to travel more sustainably (which in some cases may mean travelling more slowly). Such attitudinal changes can be encouraged by both national and local action (for instance by changing legal liability in road accidents to protect pedestrians and cyclists; through family-friendly social policies and more flexible working hours; and through the decisions of local planning committees with regard to the siting of facilities), but primarily they must be endorsed and embraced by the majority of people. In other words, only when forms of everyday travel that are both socially and environmentally just are seen as normal ('the only way') will they become the default (or majority) choice for the travelling population. It has been argued that in the past there have been (brief) periods when such aspirations have been almost achieved. Better understanding of how mobility-related social and environmental justice has been created in the past should produce more socially and environmentally just transport policies in the present.

Acknowledgements

Thanks to Jean Turnbull, Mags Adams, Dave Horton and Griet Scheldeman who have all contributed directly to the research quoted in this chapter. Thanks also to colleagues at the Universities of Leeds and Oxford Brookes (especially Miles Tight, Anne Jopson, Caroline Mullen, Tim Jones, Alison Chisholm and Emanuele Strano), who have contributed to different parts of the Understanding Walking and Cycling project. The research quoted in this chapter draws on interviews with a large number of people in seven different towns and cities: many thanks to all respondents for their willingness to give up some of their time. This research was funded at various times by The Leverhulme Trust, the ESRC and the EPSRC. Thanks to all three organisations for their support.

References

Agyeman, J. and Evans, B. (2004). 'Just Sustainability': The Emerging Discourse of Environmental Justice in Britain. *The Geographical Journal* 170, pp. 155–64.

Azetsop, J. (2010). Social Justice Approach to Road Safety in Kenya: Addressing the Uneven Distribution of Road Traffic Injuries and Deaths across Population Groups. *Public Health Ethics* 3, pp. 115–27.

Barregard, L., Bonde, E. and Öhrström, E. (2009). Risk of Hypertension from Exposure to Road Traffic Noise in a Population-Based Sample. *Occupational and Environmental Medicine* 66, pp. 410–15.

Blanke, D. (2007). *Hell on Wheels: The Promise and Peril of America's Car Culture, 1900–40*. Lawrence: University Press of Kansas.

Bruton, F. (1927). *A Short History of Manchester and Salford.* 2nd edn. Manchester: Sherratt.

Buzzelli, M., Jerrett, M., Burnett, R. and Finklestein, N. (2004). Socio-Spatial Perspectives On Air Pollution and Environmental Justice in Hamilton, Canada, 1985–1996. *Annals of the Association of American Geographers* 93, pp. 557–73.

Cerin, E., Leslie, E. and Owen, N. (2009). Explaining Socio-Economic Status Differences in Walking for Transport: An Ecological Analysis of Individual, Social and Environmental Factors. *Social Science and Medicine* 68, pp. 1013–20.

Clay, H. and Brady, K., eds (1929). *Manchester at Work: A Survey.* Manchester: Civic Week Committee.

Cooter, R. and Luckin, B., eds (1997). Accidents in History: Injuries, Fatalities and Social Relations. *Clio Medica* 41. Amsterdam and Atlanta: Wellcome Institute Series in the History of Medicine.

Currie, G., Richardson, T., Smyth, P. Vella-Brodrick, D., Hine, J., Lucas, K., Stanley, J., Morris, J., KInnear, R. and Stanley, J. (2009). Investigating Links between Transport Disadvantage, Social Exclusion and Well-Being in Melbourne – Preliminary Results. *Transport Policy* 16, pp. 97–105.

Currie, G. and Sensberg, Z. (2007). Exploring Forced Car Ownership in Metropolitan Melbourne. *Australasian Transport Research Forum* 2007. Available at: http://www.atrf.info/papers/2007/2007_Currie_Senbergs.pdf (accessed 13 May 2015).

Davis, A., Hirsch, D., Smith, N., Beckhelling, J. and Padley, M. (2012). *A Minimum Income Standard for the UK in 2012: Keeping Up in Hard Times.* York: Joseph Rowntree Foundation. Available at: http://www.minimumincomestandard.org/downloads/2012_launch/mis_report_2012.pdf (accessed 13 May 2015).

Davies, H., Vlaanderen, J., Henderson, S. and Brauer, M. (2009). Correlation Between Co-Exposure to Noise and Air Pollution from Traffic Sources. *Occupational and Environmental Medicine* 66, pp. 347–50.

Department for Transport (2012). *Reported Road Casualties, Great Britain, 2011.* London: The Stationery Office.

European Commission (2009). *EU Energy and Transport Figures: Statistical Pocket Book.* Brussels: European Communities.

Eyre, D. (1971). *Manchester's Buses 1906–1945.* Manchester: Manchester Transport Museum Society.

Frangopulo, N. (1977). *Tradition in Action: The Historical Evolution of the Greater Manchester County.* Wakefield: Manchester Education Committee.

Frost, L. (2001). The History of American Cities and Suburbs: An Outsider's View. *Journal of Urban History* 27, pp. 362–76.

Garroch, D. (2003). Sounds of the City: The Soundscapes of Early Modern European Towns. *Urban History* 30, pp. 5–25.

Gray, E., ed. (1967). *The Tramways of Salford.* 2nd edn. Salford: Trustees of Salford Transport Museum Society.

Harvard, S., Deguen, S., Zmirou-Navier, D., Schilinger, C. and Bard, D. (2009). Traffic-Related Air Pollution and Socio-Economic Status: a Spatial

Autocorrelation Study to Assess Environmental Equity on a Small Area Scale *Epidemiology* 20, pp. 223–30.

Hillman, M., Adams, J. and Whitelegg, J. (1990). *One False Move ... A Study of Children's Independent Mobility*. London: Policy Studies Institute.

Hine, J., ed. (2003). Social Exclusion and Transport Systems. *Transport Policy* 10(special issue), pp. 263–342.

Hine, J. (2012). Mobility and Transport Disadvantage. In *Mobilities: New Perspectives on Transport and Society*, ed. M. Grieco and J. Urry. Farnham: Ashgate, pp. 21–40.

Hine, J. and Mitchell, F. (2003). *Transport Disadvantage and Social Exclusion: Exclusionary Mechanisms in Transport in Urban Scotland*. Aldershot: Ashgate.

Ishaque, M. and Noland, R. (2006). Making Roads Safe for Pedestrians or Keeping Them Out of the Way? An Historical Perspective on Pedestrian Policies in Britain. *Journal of Transport History* Series 3, 27, pp. 115–37.

Johnson, V., Curie, G. and Stanley, J. (2010). Measures of Disadvantage: Is Car Ownership a Good Indicator. *Social Indicators of Research* 97, pp. 439–50.

Kenyon, S., Lyons, G. and Rafferty, J. (2002). Transport and Social Exclusion: Investigating the Possibility of Promoting Inclusion Through Virtual Mobility. *Journal of Transport Geography* 10, pp. 207–19.

Knowles, R. (1996). Transport Impacts of Greater Manchester's Metrolink Light Rail System. *Journal of Transport Geography* 4, pp. 1–14.

Ladd, B. (2009). Cars and the American City: Review Essay. *Journal of Urban History* 35, pp. 777–82.

Levitas, R., Pantaziz, C., Fahmy, E., Gordon, D., Lloyd, E. and Patsios, D. (2007). *The Multi-Dimensional Analysis of Social Exclusion*. Bristol: University of Bristol. Available at: http://webarchive.nationalarchives.gov. uk/20100407174951/http://www.cabinetoffice.gov.uk/social_exclusion_task force/publications/multidimensional.aspx (accessed 13 May 2015).

Lucas, K. (2004). *Running on Empty: Transport, Social Exclusion and Environmental Justice*. Bristol: The Policy Press.

———— (2006). Providing Transport for Social Inclusion Within a Framework of Environmental Justice in the UK. *Transportation Research A* 40, pp. 801–9.

———— (2012). Transport and Social Exclusion: Where Are We Now? *Transport Policy* 20, pp. 105–13.

Lucas, K. and Stanley, J. (2009). International Perspectives on Transport and Social Exclusion. *Transport Policy* 16(special issue), pp.19–142.

Luckin, B. (1993). Accidents, Disasters and Cities. *Urban History* 30, pp. 648–7?.

Luckin, B. and Sheen, D. (2009). Defining Early-Modern Automobility: The Road Traffic Accident Crisis in Manchester, 1939–45. *Cultural and Social History* 6, pp. 211–30.

Manchester Corporation Tramways Department (MCTramD) (1902–28). *Annual Reports*. Manchester: Manchester Corporation Minutes.

———— (1929–65). *Annual Reports*. Manchester: Manchester Corporation Minutes.

―――― (1935). *A Hundred Years of Road Passenger Transport in Manchester, 1835–1935*. Manchester: MCTranspD.

Manchester Evening News (1937–38; 1957). Manchester Central Library, transport press cuttings, *Manchester Evening News*, F388.4M1.

―――― (1938). *Manchester Evening News*, 7 June.

Mitchell, G. and Dorling, D. (2003). An Environmental Justice Analysis of British Air Quality. *Environment and Planning A* 35, pp. 909–29.

Parry, M., Canziani, O., Palutikof, J., van der Linden, P. and Hansen, C., eds (2007). *Climate Change 2007: Impacts, Adaptation and Vulnerability. Contribution of Working Group II to the Fourth Assessment Report of the Intergovernmental Panel on Climate Change*. Cambridge: Cambridge University Press.

Payer, P. (2007). The Age of Noise: Early Reactions in Vienna, 1870–1914. *Journal of Urban History* 33, pp. 773–93.

Pearce, J., Kingham, S. and Zawar-Reza, P. (2006). Every Breath You Take? Environmental Justice and Air Pollution in Christchurch, New Zealand. *Environment and Planning A* 38, pp. 919–38.

Pooley C. (2010). Landscapes without the Car: A Counterfactual Historical Geography of Twentieth-Century Britain. *Journal of Historical Geography* 36, pp. 266–75.

Pooley, C. with Jones, T., Tight, M., Horton, D., Scheldeman, G., Mullen, C., Jopson, A. and Strano, E. (2013). *Promoting Walking and Cycling. New Perspectives on Sustainable Travel*. Bristol: Policy Press.

Pooley, C. and Turnbull, J. (2000). Commuting, Transport and Urban Form: Manchester and Glasgow in the Mid-Twentieth Century. *Urban History* 27, pp. 360–83.

―――― (2005). Coping with Congestion: Responses to Urban Traffic Problems in British Cities C1920–1960. *Journal of Historical Geography* 31, pp. 78–93.

Pooley, C., Turnbull, J. and Adams, M. (2005). *A Mobile Century? Changes in Everyday Mobility in Britain in the Twentieth Century*. Aldershot: Ashgate.

Preston, J. (2009). Epilogue: Transport Policy and Social Exclusion – Some Reflections. *Transport Policy* 16, pp. 140–42.

Preston, J. and Raje, F. (2007). Accessibility, Mobility and Transport-Related Social Exclusion. *Journal of Transport Geography* 15, pp. 151–60.

Pucher, J. and Buehler, R. (2008). Making Cycling Irresistible: Lessons from the Netherlands, Denmark and Germany. *Transport Reviews* 28, pp. 495–528.

Schrag, Z. (2004). The Freeway Fight in Washington DC: The Three Sisters Bridge in Three Administrations. *Journal of Urban History* 30, pp. 648–73.

Selander, J., Nilsson, M., Bluhm, G., Rosenlund, M., Linquivst, M., Nis, G. and Pershagen, G. (2009). Long-Term Exposure to Road Traffic Noise and Myocardial Infarction. *Epidemiology* 20, pp. 272–9.

Sheller, M. and Urry, J. (2000). The City and the Car. *International Journal of Urban and Regional Research* 24, pp. 737–57.

Shergold, I. and Parkhurst, G. (2012). Transport-Related Social Exclusion amongst Older People in Rural Southwest England and Wales. *Journal of Rural Studies* 28, pp. 412–21.

Simon, E. and Inman, J. (1935). *The rebuilding of Manchester*. London: Longmans.

Simon, S. (1938). *A Century of City Government*. London: Allen and Unwin.

Stanley, J. and Vella-Brodrick, D. (2009). The Usefulness of Social Exclusion to Inform Social Policy in Transport. *Transport Policy* 16, pp. 90–96.

The Times (1934–1938). *The Times*. Available at: http://gale.cengage.co.uk/times.aspx/ (accessed 13 May 2015).

Urry, J. (2004). The 'System' of Automobility. *Theory, Culture and Society* 21(4/5), pp. 25–39.

Walker, G. (2009). Beyond Distribution and Proximity: Exploring the Multiple Spatialities of Environmental Justice. *Antipode* 41, pp. 614–36.

Walker, G. and Bulkeley, H. (2006). Geographies of Environmental Justice. *Geoforum* 37, pp. 655–9.

Websites

Cities Fit for Cycling, *The Times*. http://www.thetimes.co.uk/tto/public/cyclesafety/.

CTC: The UK's National Cyclists' Organisation. http://www.ctc.org.uk/.

Cycling Embassy of Great Britain. http://www.cycling-embassy.org.uk/.

National Travel Survey 2013. https://www.gov.uk/government/statistics/national-travel-survey-2013.

Transport for Greater Manchester, Metrolink. http://www.metrolink.co.uk/futuremetrolink/Pages/default.aspx.

(All accessed 13 May 2015)

Chapter 4

Mobility in Rural Ireland: A Study of Older People and the Challenges They Face

Aoife Ahern and Julian Hine

Rural transport policy in Ireland, north and south, has been paid little attention in the past by policy makers, with most transport investment taking place in urban areas. But in recent times there has been an acknowledgement that we need to consider the future mobility of those living in rural areas, particularly those older people who are least likely to have access to a car and, therefore, have low levels of relative mobility (Fitzpatrick Associates 2002, 2006; Weir and McCabe 2008; Nutley 2005). The National Rural Transport Survey in Ireland showed that 37 per cent of those aged over 65 in rural parts of Ireland had unmet transport needs (Fitzpatrick Associates 2002, 2006). What is particularly interesting about this group of people living in rural areas is that they are the first older generation to have experienced relatively high levels of car use and car dependency when young, so the adjustment to life without the car may be more difficult. This is particularly true of older men.

This is a generation of older people who have experienced travel in a very different way to earlier generations, and thus have higher demands of transport than in the past. Alsnih and Hensher (2003) point out that older people are now more mobile for longer, so have higher expectations of travel and transport. In today's older generation, it is generally men who are more likely to have had high levels of car ownership and use, but future older generations will also include women with higher car ownership and use levels.

This chapter describes a study that recorded the transport experiences of older people in rural Ireland: both Northern Ireland and the Republic of Ireland were included in the study. While the focus of the study was on identifying older, rural residents' travel patterns and transport problems, the study also serves as a historical record of the transport patterns and demands of an older generation that grew up with car dependency and are now making the adjustment, often unwillingly, to life without a car.

The chapter is divided into the following sections:

1. An overview of the current situation in the Republic of Ireland (ROI) and Northern Ireland (NI) regarding transport in rural areas.
2. A description of the focus groups that were conducted.

3. An analysis of the participants' answers relating to making the change from
    life with to life without a car.

Rural Transport in Ireland – The Current Situation

Ireland still has a significant proportion of its population living in rural areas:
while in relative terms the proportion of people living in rural areas has decreased,
in absolute terms there has been an increase in numbers of people in living in
rural parts of Ireland. In 2006 the census carried out in the ROI showed that
1.665 million people, or 40 per cent of the population, lived in rural areas. By
2011 this had increased to 1.741 million people, representing 32 per cent of the
population (Central Statistics Office 2011). In 2008, in rural Northern Ireland
36 per cent of the population lived in rural areas: that is approximately two-thirds
of a million (Office for National Statistics 2012). This rural population is also an
ageing population: age-dependency rates in Ireland are increasing most rapidly
in rural Ireland, with 45 per cent of those aged 65 and over living in rural areas,
while only 32 per cent of the total population live in rural areas (Central Statistics
Office 2011). In Northern Ireland the over 65s account for a growing proportion of
the population. Over the 10-year period between 2002 and 2012 the population
of this age group increased by 20.3 per cent. Households in rural Northern Ireland
are also more likely than those in urban areas to have at least one adult of a
pensionable age (Office of the First Minister and Deputy First Minister 2013).

Poor public transport provision in rural areas of Ireland has led to high car
ownership and car dependency, which in turn has decreased the likelihood of good
quality public transport being developed (Fitzpatrick Associates 2002, 2006; Weir
and McCabe 2008, Ahern and Hine 2012; McDonagh 2006). For the carless, the
difficulties of travel are worse in a society where most people have access to a
car and in rural Ireland there are few options for those without cars (Weir and
McCabe, 2008). As Hine and Kamruzzaman (2012) point out, access to services
is a function of both accessibility (how close you live to services) and mobility
(how easy it is to get to different modes of transport): for those in rural areas,
lack of access to a car when everyone else has a car leads to low levels of relative
mobility. Amongst those least likely to drive and therefore at most risk of social
exclusion in a car-dependent society are older women and the 'old-old' (those
aged over 75) (Davey 2007; Alsnih and Hensher 2003; Spinney et al. 2009). In the
Republic of Ireland the proportion of men aged 60 and over that hold a full driving
licence is 73.9 per cent, while only 39.7 per cent of women in this age category
hold a full driving licence (Central Statistics Office 2007). In Northern Ireland
89 per cent of men aged 60–69 and 42 per cent aged 70 and over hold a licence
compared to 68 per cent of women aged 60–69 and 57 per cent of women aged 70
and over (Department of Regional Development Northern Ireland 2013).

Bus is the main mode of public transport in rural Ireland (Weir and
McCabe 2008). Bus Eireann, south of the border, and Ulster Bus, north of the

border, along with some private bus operators, are the primary providers of public transport in rural Ireland (Weir and McCabe 2008; Fitzpatrick Associates 2006). On both sides of the border, community transport plays an important role.

In the Republic of Ireland the Rural Transport Programme (RTP) has been a very important part of transport policy for many rural areas. It started in 2006, following recommendations made in a report written for the government on rural transport by Fitzpatrick Associates in 2002 and has grown every year since then (Fitzpatrick Associates 2002, 2006). The scheme is coordinated and monitored by a non-profit organisation called Pobal (Fitzpatrick Associates 2006; Weir and McCabe 2008; McDonagh 2006; Pobal 2013). The RTP is delivered in each of the localities in which it operates by volunteers, who obtain funding from the government through Pobal (Fitzpatrick Associates 2006; Weir and McCabe 2008; McDonagh 2006; Pobal 2009, 2013;). The way in which the RTP runs (volunteers running the service in each area with their own vehicles) means that in each area the service is designed to meet local needs. In Northern Ireland, the Rural Community Transport Partnerships have been set up by the Department of Regional Development. As in the Republic, the services operate differently in different areas and respond to local needs. These community transport partnerships are funded through the Rural Transport Fund, a fund which also provides subsidies for socially necessary services operated by Translink. The Rural Transport Fund is designed to support transport services in rural areas which in turn will improve access to work, education, healthcare, shopping and recreational activities for rural people. Support through the fund is also provided to the Community Transport Association (CTA), a network of 17 community-transport partnerships.

In the Republic free-pass holders (those over 65) can use public transport services, including the RTP services, without charge. Most of those using the RTP services are older women, with Pobal stating that 65 per cent of its users are female and 52 per cent of users are over 66 (Fitzpatrick Associates 2006; Weir and McCabe 2008; McDonagh 2006; Pobal 2011, 2013). The programme has been very successful and consistently has experienced growing passenger numbers with 1.7 million passenger journeys being made in 2011 compared to 150,000 passenger journeys when the service first started operating in 2003 (Pobal 2011). A concessionary fares scheme has been in existence in Northern Ireland since 1978. In 2001 the scheme was extended to provide free travel to all senior citizens. In April 2007 free travel for senior citizens was extended to all-Ireland free travel, and in October 2008, free travel within Northern Ireland was made available to those aged 60–64. In rural parts of Northern Ireland concessionary travel on public transport is much lower than in Belfast (Department of Regional Development Northern Ireland 2011).

There have been criticisms by those who have reviewed rural transport policy in Ireland that focus largely has been on reducing social exclusion and not on promoting sustainability or sustainable modes. The RTP has provided local services that make sure certain vulnerable groups can access services, but the programmes do not really attempt to reduce overall car dependency or encourage active modes and sustainable travel (Fitzpatrick Associates 2002, 2006;

Weir and McCabe 2008). Fitzpatrick Associates (2006) and Weir and McCabe (2008) both point out that promoting social inclusion and promoting sustainable travel should be considered equally and that these are not mutually exclusive objectives. Similarly, in Northern Ireland emphasis has been placed on infrastructure investment. However, there is now a growing recognition of the need to promote sustainability and more sustainable modes of travel, yet it is clear that this may be more difficult to achieve in rural areas.

Focus Groups

The focus groups described in this chapter serve as a record of travel patterns and perceptions of transport held by an older generation who, when young, experienced car ownership and car use in a way that previous generations have not. Their adjustment to life without a car, in parts of Ireland where few alternatives exist, is therefore interesting not only in terms of identifying problems and challenges for rural transport but also as a record of how a car-dependent generation makes the shift to car-less life, and it also offers some hints of how future generations, which are now even more car dependent, might respond to life without a car when older.

There were 11 focus groups conducted altogether: six in the Republic of Ireland and five in Northern Ireland. Participants in the focus groups were older people: aged 65 or over in the Republic and over 60 in Northern Ireland. This reflects the age of retirement in the two countries. Some locations were classified as accessible rural areas and others as remote rural areas. In Northern Ireland three focus groups took place in accessible rural areas and two in remote rural areas according to the official classification for rural areas (The European Agricultural Fund for Rural Development 2007; NISRA 2005; Patterson and Anderson 2003). In the Republic the remoteness of the focus-group area types was defined using the remoteness index outlined in National Spatial Strategy (2000). From this, five focus groups took place in areas that were remote and one took place in an area which was accessible to an urban area/local amenities. These focus groups were in County Armagh, County Antrim, County Fermanagh, County Down, South County Leitrim, North County Leitrim, County Kildare, County Sligo, County Cork and County Longford.

A number of methods were used to recruit people to the focus groups:

1. Community Transport Organisations operational in different rural areas acted as gatekeepers for focus groups and recruited users of their transport to take part in focus groups. Six focus groups were arranged in this way.
2. Direct contact was made with social groups for older people and focus groups were arranged. Participants in these groups were not all users of transport schemes. Three focus groups were arranged in this way.
3. An advertisement was placed in the magazine of Age Action and older people in rural areas were invited to arrange focus groups. Again, members

of these focus groups were not all users of community-transport schemes. One focus group was arranged in this way.

4. Focus groups were arranged by direct contact with older people attending health centres. One focus group was arranged in this way.

Once a location had been selected and participants had chosen to take part in the focus groups, each participant was provided with background information about this research before the discussions started. This happened in a number of ways, depending on how the focus groups had been set up:

1. In some cases each participant was provided with written information about the research and the background to the project. This could be done when gatekeepers provided adequate contact details for participants.

2. It had been intended that all participants could be contacted in the way described above. However, in the Republic some gatekeepers preferred to make contact with participants themselves, as this protected the anonymity of potential participants. The gatekeepers provided those participants with the information about the research. In these cases, the written details of the research were provided to a gatekeeper (such as the community-transport organisations or the local social groups). The potential participants were contacted by the gatekeeper. The potential participants were then able to contact the researcher if necessary to discuss the research, and in some cases participants took this opportunity to speak to the researcher in advance of the focus groups.

In all cases it was made clear that participants could speak to researchers at any time, and that they could withdraw from the project at any stage. In addition it was made clear that no participants would be identified in the research reports. Therefore, in this chapter participants are only identified as male/female and as being from Northern Ireland or the Republic. In some cases, other characteristics of the participant may be described (for example, if they are a driver) when this is relevant. Focus groups were hosted in variety of different places (community centres, hotels, libraries). Topic guides were used to conduct the focus groups and all focus groups were recorded and then transcribed, with the permission of the participants. Focus groups were moderated by researchers.

There were some focus groups where people not engaged in the discussion sat in on the focus groups: sometimes the provider of the community-transport scheme sat in but this did not seem to hinder the discussion or the criticisms of community transport. In one case, in advance of the focus groups a disabled person aged under 65 years old requested to join as she experienced the same difficulties as older people. She was permitted to join and is recorded in Table 4.1 as a participant. In another group a nurse attended on behalf of older people in hospitals who could not travel to the focus groups, so that their opinions could be made known: she is not recorded as a participant in Table 4.1. The quotes included in this chapter only come from participants detailed in the table.

Table 4.1   Composition of the focus groups

Focus group	Participants	Male	Female	Drivers
1	8	2	6	6
2	10	2	8	3
3	6	3	3	0
4	12	2	10	3
5	10	1	9	4
6	4	1	3	1
7	9	2	7	0
8	7	3	4	2
9	8	3	5	2
10	5	3	2	0
11	8	0	8	0
Total	**87**	**22**	**65**	**21**

Life Without a Car – Analysis and Discussion

The findings of the focus groups demonstrated that in rural Ireland, life without the car is extremely difficult. Health trips become more complicated, social trips are less likely to happen and older people are excluded, both spatially and in time, from the activities in which they wish to engage. While alternatives to the car, like rural transport schemes, provide for some trips it was evident that this generation of older people found car-less life harder than life with the car.

Unlike previous generations, they, particularly the men, are unused to organised, public forms of transport and appeared not only to dislike the inflexibility of public transport but also the lack of private space on community-transport and public-transport systems. Examining the impacts of losing access to a car on this first generation of car dependent older people is important in terms of providing good transport for them, but also in better understanding the challenges that might be faced in the future when today's car dependent children and adults become older.

For participants of the focus groups the car was still a mode they wanted to use – those who were still driving wanted to continue to do so for as long as they possibly could. For those who could no longer drive, they still liked to get lifts with neighbours and family living nearby. However, they did not like to be overly reliant on others or to annoy them with too many requests. Participants made a distinction between one-off important trips, more regular scheduled trips, and 'unnecessary' trips. They would ask for lifts for the first of these trip types: vital, scheduled, one-off trips (like accessing health services). However, many participants did not like to ask for lifts for the other two trip types: regular trips, like the weekly trips to the shops, a club or society; or trips that are seen as unnecessary, like social trips. Therefore, community-transport schemes are important to older people as they allow participation in some social activities, although not as often as many in the focus groups would like, and also allow them to make regular trips to towns to access shops, clubs and services every week.

Focus group participants described how losing the ability to drive themselves, or losing a spouse who would drive them consistently, had negative impacts upon their lifestyles. Opportunities for social interaction reduced:

> I know about that shock. My husband used to drive me everywhere – to the hairdressers and everything. We used to go into town every Friday to do the shopping and we would often go to Sligo on a Saturday. I missed it terribly when he died, I did. Then my brother used to drive me. He died after that. I really miss the car. I never drove myself but I really miss the car. (Female)

One gentleman who no longer drove for health reasons stated that in rural Ireland 'life was for the car'. In rural Ireland, people without cars have little or no access, according to the members of the focus groups, to essential services, to shops or even to public transport, which is often located in larger towns and is inaccessible to those living outside of those towns without a car to drive to the bus stops:

> I think not driving really affects me. Where I live, which is outside the village. A little too far to walk in. Although I understand there are various private bus services that run on a reasonably regular level it is very hard to find information about them. And even when you do use them, they drop you back into the middle of the village. And you are dropped back with a bag of shopping. I might as well as be 10 miles from home as half mile. (Male)

While all members of the focus groups who could not drive described difficulties with their trips, the greatest difficulties were experienced by men. Women's lives and social opportunities lessened when they became older but less so than those of men in the focus groups who could no longer drive, who found the adjustment from car dependency to car-less life particularly difficult. This may in part be due the fact that in this generation older men were much more likely than older women to have driven for most of their adult lives and so were more car-dependent. For older men, the car had become the normal mode of transport and other alternatives were not considered until this was absolutely necessary. They were unused to travelling with others or to using public transport, whereas many of the women, when they wished to travel independently as younger women, had used public transport. This was particularly evident when it came to speaking of the community-transport schemes. It was felt by the male focus group participants that these schemes are very much feminised. Male participants of the focus groups felt that the destinations offered by the community transport schemes are where females wish to go, rather than where men wish to go. Community-transport schemes went to towns during the day for shopping or to social clubs, which were predominantly frequented by women, whereas focus group participants stated that men would prefer trips at night and to local public houses. But more than this, older men in the focus groups spoke of how some men are uncomfortable using community-transport schemes. They did not like to share space with others.

For these men, the car represented freedom to travel when and where they wanted. In the focus groups described here, many of the men were using community transport but spoke about male friends and acquaintances that had chosen social isolation above using community-transport schemes, and also of older men who would continue to drive no matter what in order not to lose what they saw as their own control over their lives.

For the student of transport history, this is a generation of particular interest as we see the impacts of car dependence in adult life on choices and decisions made when older. At present it is older males who are least prepared for giving up the car, a view also found by other researchers (Glasgow and Blakely 2000; O'Neill 1997; Davey 2007); but as car dependency increases and as the travel patterns of young women become more similar to those of young men, and as children become more car dependent and less likely to use public transport for school trips, perhaps future generations of older women will also find the shift from car dependency to life without a car as difficult as older men today.

Those who still drove and took part in the focus groups – especially men but also those women who drove – spoke of their concerns regarding what they saw as the inevitability of ceasing to drive in the future. Many knew that the day was coming when they would have to give up the car but they knew little about alternatives available and generally had very negative views of those alternatives: 'For those of us who can drive, we get worried about when we won't be able to drive any more. Either we'll have to move somewhere else or you are depending on somebody to ... you know ... they are the only options' (Female).

Car dependency in rural Ireland is now what is seen as normal life and so to be without a car is 'odd'. Indeed, one participant stated that in rural Ireland he saw life without a car in rural areas as 'a disability'. While some ex-drivers had begun to adjust to life without cars, and were using community transport where it existed, these ex-drivers stated that if they could drive they would. Participants had not moved from car to community transport or public transport out of any great desire to become more environmentally friendly or to travel using more sustainable modes. They still saw car use as the norm and desirable, and use of the alternatives only as something that must be done if the car was no longer an option.

Conclusion

As other researchers have also commented, the emphasis in rural transport in Ireland has been on developing services that help tackle social isolation and exclusion and that provide particular vulnerable groups, such as older people, with transport (Fitzpatrick Associates 2002, 2006; Weir and McCabe 2008). This has led to the setting up of community-transport schemes in both the Republic and Northern Ireland. These schemes work well and focus group participants talked about how these schemes offered a vital service to older people in rural areas without cars. However, while these specialist schemes may help to reduce social isolation, they do not attempt to tackle the problem of increasing car dependency in rural areas. This has all led to a rural society where car dependency and car use is the norm. In the focus groups, ceasing to drive or loss of access to a car every day was seen as having a detrimental impact upon lives, both in terms of the possibilities to access services and to participate in an active social life.

While participants were loath to give up their cars, or regretted that they already had given up their cars, some groups were more vulnerable to the impacts of ceasing to drive than others. Even in locations where community transport was active, it is evident that some older men did not wish to make the transition from car to community transport. Indeed, community-transport schemes in the locations where focus groups were carried out were underused, despite the fact that participants felt that there was a need for more community transport.

While at present older women seem to make the adjustment to travelling in shared spaces and on community-transport schemes more easily than men, it is a question that we must look at for future generations. Young women today have more complicated patterns than their predecessors and are more likely to drive. Will current generations of younger, car-dependent women experience the same difficulties that older men appear to experience when moving from car to public transport? If this is the case, reducing car dependency among younger people in rural areas is important for a number of reasons. Not only is it is important in terms of ensuring we travel more sustainably and use more environmentally friendly modes today, but also for future older generations to be better able to cope with life without a car it is important that they are better prepared for that life. We need to provide not only specialist services for particular groups, but also more good quality public transport in rural areas that everyone can use. In this way we may normalise the use of public transport and alternative modes in rural areas, and reverse the normalisation of car use.

Acknowledgement

The work described in this chapter has been funded by CARDI, the Centre for Aging Research and Development in Ireland.

Note

Since April 2012, responsibility for the RTP in Ireland has been taken over by the National Transport Authority (NTA). Pobal continued to manage the RTP on the behalf of the NTA in 2012 and 2013. The NTA announced changes to the management and implementation of the scheme in 2013, to take place in 2014. This was subsequent to the focus groups described in this chapter.

References

Ahern, A. and Hine J. (2012). Rural Transport – Valuing the Mobility of Older People. *Research in Transportation Economics* 34, pp. 27–34.

Alsnih, R. and Hensher, D. (2003). The Mobility and Accessibility Expectations of Seniors in An Ageing Population. *Transportation Research Part A* 37 pp. 903–16.

Banister, D. and Bowling, A. (2004). Quality of Life for the Elderly: The Transport Dimension. *Transport Policy* 11, pp. 105–15.

Care of the Aged (1968). *Report of an Inter-Departmental Committee*. Dublin: Stationery Office.

Central Statistics Office (2007). *Ageing in Ireland*. Dublin: Stationery Office.

————(2011). *This is Ireland. Highlights from the 2011 Census Part 2*. Dublin: Stationery Office. Available at: http://www.cso.ie/en/media/csoie/census documents/census2011pdr/Table,of,Contents,Foreword,and,Appendices.pdf (accessed 10 May 2015).

Davey, J. (2007). Older People and Transport: Coping Without a Car. *Ageing and Society* 27, pp. 49–65.

Department for Regional Development Northern Ireland (2011). *Northern Ireland Concessionary Fares Users' Survey*. Belfast: DRDNI. Available at: http:// www.drdni.gov.uk/ni_concessionary_fares_users_survey_may_2011.pdf (accessed 10 May 2015).

———— (2013). *Northern Ireland Travel Survey. In Depth Report 2010–2012*. Belfast: DRDNI. Available at: http://www.drdni.gov.uk/final_-_tsni_indepth_ report_2010–2012.pdf (accessed 10 May 2015).

European Agricultural Fund for Rural Development (2007). *Northern Ireland Rural Development Programme 2007–2013*. Belfast: Department of Agriculture and Rural Development.

Fitzpatrick Associates (2002). *Report of the Interdepartmental Committee on Rural Public Transport*. Dublin: Department of Transport.

———— (2006). *Progressing Rural Public Transport in Ireland – A Discussion Paper*. Dublin: Department of Transport.

Gilhooly, M., Hamilton, K. and O'Neill, M. (2003). *Transport and Ageing: Extending Quality of Life for Older People via Public and Private Transport*. ESRC End of Award Report L480254025. Swindon: ESRC.

Glasgow, N. and Blakely, R. (2000). Older Nonmetropolitan Residents' Evaluations of Their Transportation Arrangements. *Journal of Applied Gerontology* 19, pp. 95–116.

Hine, J. and Kamruzzaman, M. (2012). Journeys to Health Services in Great Britain: An Analysis of Changing Travel Patterns 1985–2006. *Health and Place* 18, pp. 274–85.

McDonagh, J. (2006). Transport Policy Instruments and Transport-Related Social Exclusion in Rural Republic of Ireland. *Journal of Transport Geography* 14, pp. 355–66.

National Spatial Strategy (2000). *Irish Rural Structure and Gaeltacht Areas*. Dublin: Centre for Local and Regional Studies, NUI Maynooth and Brady Shipman Martin. Available at: http://www.irishspatialstrategy.i.e./docs/report10.pdf (accessed 10 May 2015).

Office for National Statistics (2012). *Country Profiles – Key Statistics Northern Ireland*. Belfast: Office for National Statistics. Available at: http://www.ons.gov.uk/ons/dcp171780_275448.pdf (accessed 10 May 2015).

Office of the First Minister and Deputy First Minister (2013). *A Profile of Older People in Northern Ireland – 2013 Update*. Belfast: NISRA. Available at: http://www.ofmdfmni.gov.uk/a-profile-of-older-people-2013-update.pdf (accessed 10 May 2015).

O'Neill, D. (1997). Prediction and Coping with the Consequences of Stopping Driving. *Alzheimer Disease and Associated Disorders* 11, pp. 70–72.

Pobal (2011). *Annual Report*. Dublin: The Stationery Office.

——— (2013). Rural Transport Programme website. Available at: https://www.pobal.ie/FundingProgrammes/RuralTransportProgramme/Pages/Rural%20Transport%20Programme.aspx (accessed 10 May 2015).

Spinney, J., Scott, D. and Newbold, K. (2009). Transport Mobility Benefits and Quality of Life: A Time-Use Perspective of Elderly Canadians. *Transport Policy* 16, pp. 1–11.

Weir, L. and McCabe, F. (2008). *Towards a Sustainable Rural Transport Policy*. Dublin: Comhar, Sustainable Development Council.

Chapter 5

Have Consumer Movements Enhanced Transport Justice? Passenger Representation on Britain's Railways before 1947

Hiroki Shin

In today's UK, transport policy passenger representation occupies only a minor place. Certainly, there is an official passenger watchdog, Transport Focus (until March 2015, Passenger Focus), covering the entire country, though there are some areas, such as London, where more regionally based TravelWatch organisations operate. Despite being a national organisation, Transport Focus has a fairly low profile. The relative neglect of passenger representation, especially when one compares this to the high profile given to infrastructural programmes, is a growing trend. The coalition government's halving of the budget of Passenger Focus in 2011 significantly weakened the position of the organisation since it was forced to reduce the level of liaison with the Train Operating Companies (TOCs) (Passenger Focus 2011: 6). The predecessors of Passenger Focus did not fare well either. The user consultative bodies established by the 1947 Transport Act have never had sufficient political leverage to tangibly affect transport policy making (Dudley and Richardson 2001: 40).

The current situation and history of passenger representation in the UK are reflected in the academic treatment of this topic. As Martin Shiefelbusch (2005) rightly pointed out, passenger representation is a long-neglected topic. With a few exceptions, passenger representation on the railways has been relegated to the sideline of transport studies and history. The pressure groups in other modes of transport are treated relatively better (Bickerstaff, Tolley and Walker 2002; Grant 1977; Tyme 1978). They sometimes appear as an interest group involved with infrastructure planning. In the case of railways, new construction programmes have been fairly rare since the early twentieth century, thereby limiting the potential of public involvement in the transport policy via infrastructure planning. The scarcity of new infrastructure plans does not, in theory, preclude passengers' involvement in transport policy. There is no fundamental reason to exclude public involvement in the discussion of perennial passenger concerns of, say, fares, congestion and service.

From the perspective of transport justice, the neglect of passenger representation becomes more problematic. Service provisions of train operating companies are largely determined by the companies' views on profitability. Generally speaking, profitable lines tend to be better served while unprofitable lines are not. And the latter lines generally serve lower-income communities. If profit consideration is taken too far, it can even deprive a disadvantaged community of a means of transport, whether taking the form of a drastic reduction of services at a station or a line closure in the extreme case. The similar argument applies to fares and other facilities, the level of which can pose a sizable deterrent effect on passengers' use of trains. To be fair to the transport operators, they need to strike a balance between satisfying customers and maintaining profitable business. This ideal, however, is not always realised, and profitability often reigns supreme. As such, business policy seems to have generally been on the side of regular, higher paying passengers who bring in constant revenue, such as business travellers moving between large urban centres like Birmingham and London. The problem of transport providers favouring already active members of society is not peculiar to privatised transport. It was also recognised and criticised during the period of nationalised railways (Grey 1975: 11), a recognition that has brought little fundamental change in how rail transport is planned and operated.

In a more fundamental discussion, the existence of diverse passenger groups and individuals, who have different needs and wants, has led some people to doubt the very possibility of passenger representation (Glaister, Burnham, Stevens and Travers 2006: 174). How can it be possible to represent such heterogeneous groups of people and satisfy all of them? So far, the widely adopted solution to this question is to guarantee a basic level of passenger rights. In the UK, passenger rights are set out in the National Rail Conditions of Carriage as well as the Passenger Charters. In other EU countries, the EU passenger rights policy is enforced as a cross-border framework[1] (Butcher 2012: 2–3). However, these basic passenger rights do not give a group of passengers powers to influence TOCs' business policy. Nor is their right of representation clearly recognised; passengers are generally treated as atomised, individual customers. Passenger watchdogs such as Transport Focus are supposed to enforce as well as complement basic passenger rights, but there is little scope for such organisations to be proactive in improving passenger service.

The current system of passenger representation is formulated around, and at the same time reinforcing, the idea that the national or official representation of passengers' interest is the norm. The existing literature on the topic also seems to take this for granted. In the UK, it is generally believed that the beginning of modern passenger representation started with the creation of user consultative bodies in 1947 (Schiefelbusch and Smale 2009). As this chapter will show, passenger representation has a longer history. Moreover, taking the national/ official representation as the norm has two obvious problems. First, this approach tends to minimise the role of voluntary or unofficial user groups – a number of such groups undoubtedly exist in the UK today – placing them outside the sphere of policy making. Second, the same approach makes it difficult to see the complex

---

1   Murillo points out that passenger representation in the EU policy is also insufficient (Murillo 2008: 98).

relationship between state, transport providers and passengers; the interactions between them do not necessarily take place within the official representation framework. Thus, there are practical as well as conceptual barriers for policy makers to grasp the wider situation surrounding passenger issues and passenger representation.

The historical approach enables us to keep an informed distance from the contemporary framework. The same approach would allow us to consider different options we actually have, but which many of us do not see, because of the preconceived idea of how passenger representation has been, or ought to be achieved. The following sections will show some historical variations of passenger representation. The long history of the railways in the UK, where the world's first commercial passenger rail service appeared, sheds light on the development of passenger representation in this country, as well as on the historical background which formed the foundation of today's passenger representation machinery.

The Emergence of Passenger Issues: Gladstone's Act of 1844

The first decade of railway passenger service began in 1830 with the opening of Liverpool and Manchester Railway. Rail travel was largely confined to relatively wealthy travellers. The fares were prohibitively high for most working people and their families, and the railway companies did not see much potential in providing them with affordable travel means – some people thought it even conducive to social unrest (Headicar 2009: 70). The situation, however, changed with the expansion of railway system, whose creation was left to private enterprises. Aided by speculative booms, numerous schemes were promoted, sometimes without considering the potential transport demand. As a consequence, a number of places came to be served by parallel lines operated by rival companies, creating the problem of overcapacity (Cain 1991; Casson 2009). The companies were desperately in need for passengers in order to survive the excessive competition which arose from the scarcely planned line building. Still, the dominant contemporary thinking was yet to embrace the idea of high-volume, low-margin business. Hence, within the early passenger service, consisting of three to four classes, the provisions for third-class passenger service – let alone fourth class – were very poor. While first-class passengers enjoyed leisurely travel in compartments reminiscent of horse carriages, third-class passengers were carried in uncomfortable carriages barely equipped with technologies and amenities to mitigate the jars and jolts that inevitably accompanied the early rail journey. The use of open carriage for the third class was quite common (Select Committee on Railways 1970b: 37–8; Schivelbusch 1986: 72). In most cases this was not an enjoyable experience. The passengers were not protected from bad weather, and there was always the risk of passengers being thrown out of the vehicle if an accident occurred or if they were extremely careless.

A serious accident was waiting to happen, and it did happen on Christmas Eve in 1841. At Sonning Cutting near Reading, a train crashed into a landslip caused by heavy rain the previous night, killing eight passengers and injuring 17 (Parris 1965: 44; Rolt 2007: 20). It was one of the earliest rail disasters, which understandably caused national anxiety about the danger accompanying this relatively new means of travel. What funnelled the anxiety into a public rage was the fact that the unfortunate victims – most of them were stonemasons working on the new Houses of Parliament on their way home for Christmas – were carried in an open carriage. It was pointed out that if they had been carried in an enclosed carriage, some or most of their lives could have been saved. The legal system at the time was ill prepared to deal with such a case, and the company responsible for the accident, the Great Western Railway, got away almost unpunished. A critic wrote that the railways were profiting from a business that was sacrificing the lives of its customers, who had 'a right to demand ... every care and protection for which they pay' (The Times 1841).

The accident possibly precipitated the regulation of the railways. W.E. Gladstone, who had been appointed vice president of the Board of Trade a few months prior to the Sonning accident, took up the issue. There was also a general feeling that some sort of regulation was needed for the railway system which for some time had been left to self-control. From 1838 a parliamentary committee had been investigating the current practice of railway business. Gladstone managed to make some input in this inquiry. The Railway Regulation Act of 1842, based on the committee's work, gave the Board of Trade some foothold to intervene, albeit to a fairly limited degree, with the workings of railways when public comfort and convenience were neglected (Hyde 1934: 152).

In 1844 Gladstone moved the parliament to set up a select committee to consider further changes in railway administration. The investigation was wide ranging, including the treatment of third-class passengers. There was a growing concern about the unfettered railway power to which passengers were subjugated. Gladstone met strong opposition, mostly from the railway interest, when he tried to introduce his regulatory ideas (Hyde 1934: 165). Despite this, in the third report of the committee, published in April 1844, the idea of what was later to be known as the 'parliamentary train' was set out (Select Committee on Railways 1970a: 6). This was, almost *in verbatim*, incorporated in the Railway Regulation Act of 1844 (7 & 8 Vict. c.85). Section 6 of the same act obliged railway companies to run at least one daily service on 'covered carriages' at a cost not exceeding one penny per mile. In return, the companies were granted some benefits, notably the exemption of tax payment on this low-fare service (Section 9).

Historians' opinions about the 1844 Act are still divided. There are different interpretations of Gladstone and his supporters' efforts to improve passenger conditions and different evaluations of the effects of the act (Mclean and Foster 1992). In any case by setting the minimum requirement for passenger carriages the 1844 Act guaranteed a degree of travel safety. As such, the act is regarded as an early instance of consumer protection (Glaister 2006: 3).

The use of covered carriage meant that most passengers were thenceforward protected from bad weather, thereby establishing a minimum level of comfort. Importantly, the act clearly stated that the parliamentary train was intended to secure the 'poorer Class of Travellers the Means of travelling at moderate Fares'. Although one might detect some degree of rhetorical ornamentation and Victorian paternalism, the act can well be seen as an embryonic social transport policy, even if it was still firmly located in the culture of paternalistic, top-down social reform. From a wider perspective the 1844 Act came out of the struggle over the supremacy in railway regulation, between the newly created state regulatory body, the Railway Department of the Board of Trade, and the railway industry. In this context, it was probably essential for the former to claim that it represented the public interest in order to justify its interference into private enterprise (Mclean and Foster 1992: 329). Public interest in this context did not directly come from the passengers, as they were yet to consolidate their collective interest.

Passenger Issues beyond Parliament: Passenger Tax

For the next two decades or so the 1844 Act had only a limited impact on the general travelling public. The fare of one penny a mile was not sufficiently cheap for ordinary people and workers to travel regularly, when the average yearly wage for workers was about £50 (Mitchell 1988: 153). A return journey of 190 miles each way – roughly the distance between London and Manchester – would have cost about two-thirds of one's weekly earnings. Many people only used railways for occasional movements, such as seasonal migration of workers and family visits (Mokyr 2009: 278). Having said that, railway travel, especially third class, was rapidly increasing from the 1840s. Excursions, with which Thomas Cook and the 1851 Great Exhibition are often associated, were making rail travel a fairly widely shared experience, if not an everyday or regular event (Hoppen 1998: 366–8). Also, the changing pattern of occupational mobility possibly encouraged, and was encouraged by, rail travel. Somewhat ironically, the popularisation of rail travel came to highlight the limitations of the 1844 Act.

In order for a passenger service to be designated as a parliamentary train, hence to be granted tax exemption, it needed to fulfil several requirements. Apart from the penny-a-mile fare and covered carriage, there was a requirement for the train to stop at 'every station' en route. On the one hand, this rule ensured maximum access for the passengers on the route, but on the other hand, it made the train journey less attractive, especially when one was travelling a long distance (Hermes 1899: 1). Stopping service necessarily slowed the journey, and even with the basic facilities provided by the 1844 Act, rail travel in a low-fare compartment was anything but a leisurely journey. In addition, railway companies only ran a limited number of parliamentary trains – usually mornings and evenings, since the legal obligation was to run only one train each way per day (Lee 1946: 19). The limited number of parliamentary service made it extremely difficult for passengers to travel across different routes by connecting one parliamentary train journey with another (Lee 1946: 21). The parliamentary train was run as a special service, distinct from ordinary services which were generally faster. Third-class passenger service was similarly limited, albeit it was part of regular service, forming a section of a train along with first and second class. Low-cost conveyance was usually a feature of slower trains, and only a small number of companies offered third class on express trains.

Some companies certainly regarded the express train as a value-added service, hence only higher-paying customers should be allowed such luxury. But the discrimination against low-fare passengers on faster services was chiefly the result of the 1844 Act. Express service could not be provided for by parliamentary train, as the act required the latter to call at every station on the route. Third-class express service was not bound by that rule, but general improvements to facilities in carriages lowered the profit margin of third-class service, making railway companies generally reluctant to extend it to faster trains. The Board of Trade gave some encouragement to the companies to increase the availability and convenience of low-fare services by administering the 1844 Act flexibly, allowing some companies to run parliamentary trains which did not stop at every station. The enticement for the train operators was that such service was exempt of the passenger duty that was normally levied on the ticket revenue at 5 per cent. The Board of Trade's generous administration of the parliamentary train was questioned by the Inland Revenue, which saw that the Board of Trade overstepped its authority by giving tax exemption beyond the terms stipulated by the 1844 Act.

This issue came to the fore in 1872, when the Midland Railway started to admit third-class passengers on all its trains, including express services (Lee 1946: 43). The company claimed that all of its third-class services should be exempted from the payment of passenger duty, as the fares were less than one penny per mile. Some of the Midland Railway's rivals saw the Midland's low-cost express service as a threat to their business, and some others perceived the same service as a new business model. A number of similar services were, therefore, introduced on other lines, making the same claim of tax exemption (Lee 1946: 43; MacDermot 1964: 208).

Seeing that the floodgate of tax-exempted services was opening, the Inland Revenue had recourse to the court in 1874. The Court of Exchequer and then the House of Lords ruled that the stopping-service requirement could not be waived by the Board of Trade, let alone by the railway companies (Railway Passenger Duty n.d.). With the Board of Trade no longer in position to support their new services, the Railway Companies Association (RCA) – representing the majority of railway lines in Britain – turned to harness its political pressure for the abolition of passenger duty (RCA 1872). More specifically for the purpose, the Passenger Duty Repeal Association was formed within RCA, but it failed to mobilise sufficient support in parliament. Changing its tactics, RCA decided to transfer the burden to passengers by increasing third-class fares by 5 per cent (RCA 1874).

The RCA's decision of a fares increase might have been a strategy to arouse public opinion. In fact, one of its leading members, Edward Watkin, was at the time exploring ways to create an extra-parliamentary movement over passenger duty (Hodgkins 2002: 436). His instigation was taken up by a group of political reformers; chief among them were C.D. Collet and George Holyoake, who had successfully led a movement against taxation on knowledge in the 1840–60s, resulting in the abolition of the newspaper stamp duty. These reformers saw the taxation on rail travel as another state injustice to the general public by hindering people's mobility (Holyoake 1905: 42). Without requiring much persuasion from Watkin, about thirty political reformers organised themselves into the Travelling Tax Abolition Committee in 1877 (Travelling Tax Abolition Committee 1878; Grugel 1976: 151). The Abolition Committee immediately started its propaganda campaigns, from issuing pamphlets and newsletters to organising and participating in public meetings (Alderman 1973: 90; Dyos 1982: 232). It is difficult to say to what extent the committee's cause was publicly supported. But there is evidence that at least some part of the cooperative societies, in which Holyoake had deeply been involved, responded to its appeal. It is clear that this extra-parliamentary movement succeeded in expanding the horizon of passenger issues beyond parliament and business (Alderman 1973: 93).

However, it was not the Abolition Committee that eventually brought about a change. It was a social problem, rather than public opinion, which moved the government to revise the passenger duty. By the 1880s the insufficient urban housing problem was felt so acutely that the government recognised the urgent need to take some actions (Polasky 2001). One of the ways to alleviate the housing problem was, it was thought, to affect workers' emigration from the urban centres to the suburbs and make them commute to their workplace (Alderman 1973: 91; Haywood 2009: 31; Headicar 2009: 71; Smith 1988: 36). This called for affordable means of daily transport. To solve this issue, the government was prepared to make some concessions to the railway companies. The force of change came from the government's attempt to solve a social problem, rather than from the consideration of passengers. Thus the political negotiation over the passenger duty was carried out almost exclusively between the government and RCA, leaving out the extra-parliamentary movement by the Abolition Committee (Alderman 1973: 92–4). The Cheap Trains Act of 1883 was enacted as the result of this negotiation and abolished the tax on penny-a-mile fares and granted further tax reductions to urban train services. With this change, the parliamentary train was now re-formed into workmen's trains, which existed until 1962 (Gibbins 2000: 9).

As a later historian concluded, Holyoake probably exaggerated the achievement of the Abolition Committee when he claimed that its campaigns were instrumental to the partial abolition of passenger duty – the tax on first and second class remained in place until 1929 (Alderman 1973: 90; Holyoake 1905: 43; Lee 1946: 61). After all, the practical arrangement of workmen's trains was made behind the closed door of business–government negotiation. On the one hand, this shows the limitations of extra-parliamentary movements at the time (Smith 1988: 34). On the other, the exclusion of the Abolition Committee from the negotiation was a reflection of the committee's ambiguous position as the self-appointed guardian of passenger interest. The Abolition Committee consisted of political reformers, whose action was based on the passenger interest as they perceived it, not as expressed by the people whom they claimed to be representing. Also, there was a suspicion that the Abolition Committee was representing business interest, rather than public interest. Even if the motives were different, the Abolition Committee and the railway companies were pursuing the same goal, the abolition of the passenger tax. The abolition of the tax, if it did not accompany a reduction of fares, would simply benefit the companies, rather than passengers. In parliament, invoking the working-class interest was similarly questioned, and an MP went as far as to say that it was used as 'a sort of stalking-horse' (House of Commons 1876).

Even if it was not the driving force in the revision of the passenger duty, it is significant that the activity of the Abolition Committee helped bring the passenger issues out of the confines of a politico-business platform into public discussion. The committee certainly had its limitations, not least its claim to be the representative of passengers. But the very fact that it could appeal to some part of the travelling public seems to show that an increasing number of travellers were starting to take the issues concerning rail service as their own problem to tackle.

Direct Representation: Commercial Travellers

In the last quarter of the nineteenth century some passengers were beginning to see shared interest among their fellow travellers. Some voluntary passenger associations emerged in this period, albeit their scope was generally very limited. One of the earliest examples, the Metropolitan Association for Procuring Cheap and Regular Railway was established in 1868 and held public meetings to promote their cause (Dyos 1982: 232; Lee 1946: 54). There was also a case of a group of season-ticket holders organising a 'passenger strike' in 1879 in protest against a fare increase. The disgruntled season-ticket holders declared that they would only purchase second-class tickets instead of their usual choice of first class! (Pall Mall Gazette 1878; Morning Post 1879). The Southend Season Ticket Holders' Association was already in existence in 1894 (Schiefelbusch and Smale 2009: 252), and was later to become a major passenger association. Evidence is far and few between, but there were probably more passenger groups emerging around the turn of the century. Whereas the increase in the number of such voluntary associations shows growing awareness of passengers' interest by passengers themselves, only a limited number of groups could actively seek their collective interest. And the association organised by commercial travellers – travelling salespersons in a modern term – was a case in point.

Since well before the arrival of rail travel, commercial travellers had been moving around the country using various means of transport. By 1872 they had come to possess a degree of solidarity enough to establish an organisation, the Commercial Travellers' Christian Association. In 1883, the same year as the passing of the Cheap Trains Act, they reorganised the association under a more secular title, the United Kingdom Commercial Travellers Association (UKCTA) (French 2005, 2010; Hosgood 1994; Hancox 1953: 3). From the start, improving the conditions of rail travel was a chief objective of the association, as they frequently travelled on trains, sometimes describing themselves as the 'best customers' of the railways (The Times 1884).

The strategy of the UKCTA was to negotiate directly with the railway industry, represented by the Railway Clearing House (RCH). The RCH was an industry association with significant influence on railway companies' policy and practice (Bagwell 1968; Campbell-Kelly 1994; Edwards 2008). The UKCTA's initial efforts met the obstruction of the RCH's high-handed attitude (Hancox 1953: 32). However, as the membership of the UKCTA grew, the railway officials started to realise that they could no longer ignore the collective demands of commercial travellers. The price of doing so was made clear in October 1887, when the UKCTA decided to divert all traffic from the London & North Western Railway. The direct action was organised in response to the railway company's refusal to allow commercial travellers extra luggage allowance (On the Road 1887: 187; Hancox 1953: 17). This threatened boycott was barely avoided by the company yielding to the demand of commercial travellers. Invigorated with the success, the UKCTA continued its campaigns into the twentieth century to achieve better deals for its members, some of which, such as special weekend ticket, were realised in the 1890s.

The direct negotiation with the railway industry was not the only stratagem the UKCTA employed. Using its parliamentary agents, the association sought to influence the legislation. It is significant that a voluntary passenger organisation such as the UKCTA had come to possess influence over the railway business and legislature, though we should not overstate the extent of its power. Unlike the Abolition Committee, the UKCTA was a legitimate body to represent a group of passengers, feeding their demands into the business and political process, backed by the threat of direct action. Still, from a wider perspective, the case of the UKCTA also poses some questions. Was not the UKCTA's direct dealing with the railway industry necessitated by the absence of a formal mechanism to improve travel conditions? Commercial travellers could mobilise a fairly large pressure group and act directly against the railways, but what could smaller, weaker groups do when they felt their needs and wants were neglected? Potentially, giving a particular group a better deal could be seen as unfair, especially when powerful groups seemed to be getting what they want, while the voices of the less powerful were unheeded (White 1995: 16; Becket 1910: 109–11; Gurney 1996: 83). The 1844 and 1883 Acts addressed some passenger issues, but these acts only set out the minimum quality obligation of rail passenger service. Improvements beyond the minimum requirements were still left to the railway companies. If the railway were a public service, as often described by the railway directors of the period (Alborn 1998: 217), the differential treatment was problematic, but the issue remained unaddressed before the First World War.

Failed Attempt at Consumer Participation: Interwar Years

During the war Britain's railways came under state control. To open the capacity for military movement and discourage civilian travel, most of the concessionary fares were withdrawn (Hancox 1953: 54). The end of the war did not immediately bring back the pre-war travel condition. Quite contrarily, the fares were kept high, to the great frustration of the general travelling public. During the discussion that led to a substantial reorganisation of the railway industry – eventually bringing about four railway groups – the possibility of introducing direct consumer representation to the railways' regulatory framework was briefly considered. However, the political discussion soon lost momentum (Divall 2009: 112). The passenger issues as a consequence were largely to be left to the Railway Rates Tribunal, with the Ministry of Transport (created in 1919) maintaining a hands-off stance.

The Railway Act of 1921 had provisions for the so-called Local Joint Committees, in which railway companies and their users were supposed to have regular contact (Gorst 1927: 67). The Tribunal was to decide upon the committees' basic terms of reference but it was apparently not very keen on the idea. The initiative finally came from outside the Tribunal in January 1923 when the Bradford Chamber of Commerce made an application to establish and to participate in such a committee (Railway Rates Tribunal 1922: 19, 30–31; Cameron, 1953: 55). Seeing that the Tribunal was still not forthcoming in formulating the organisation of Local Joint Committee, delegates from railway companies, the Association of British Chambers of Commerce and the Federation of British Industries started to discuss the shape and role of the Committee outside the Tribunal (Railway Rates Tribunal 1923: 2). As a result, 28 Local Joint Committees – later called Railway and Traders Conferences – were established. The Local Joint Committees thus set up were much less ambitious institutions than the 1921 Act had originally intended. The committees were voluntary bodies and their relationship with the Railway Rates Tribunal was rather ambiguous (Ministry of Transport 1947). Furthermore, the committees were regarded and acted, as a conciliatory body for railways, traders and industry (Railway Gazette 1923: 141). There were hardly any members from the general travelling public. Under the circumstances, it was not surprising that the committees focused chiefly on freight rates. The Local Joint Committees did not even become a regular feature of Britain's railway system, and in some areas, the committee had simply disappeared by the outbreak of the Second World War.

Ordinary passengers without trade or industry affiliation were almost completely left out from the scheme. Not all the passengers, however, acquiesced to this institutional alienation. In 1919 a fairly large group of passengers set up an organisation called the National Association of Railway Travellers (NART) (The Times 1919). This voluntary organisation seems to have been founded during an annual meeting of the British Association for the Advancement of Science (British Association for the Advancement of Science 1920: 177). The background of the association's establishment is unclear, but possibly the initiative came from the people who regarded travel as a crucial part of their intellectual communication. Charles Higham MP became the first chairman of the association, which claimed around half a million membership, including 40 MPs. NART immediately began its campaigns aiming at reducing rail fares down to the pre-war level. Its activity was supported by affiliate organisations, including the UKCTA (Railway Yearbook 1924: 95).

It is difficult to evaluate the impact of NART's campaigns on the reduction of rail fares. Indeed, the fares were subsequently reduced, but this seems to have resulted from the railways' competition with the increasing road traffic (Bagwell 1988; Barker 1986; Butterfield 1986). Whereas the ongoing intermodal competition worked to some passengers' advantage, the reduction of fares was hardly grounded on social consideration. The drive for cheaper rail travel, and better service in some cases, came chiefly from the railways' commercial motivation. The railways were desperately in need of attracting passengers, so they were willing to respond to passengers' needs and wants. But fundamentally 'it was left to the railways to develop an understanding of consumers and kinds of services which might appeal to them' (Divall 2009: 113). This was not entirely to the advantage of passengers. The railway companies did not make much effort to cater to minor groups of passengers on unremunerative lines. Behind the general reduction of fares and upgrading of services, some companies were considering – and in some cases carrying out – line closures, foreboding what was to come in the 1960s (Loft 2006: 19).

During the interwar period, there was a missed opportunity to reconfigure Britain's railway system and to incorporate a mechanism of passenger representation. At the same time, the Local Joint Committee, by giving membership only to trade and industrial users, consolidated and perpetuated the exclusion of the general travelling public. Although this was to some extent mitigated by the railways' need to sustain its passenger business in the face of road competition, passengers' position was precariously dependent upon the railways' goodwill that could easily disappear with a change of business condition. What could have changed the situation was the recognition of spontaneous passenger voices in a wider framework of transport policy, with some sort of mechanism to allow such voices constant inlet into official or business institutions. It did not happen, and the specific configuration of passenger issues during the interwar years was to reverberate in the later period.

Nationalised Railways and Passenger Representation

Britain's railways were, again, brought under state control during the Second World War. This time, the railways were not returned to private ownership with the end of the war. By the Transport Act of 1947 they became nationalised as British Railways (BR). The act, created by the Labour government, made a more serious attempt to address consumer participation than the half-hearted attempt by the 1921 Act by incorporating provisions for official consultative bodies of transport users. The consultative machinery consisted of a Central Transport Consultative Committee (CTCC) and 11 Transport Users' Consultative Committees (TUCC) (Gourvish 1986: 100; Hilton 2003: 147; Robson 1962: 246–51). The former was the central board overseeing the latter, its regional offshoots (Cameron: 1953: 55). During the parliamentary discussion over the Transport Bill, Minister of Transport Alfred Barnes stated that such a mechanism was proposed 'to enable the public adequately to represent their views' (Barnes 1946). This sounds very well, but Barnes' 'public' was still closely following the tradition of the Local Joint Committee. In fact, the Bill defined the membership of the consultative committees as representatives of 'agriculture, commerce, industry, labour and local authorities' (10 & 11 Geo. 6 c.49, 6 (4) (b)).

When the bill was examined by the House of Lords the lack of representation of the general public came under severe criticism. In the same vein as the 1921 Act, the government insisted that the local authorities could sufficiently represent the interest of the general public. Some members of the House disagreed. They advocated a more direct representation of ordinary travellers, the 'daily breader' or 'Billy Brown of London Town' (House of Lords 1947a). It was also argued that it was unfair to allow representation only from already organised interests, a point countered by the government's claim that there was no body 'fully representative of the interests of the travelling public'. There were more practical suggestions to allow representation from commercial travellers or to insert the words 'the interests of the travelling public' in the bill (House of Lords 1947b), but while the eventual legislation named local authorities as one of the interested parties to be represented in the TUCCs, the general public could find their way into the consultative machinery only through two – rather obscurely termed – 'additional' members of each TUCC (10 & 11 Geo. 6 c.49, 6 (4) (iii)).

The implicit model of the TUCCs was the Local Joint Committees, on which the Ministry of Transport gathered information in June and July 1947 (Ministry of Transport 1947). When compared with the Local Joint Committees, the TUCCs had representations from wider interests, but they were still dominated by trade and industry. The 'additional members' were included, such as Mrs M.H. Neal of the East Anglia TUCC, who was a member of the East Suffolk County Federation of Women's Institutes Executive Committee (Railway Gazette 1951: 278). It is nevertheless doubtful that members like Mrs Neal could attain an influential position in the consultative machinery in the face of strong trade and industry interests.

The power and influence of the CTCC and TUCCs have subsequently been curtailed both by legislation and practice (Haywood 2009: 67; Howe 1964; Wistrich 1990: 49). By the mid-1960s, some user groups had already been dismayed by the consultative bodies' very restricted terms of reference (Odell 1965). In its reports published in 1968 and 1976, the National Consumer Council (1976: 9) criticised the TUCCs as representing only a limited portion of passengers. The lack of mechanism to channel through the needs and wants of ordinary passengers was, once again, filled by the transport provider's goodwill, but customer input had to make some sort of business sense in the eyes of BR. And it was more likely that a group's voice was heard when it had connection or presence that the BR could not lightly push aside. The Orpington & District Rail Passengers Association (ODRPA) was one such case, being organised in a place where a sizable commuter population into the city of London existed. The association, after an unsuccessful attempt through official channels to improve local rail service, decided to make a direct appeal to BR (Orpington & District Rail Passengers Association 1964–67). The strategy brought some tangible results, but its impact was only to be felt in the association's immediate locality.

Like the interwar period, a fairly wide-scale private initiative was activated, and the National Association of Rail Passengers (NARP) was established in October 1976 (British Railways Board 1976). Despite its claim of 20,000 members, NARP failed to grow into an organisation to match the official consultative machinery. NARP existed in the shadow of the CTCC and TUCCs, like many other user groups that emerged in post-war Britain. The official consultative bodies were the only ones recognised by the transport policy makers. It is questionable that official bodies deserved such exclusive attention, and there were certainly a number of people, including those inside the machinery, who were almost entirely unhappy with the system. Eric Midwinter, chairman of the London Regional Passengers Committee in the mid-1980s,[2] clearly recognised that there was almost no consumer participation at the point of service delivery (Midwinter 1986: 195). He also lamented that the TUCCs did not possess the capacity 'to organise and make coherent the views of localised groups of customers' (Midwinter 1986: 197).

The limitation of the official consultative machinery was deeply rooted. The system created in 1947 had only an extremely limited scope in incorporating the views and voices of the ordinary passengers. To put it bluntly, the TUCCs were not designed to make coherent views of localised passenger groups. The consultative committees were firmly located in the tradition of the Local Joint Committees, dominated by trade, industry and the railways. In spite of its fundamental problem, it would be unfair to ignore a number of battles fought by the TUCCs against line closures (Haywood 2009: 61; Joy 1973: 115–32). Similarly, it would be simply wrong to say that all the passenger issues were neglected (Boggis 1990; Giblin 1986). Without doubt, however, there has been constant frustration of the

---

2   This was the successor to the London TUCC, later to become London TravelWatch (Schiefelbusch and Smale 2009: 255). See also (White 1995: 16).

insufficiency of the official consultative system and the sense that passenger voices were not much heeded (Robson 1962: 250). The emergence of spontaneous user groups was partly an expression of this long-standing frustration. But to explain their existence only in terms of negative response to the shortcomings of the existing system may not be productive.[3] From a long-term historical perspective, the appearance of voluntary associations, some of which had longer lineage than the official bodies, looks as though it is a perennial feature of transport. It is possibly because the needs and wants of passengers are variable over time and in different circumstances. If so, spontaneous passenger associations can be a legitimate part of transport, rather than an external factor only occasionally taken into consideration.

Conclusion

This chapter traced the history of passenger representation in Britain, delineating the general course of development while shedding light on some of the problems that were brought forward to the official consultative machinery created in 1947. Although some readers may feel that the narrative structure adopted here highlights the shortcomings and missed opportunities, the intention of this chapter is by no means to suggest that consumer participation in all areas of transport service is the solution or desirable: customers are not always right. But when passengers' voices are unheeded, or only selectively picked up, there is a risk of unfair discrimination against certain groups of passengers. If official representation tries to totally replace passengers' direct participation and relegate the ordinary travelling public or voluntary associations outside the purview of transport policy, it might help creating such injustice, perpetuating a hierarchy among passenger groups.

Hence, relying too much upon the official representative machinery while neglecting spontaneous passenger movements is probably not a wise policy. Doing so would unnecessarily limit policy options and might even lead to injustice to some groups of passengers. Policy makers need to keep in mind that the transport system is a changeable ecology, in which a healthy balance of all the actors needs to be maintained. By fine-tuning the balance, transport justice, various passenger interests and business performance can be maximised (Dienel 2009).

If passenger representation is a fluid entity, the search for a single representative body of passengers is possibly a futile exercise. Even so, or because of that very reason, the non-existence of such an idealised passenger representative should not exonerate policy makers from taking passenger voices seriously (Webler and Renn 1995: 28). Careful consideration needs to be given to passenger representation not simply because we need to hear users' voice, but also because fair treatment is required for various and varying passenger voices.

---

3   See, for example, the views of the Monopolies and Mergers Committee in the 1980s (Redwood and Hatch 1982: 142).

References

Alborn, T.L. (1998). *Conceiving Companies: Joint-Stock Politics in Victorian England*. London: Routledge.

Alderman, G. (1973). *The Railway Interest*. Leicester: Leicester University Press.

British Association for the Advancement of Science (1920). *Report of the British Association for the Advancement of Science*. London: J. Murray.

Bagwell, P. (1968). *The Railway Clearing House in the British Economy 1842–1922*. London: Allen & Unwin.

——— (1988). *The Transport Revolution*. 2nd ed. London: Routledge.

Barker, T.C. (1986). Some Thoughts on the Railways' Competitors in General and Road Transport Competition in Particular, Part I. *Journal of the Railway and Canal Historical Society* 28(8), pp. 328–37.

Barnes, A. (1946). *Hansard*. 16 December.

Beckett, C.J. (1910). *Darwen Industrial Co-operative Society Ltd*. Manchester: Co-operative Wholesale Society's Printing Works.

Bickerstaff, K., Tolley, R. and Walker, G. (2002). Transport Planning and Participation: The Rhetoric and Realities of Public Involvement. *Journal of Transport Geography* 10(1), pp. 61–73.

Boggis, F. (1990). Customer Care: a 'Bottom-Up' View of a 'Top-Down' Policy. *European Journal of Marketing* 24(12), pp. 22–34.

British Railways Board (1976). Secretary's Department Files. TNA, AN 192/1238.

Butcher, L. (2012). *Transport: Passenger Rights, Representation and Complaints*. Parliamentary Briefing Paper (SN03163). Available at: http://www.parliament.uk/briefing-papers/SN03163.pdf (accessed 13 May 2015).

Butterfield, P. (1986). Grouping, Pooling and Competition: The Passenger Policy of the London and North Eastern Railway, 1923–39. *Journal of Transport History* Series 3, 7(1), pp. 21–47.

Cain, P.J. (1991). Railways 1870–1914: The Maturity of the Private System. In *Transport in Victorian Britain*, ed. M.J. Freeman and D.H. Aldcroft. Manchester: Manchester University Press, pp. 93–133.

Cameron, M.A. (1953). Transport Users' Consultative Committees. *Journal of the Institute of Transport* 26(2), pp. 54–8.

Campbell-Kelly, M. (1994). The Railway Clearing House and Victorian Data Processing. In *Information Acumen: The Understanding and Use of Knowledge in Modern Business*, ed. L. Bud-Frierman. London: Routledge, pp. 51–74.

Casson, M. (2009). *The World's First Railway System: Enterprise, Competition, and Regulation on the Railway Network in Victorian Britain*. Oxford: Oxford University Press.

Dienel, H.-L. (2009). Introduction. In *Public Transport and Its Users: The Passenger's Perspective in Planning and Customer Care*, ed. M. Schiefelbusch and Hans-Liudger Dienel. Aldershot: Ashgate, pp. 1–3.

Divall, C. (2009). The Modern Passenger: Constructing the Consumer on Britain's Railways, 1919–1939. In *Railway Modernization: an Historical Perspective (19th and 20th Centuries)*, ed. M. Pinheiro. Lisbon: CEHCP, pp. 109–22.

Dudley, G. and Richardson, J. (2001). *Why Does Policy Change? Lessons from British Transport Policy, 1945–99*. London: Routledge.

Dyos, H.J. (1982). Workmen's Fares in South London, 1860–1914. In *Exploring the Urban Past: Essays in Urban History*, ed. D. Cannadine and D.A. Reeder. Cambridge: Cambridge University Press, pp. 87–100.

Edwards, R. (2008). 'Minutes Most Innocuous and Neat': The Records of the Railway Clearing House, 1923–63. *Business Archives* 96, pp. 1–14.

French, M. (2005). Commercials, Careers, and Culture: Travelling Salesmen in Britain, 1890s–1930s. *Economic History Review* 58(2), pp. 352–77.

——— (2010). On The Road: Travelling Salesmen and Experiences of Mobility in Britain Before 1939. *Journal of Transport History* Series 3, 31(2), pp. 133–50.

Gibbins, E.A. (2000). *The Railway Closure Controversy*. Alsager: Leisure Products.

Giblin, D. (1986). Customer Care in British Rail. In *Are They Being Served? Quality Consciousness in Service Industries*, ed. B. Moores. Oxford: Philip Allan, pp. 57–66.

Glaister, S., Burnham, J., Handley S. and Travers, T. (2006). *Transport Policy in Britain*. 2nd ed. Basingstoke: Palgrave Macmillan.

Gorst, E.M. (1927). *A Guide to the Railway Rates Tribunal*. London: Solicitors Law Stationery Society.

Gourvish, T.R. (1986). *British Railways, 1948–73: A Business History*. Cambridge: Cambridge University Press.

Grant, J. (1977). *The Politics of Urban Transport Planning*. London: Earth Resources Research.

Grey, A. (1975). *Urban Fares Policy*. Farnborough: Saxon House.

Grugel, L.E. (1976). *George Jacob Holyoake: A Study in the Evolution of a Victorian Radical*. Philadelphia: Porcupine Press.

Gurney, P. (1996). *Co-operative Culture and the Politics of Consumption in England, 1870–1930*. Manchester: Manchester University Press.

Hancox, T.W. (1953). *Seventy Years, 1883–1953: History of the United Commercial Travellers' Association*. London: United Commercial Travellers' Association of Great Britain and Ireland.

Haywood, R. (2009). *Railways, Urban Development and Town Planning in Britain: 1948–2008*. Farnham: Ashgate.

Headicar, P. (2009). *Transport Policy and Planning in Great Britain*. London: Routledge.

Hermes (1899). *Taxes on Travelling: Interview with Mr George Jacob Holyoake*. London: Columbus.

Hilton, M. (2003). *Consumerism in Twentieth-Century Britain: The Search for Historical Movement*. Cambridge: Cambridge University Press.

Hodgkins, D. (2002). *The Second Railway King: The Life and Times of Sir Edward Watkin, 1819–1901*. Cardiff: Merton Priory Press.

Holyoake, G.J. (1905). *Bygones Worth Remembering*. London: T. Fisher Unwin.

Hoppen, K.T. (1998). *The Mid-Victorian Generation, 1846–1886*. Oxford: Oxford University Press.

Hosgood, C.P. (1994). The 'Knights of the Road': Commercial Travellers and the Culture of the Commercial Room in Late-Victorian and Edwardian England. *Victorian Studies* 37(4), pp. 519–47.

House of Commons (1876). *Hansard*. 7 March.

House of Lords (1947a). *Hansard*. 12 June.

——— (1947b). *Hansard*. 9 July.

Howe, M. (1964). The Transport Act, 1962, and the Consumers' Consultative Committees. *Public Administration* 42(1), pp. 45–56. Available at: http://onlinelibrary.wiley.com/doi/10.1111/j.1467–9299.1964.tb01733.x/abstract (accessed 13 May 2015).

Hyde, F.E. (1934). *Mr Gladstone at the Board of Trade*. London: Cobden-Sanderson.

Joy, S. (1973). *The Train that Ran Away: A Business History of British Railways, 1948–1968*. London: Ian Allan.

Lee, C.E. (1946). *Passenger Class Distinctions*. London: The Railway Gazette.

Loft, C. (2006). *Government, the Railways, and the Modernization of Britain: Beeching's Last Trains*. London: Routledge.

MacDermot, E.T. (1964). *History of the Great Western Railway*. Rev. ed., vol. 2. London: Ian Allan.

Mclean, I. and Foster, C. (1992). The Political Economy of Regulation: Interests, Ideology, Voters, and the UK Regulation of Railways Act 1844. *Public Administration* 70(3), pp. 313–31.

Midwinter, E. (1986). Looking After the Passenger. In *Passenger Transport: Planning for Radical Change*, ed. J.D. Carr. Aldershot: Gower, pp. 193–200.

Ministry of Transport (1947). Consultative Committees Policy. TNA, MT 45/474.

Mitchell, B.R. (1988). *British Historical Statistics*. Cambridge: Cambridge University Press.

Mokyr, J. (2009). *The Enlightened Economy: An Economic History of Britain 1700–1850*. New Haven: Yale University Press.

Morning Post (1879). *Morning Post*. 20 January.

Murillo, N.R. (2008). New Rights for Rail Passengers in the European Union. *International Travel Law Journal* (2), pp. 91–9.

National Consumer Council (1976). *Consumers and the Nationalised Industries*. London: HMSO.

Odell, P. (1965) Letter, P. Odell to S. Swingler, 13 December. In Orpington & District Rail Passengers Association papers. Bromley Local Studies Library, ref. 706/1.

On the Road (1887). *On the Road*. November–December.

Orpington & District Rail Passengers Association (1964–67). ODRPA papers. Bromley Local Studies Library, ref. 706/1–3.

Pall Mall Gazette (1878). *Pall Mall Gazette*. 31 December.

Parris, H. (1965). *Government and the Railways in Nineteenth-Century Britain.* London: Routledge and Kegan Paul.

Passenger Focus (2011). *Annual Report and Accounts, 2010–11.* London: The Stationery Office.

Polasky, J. (2001). Transplanting and Rooting Workers in London and Brussels: a Comparative History. *Journal of Modern History* 73(3), pp.52–60.

Railway Companies Association (1872). RCA, Minutes, 30 July. TNA, RAIL 1098/2.

———— (1874). RCA, Minutes, 14 October. TNA, RAIL 1098/2.

Railway Gazette (1923). *Railway Gazette.* 2 February.

———— (1951). *Railway Gazette.* 9 March.

Railway Passenger Duty Historical File (n.d). TNA, RAIL 1007/573.

Railway Rates Tribunal (1922). *Annual Report.*

———— (1923). *Annual Report.*

Railway Yearbook (1924). *Railway Yearbook.*

Redwood, J. and Hatch, J. (1982). *Controlling Public Industries.* Oxford: Basil Blackwell.

Robson, W.A. (1962). *Nationalized Industry and Public Ownership.* 2nd ed. London: Allen & Unwin.

Rolt, L.T.C. (2007). *Red for Danger: The Classic History of British Railway Disasters.* New edn. Stroud: Sutton Publishing.

Schiefelbusch, M. (2005). Citizens' Involvement and the Representation of Passenger Interests in Public Transport: Dimensions of a Long-Neglected Area of Transport Planning and Policy with Case Studies from Germany. *Transport Reviews* 25(3), pp. 261–82.

Schiefelbusch, M. and Smale, A. (2009). United Kingdom. In *Public Transport and Its Users: The Passenger's Perspective in Planning and Customer Care*, ed. M. Schiefelbusch and H.-L. Dienel. Aldershot: Ashgate, pp. 248–59.

Schivelbusch, W. (1986). *The Railway Journey: The Industrialization of Time and Space in the 19th Century.* New edn. Oxford: Blackwell.

Select Committee on Railways (1970a). *Third Report from the Select Committee on Railways.* Orig. 1844. Shannon, Ireland: Irish University Press.

———— (1970b). *Fifth Report from the Select Committee on Railways.* Orig. 1844. Shannon, Ireland: Irish University Press.

Smith, D. (1988). *The Railway and Its Passengers: A Social History.* Newton Abbot: David & Charles.

The Times (1841). *The Times.* 27 December.

———— (1884). *The Times.* 22 January.

———— (1919). *The Times.* 13 June.

Travelling Tax Abolition Committee (1878). *Gazette of the Travelling Tax Abolition Committee,* September.

Tyme, J. (1978). *Motorways versus Democracy: Public Inquiries into Road Proposals and Their Political Significance.* London: Macmillan.

Webler, T. and Renn, O. (1995). A Brief Primer on Participation: Philosophy and Practice. In *Fairness and Competence in Citizen Participation: Evaluating Models for Environmental Discourse*, ed. O. Renn, T. Webler and P.M. Wiedemann. Dordrecht: Kluwer Academic, pp. 17–33.

White, P. (1995). *Public Transport: Its Planning, Management, and Operation.* 3rd ed. London: UCL Press.

Wistrich, E. (1990). Transport. In *Consuming Public Services*, ed. N. Deakin and A. Wright. London: Routledge, pp. 35–55.

Chapter 6

High Speed 2 Where? A Historical Perspective on the 'Strategic Case' for HS2

Colin Divall

High Speed 2 (HS2) is a £50 billion passenger railway scheduled to open from Birmingham to London in 2026 and from Manchester and Leeds in 2033. The route might turn into the backbone of a trunk network supplementing the one built largely in the nineteenth century: the government has mooted both an extension to the Scottish central belt and a new line across the north of England (HS3). In any case services using HS2 are planned to link eight of the UK's largest conurbations, either throughout by high-speed trains or by trains that also run on the existing railway.

The Labour government made construction of HS2 official policy in 2009 and the project has since enjoyed widespread, if not universal, political support at national and regional levels: some tens of millions of pounds were spent on preparatory works in advance of final parliamentary approval. However, this does not mean that the 'strategic case' – to adopt the official terminology – for HS2 has been well made. Indeed the Labour government's decision was in some ways surprising given that just three years earlier Sir Roy Eddington's review of UK transport policy, widely regarded as the most authoritative for many years, warned against this kind of large-scale investment; he argued that Britain's economic geography, the strength of airline competition and the 'surprising low' market for inter-urban business travel meant that it would be 'difficult' to demonstrate that high-speed rail (HSR) would be the best way of meeting the UK's economic, environmental and other policy goals (Eddington 2006).

This chapter draws upon history to question the wisdom of this political U-turn and to suggest further avenues of historical research that might help to inform debate over HS2. The past is always in some degree a foreign country and so cannot tell us whether either Eddington or the current political consensus is 'right' about HS2 – that is a task for future historians. So too is the job of analysing in detail the political and policy machinations that have produced that consensus. But an understanding of the way in which similar mega transport projects have developed in the recent past, of the experience of high-speed railways overseas, and of the UK's record over more than 150 years of planning rail infrastructure cautions against some of the key assumptions underpinning HS2. To take the last point first: the short history of the HS2 project to date suggests that the nineteenth-century's failure to develop a strategic plan for Britain's railway network is being repeated, despite claims to the contrary. History also warns that predictions of the long-term need for future rail capacity might be less reliable than is assumed. Finally som of the arguments for HS2 based upon economic growth and regional development are not widely supported by what has happened over the half-century's experience of HSR outside the UK. In sum the project already bears many of the hallmark of the kind of megaproject that academics such as Bend Flyvbjerg (2009) argue rich countries can afford but that do not always add much to the sum of economic well-being let along social equity or ecological sustainability.

The 'Strategic Case', Mega Transport Projects and History

If it is built HS2 will be a mega transport project (MTP), defined by the OMEGA study of 30 such schemes as:

> land-based transport infrastructure investments within and connecting major urban areas and metropolitan regions in the form of bridges, tunnels, road and rail links, or combinations of these. They are projects that entail a construction cost of over US$1 billion (at 1990 prices), completed since 1990 and are frequently perceived as critical to the 'success' of major urban, metropolitan, regional and /or national development. (OMEGA Centre 2012: iii)

MTPs are often characterised by a fluid set of strategic objectives that shift along with their political, economic, social, cultural and environmental contexts. This i unavoidable: because MTPs are conceived, planned, constructed and operated (and to anticipate, disposed of) over many tens of decades – perhaps a century or more the geographical regions, economic sectors, communities and environments the serve will alter, perhaps radically. Indeed as 'agents of change' MTPs can be partl responsible for such transformations. It is therefore reasonable to assess a MT against a wider range of objectives than those that originally inspired or were use to approve it. Other criteria might legitimately emerge during the project lifecycle thus for example the fact that HS1 (the Channel Tunnel link) was not originall planned to stimulate urban and regional regeneration or to provide extra capacit for long-distance commuting does not mean that these factors should be ignore in appraisals (OMEGA Centre 2008). However many MTPs have been develope without sufficient regard for the wide range of stakeholders that will inevitabl be affected and without thoroughly considering alternative proposals (OMEGA 2012: 16–23; OMEGA 2008; Priemus, Flyvbjerg and van Wee 2008: 2–1: de Bruijn and Leijten 2008: 84).

How open has the Department for Transport (DfT) and its arm's-length deliver vehicle, HS2 Ltd, been in formulating HS2's strategic goals? A comprehensiv analysis is not possible here but the evidence is not encouraging. The strategic cas has gone through several iterations of the same basic objectives (DfT 2011, 201: with the latest (October 2013) version based on the premise that the government task is 'to build a stronger, more balanced economy capable of delivering lasting growth and widely shared prosperity' (DFT 2013: 3.1.1). Thus since transport is a key to economic development and Britain's domestic air, road and rail networks are increasingly congested HS2 is needed:

- to provide sufficient capacity to meet long-term demand, and to improve resilience and reliability across the [rail] network; and
- to improve connectivity by delivering better journey times and making travel easier (DfT 2013: 3.1.2).

Supplementing these key transport objectives the DfT argues that it is important to assess 'how the new railway will contribute to the economy at local, regional and national level' (DfT 2013: 69); a consistent goal has been regenerating regions outside London and the south east (DfT 2013: 72–4, 5.2.1–5.3.5).

Discussion of these objectives in the public realm has made remarkably little use of the last half-century's global experience of high-speed rail (HSR).[1] There are probably three reasons for this: the lack of detailed studies; methodological difficulties; and the weak evidence for some of the key claims made for HS2. First, given the huge capital sums involved it is striking that there are so few studies of HSR's successes and failures in meeting economic, social and environmental goals (Preston 2009: 12; Priemus, Flyvbjerg and van Wee 2008: 10–11). The demand for such work seems obvious; as one academic appearing before the House of Lords Economic Affairs Select Committee remarked in 2014:

> There is a need for more ex-post appraisal. That is, to look back at investments we have made in the past, not just in this country but borrowing evidence from other European countries and other countries more generally, and asking what impact did they really have … We need to look back at the past. We need to do that to inform us about whether the cost-benefit numbers we have are of the right order of magnitude … (Graham and Venables 2014: 252)

However, there are methodological difficulties in doing this: as a rather more sceptical witness argued, '[g]iven the extent to which each large-scale [transport] infrastructure project is unique, it is very difficult to calibrate models on past experience' (Vickerman 2014: 697; see also Overman 2014: 577, 583).

Difficult – but not impossible. For example, the OMEGA study of MTPs demonstrates that analyses sensitive to differences between places and times can discern general trends. But past experience has always been open to being used selectively by a project's proponents and opponents. For example, lengthy debates in the 1930s and 1940s within elite political, policy and professional circles over the wisdom of building motorways in the UK drew in a partial way upon

---

1   There is anecdotal evidence that the perceived success of the Japanese Shinkansen inspired early support for HS2 within the senior ranks of the Labour government.

overseas evidence from US parkways, Italian autostrade and German autobahnen (Merriman 2007: 23–59; Mom 2005). This *rhetorical* use of history – both in the past and nowadays – alerts us to the ways in which participants in the policy process sometimes frame their use of evidence: asking certain questions but not others, or citing one fact while ignoring another shapes the conclusions that are drawn. The point needs to be kept in mind as the HS2 project evolves: enthusiasm for 'evidence-based policy' should be taken as an alert to be on the lookout for 'policy-based evidence'.

Bearing these caveats in mind what does history suggest about the factors underlying the 'success' or 'failure' of HSR? We must be clear about the criteria being used – are they those of the project's promoters, of other stakeholders or those of comparatively disinterested analysts (of which there are few when it comes to HS2)? For example, there is little doubt that Spain's HSR network is poorly used and hopelessly uneconomic: but in an important sense this is irrelevant when we understand that the Spanish political elite regards HSR chiefly as a symbol of national political integration – its mere existence, linking the provinces to the capital, is more important than usage (Albalate and Bel 2014: 95–111). Nonetheless, most HSR projects have been aimed at some combination of the factors at play with HS2: improving transport networks and economic growth. Let us take these in turn.

Travel Demand

HSR is at its best when boosting the efficiency of transport corridors with a proven high demand, particularly by providing additional capacity on a railway that is congested or is likely to become so. A fairly comprehensive historical overview by two Spanish economists, Daniel Albalate and Germà Bel (2014), of Japan, France, Germany, Spain and China (with brief asides on Italy, Korea and Taiwan) shows that such HSR lines have often been highly successful. Indeed, within a few years of opening, the pioneering routes in Japan (Toyko–Osaka, 1964) and France (Paris–Lyon, 1981–83) had generated sufficient income to pay off construction costs. However, these are the exceptions: while HSR on heavily trafficked routes generally covers operating costs, it can take many decades to pay back the very high capital investment, if indeed this is achieved at all. The narrow financial case for investing in HSR is therefore almost always weak or even unfavourable.

This is not unusual with MTPs, because the benefits to both users and society as a whole are not captured by the revenue generated. HSR is therefore commonly justified on the basis of social cost–benefit analysis (CBA), weighing monetarised estimates of a project's general costs against those of its value to users and, increasingly, the wider economy. Although CBA has existed for well over 50 years the technique is still evolving and results are, like any modelling exercise, subject to decisions about what to include or exclude (the system boundaries), as well as to uncertainties about the future behaviour of the model's elements – for instance, the value of time saved by travelling faster, or the relationship between economic growth and the demand for travel – and the choice of the period over which the costs and benefits are to be reckoned (Wee and Tavasszy 2008). But whatever the exact details, even in Japan and France network extensions have increasingly relied on CBA, and not surprisingly returns have tended to diminish as HSR is built along less busy corridors (Abalate and Bel 2014; Meunier 2002; Hood 2006: 91–129).

The prediction of congestion by the 2020s is a key factor in the argument for HS2 and so it would be useful if historical experience could offer guidance about the level of traffic needed to generate a positive benefit–cost ratio (BCR). This is not easily done, partly because countries use different methods of CBA even for the narrowly defined transport elements. The problem is compounded by the now-standard inclusion of wider economic benefits into CBA, which introduces yet more methodological difficulties in comparing like with like (Olsson, Økland and Halvorsen 2012; van Wee and Tavasszy 2008: 61–2; Vickerman 2008). Nevertheless, despite these caveats various estimates based upon European experience suggest that a 500 km (312 mile) HSR route needs between six and nine million passenger journeys in the first year of operation to generate a positive BCR, with the upper limit regarded as closer to the norm (Albalate and Bel 2014: 25).

Perhaps wisely in terms of the project's perceived credibility the DfT's strategic case does not offer a global figure for the predicted usage of HS2 in the first year of operation, concentrating instead on very long-term predictions and, in the short-term, on the relief of over-crowding on commuter trains and peak-hour, long-distance services. It does however give positive BCRs, estimated over the Treasury's standard 60 years for major projects, of 1.4 (excluding wider economic benefits) for the first stage and 1.8 for the second (DfT 2013: 5.4.15). Although favourable these are not ratios that would normally attract high levels of public investment in transport infrastructure in the UK without pressing additional reasons for a project to go ahead: they are however comparable with the BCR of 1.1 to 1.5 that underpinned government approval for HS1 (OMEGA 2008: 116–17).[2]

In historical terms the predictions of costs and traffic estimates upon which BCRs are based have often been badly wrong despite the increasing sophistication of modelling. For example, international passenger volumes over HS1 and through the Channel Tunnel have been consistently much lower than initially predicted (OMEGA 2008: 117–18; Gourvish 2006: 366–73; Anguera 2006). The key study is Bent Flyvbjerg's analysis of 58 major rail infrastructure projects (not all of them HSR) completed over a 70-year period; the average cost overrun was 44.7 per cent. Similarly, for 25 rail projects over a 30-year period, traffic was on average 51.4 per cent lower than predicted.[3] In neither case did the quality of forecasting improve significantly over the decades (Flyvbjerg 2009: 346–7, 2008).

---

2   HS2's BCRs have generally worsened as the project has developed (Hall 2013: 342–9).

3   The standard deviations were 38.4 and 28.1 respectively – which means that there was quite a wide spread to the degree by which estimates were out.

However, since 2004 all major publicly funded infrastructure projects in the UK have been assessed in a way that tries to take account of the systematic errors, or 'optimism bias', that distort insiders' estimates of costs and traffic levels. Reference-class forecasting adds often substantial correcting factors based upon the historical experience of similar projects (Flyvbjerg 2004, 2008: 133–6). The technique has limitations, particularly when data on similar projects are scanty (an issue, as we have already seen, with HSR), but nevertheless the cost estimates for HS2 include contingencies based on the historical outturns of 'major infrastructure projects in the UK and overseas' (DfT 2012: 60) – although these contingencies have been reduced in scope and size as the DfT claims to have gained a better understanding of costs. For example, in January 2012 the DfT added a 64 per cent contingency against the base infrastructure costs for the Birmingham route while by 2013 this had been reduced to 38 per cent, giving a total of £21.4 billion (with a 95 per cent degree of confidence that this figure can be met) or £19.4 billion (with a lower confidence level of 50 per cent) (DfT 2012: 4.3.1, 7.2.2, 10.7.1–5; DfT 2013: 5.4.9–12 n.157, 7.2.2, 7.2.16–21).

The DfT also acknowledges that long-term predictions of travel demand is 'inherently challenging' and are seldom very accurate (DfT 2013: 5.4.29). Thus, although HS2 has been appraised over a 60-year lifecycle, passenger figures are capped at the level predicted for 2036 (DfT 2013: 5.4.21). However, it is still questionable whether this attempt to forecast over roughly two decades sufficiently acknowledges the historical volatility of passenger trends in the UK or of the experience of HSR overseas. As the analysis for HS2 recognises, this is not just a question of aggregate demand. In the UK different market sectors – such as long-distance commuting, business trips or leisure travel – have developed in distinctive ways over the last few decades and it is not clear that for all the long history of passenger-demand modelling in the UK (Nash, Wardman, Button and Nijkamp 2002: 261–452) and the sophistication of current models that we fully understand how and why this has occurred and thus how trends might develop. As a member of the academic team responsible for the modelling techniques used for HS2 has remarked, 'there has to be a caveat that 20 years ago we would not necessarily have predicted the kind of rail growth that we have seen over the last 20 years' (Mackie, Niblett and Vickerman 2014: 518).

Although such trends seem to support the arguments of those who justify HS2 in terms of rising demand, their real import is more subtle: that infrastructure planning has very long-term implications whereas knowledge of the flows that will have to be accommodated (and which might in part be generated by a MTP) is perhaps little better than a guess. This lesson is not lost on some of HS2's proponents: according to Rod Smith, a former scientific advisor to the DfT, HS2 is not about 'counting beans' with CBA but making an imaginative commitment to infrastructure that will serve the UK for 50 years or more (Smith 2014). Or as the DfT argues more prosaically, HS2 would provide the '[f]lexibility to respond to uncertain future economic circumstances' in ways that cannot be easily captured by CBA (DfT 2013: 5.4.19). The distinguished planner the late

Sir Peter Hall made the point more forcibly still: CBA 'becomes the enemy of good strategic policy' precisely because it cannot capture the potentially transformative, dynamic effects that MTPs have on economic activity and hence on travel demand (Hall 2013: 349–50). These points are well taken, but they also suggest that HS2 should be tested against a much wider range of scenarios than apparently informs the DfT's long-term appraisal. The 'most pessimistic' of these, projecting 36 years into the future from a 2013 base, still predicts rising levels of travel demand that stay comfortably within conventional assumptions of growing population and economic activity (DfT 2013: 5.4.21–23, 5.4.35). We shall return to this important point.

Wider Economic Benefits and Regional Regeneration

HS2's wider benefits in terms of national economic growth and regional regeneration were critically important for the October 2013 iteration of the strategic case, raising the estimated BCRs by around a fifth to 1.7 for the Birmingham leg and 2.3 for the entire network, and seem likely to become increasingly significant for the debate (DfT 2013: 5.4.5–6, 5.4.15; Hall 2013: 350). There are good theoretical reasons and empirical evidence to suggest that MTPs can have these kinds of impact. For example, 'agglomeration effects' boost GDP at both the national and regional level because businesses will be better connected to each other and are able to draw upon larger, more geographically dispersed pools of labour (Vickerman 2008; Hall 2013: 349–51). However, the aggregate size of these effects and their regional distribution is very controversial and became more so when in 2013 a novel way of assessing them was added to HS2's strategic case. The consultants KPMG estimated that by 2037 they might add £8–15 billion annually to the UK economy, with the English midlands and north taking a greater share than London and the south-east (DfT 2013: 5.3.4–5; Hall 2013: 351; Graham and Venables 2014: 251–2).

What does the history of HSR suggest about economic growth in general and regional development in particular? The picture is mixed but not, on balance, very favourable. An early overview commissioned by HS2 Ltd (but given little publicity) from Terry Gourvish, the Channel Tunnel's official historian (Gourvish 2006), concluded that it would be 'unwise to pin much faith in new [high-speed] railways as an engine of growth' although he noted that across Europe HSR might have been responsible for 'modest' increases in GDP of between 1 and 3 per cent (Gourvish 2010: 26). Albalate and Bel's more recent metastudy (2012, 2014) comes to broadly the same conclusion: generally speaking HSR has done little to stimulate entirely fresh economic activity or investment but has helped to consolidate and sustain existing trends.

Neither is the evidence on regional regeneration very encouraging, although here the problem of the lack of detailed studies is particularly pressing since the geographical distribution of agglomeration and other effects depends upon the make-up of a region's economy: it is dangerous to generalise from a limited number of cases (Vickerman 2008: 67–76). Albalate and Bel provisionally conclude (2014: 158) that attempts to use HSR to promote regional development and inter-regional equity 'only seems to result in economic failure of the project' to borrow Chia-Lin Chen and Peter Hall's evocative language (2013: 355), on balance HSR has 'desertified' rather than 'irrigated' the regions. Albalate and Bel do however observe some regional effects: because HSR provides fast and reliable transport for businesses that depend on inter- and intra-organisational mobility – predominantly those in service industries – HSR can benefit city regions with economies already weighted in this direction. Even so, there is a high risk that in any given city-pair, the bulk of the benefits will accrue to the one that is already stronger; 'the most important nodes are those that benefit most' (Albante and Bel 2014: 27–9, 168–9, quote on 28). The economic geographer John Tomaney comes to a similar conclusion (Tomaney 2011), and a rare retrospective appraisal of the Channel Tunnel about a decade after opening concluded that there were few significant benefits to the regions close to the tunnel portals (Hay, Meredith and Vickerman: 2004).

However, a more recent study that looks in considerable detail at regional characteristics is more positive. While Chen and Hall argue that HSR neither guarantees the reduction of regional inequalities nor the irrigation of sub-regions beyond a provincial capital, they show that since the early 1980s Manchester in the UK and Lille in France have exploited HSR connections with their capital to do better economically than other urban regions (but *not* significantly to close the wide gap with the national metropolis).[4] The key seems to lie in widening access to the HSR hub through local and regional transport improvements combined with a whole range of non-transport initiatives in fields such as education, housing and the transformation of the physical environment. Chen and Hall conclude that France's decentralised and integrated approach to strategic land-use and transport planning is much more likely to produce regional benefits than the UK's centralised and disaggregated governance of these issues (Chen and Hall 2013: 355–60, 365–7; see also Banister and Givoni 2013: 330–35). In sum, historical experience does *not* demonstrate that HS2 will inevitably fail to contribute to regional regeneration: but it does suggest that successes will be limited, particularly in closing the gap between London and the regions, and highly dependent on sustained and concerted effort by politicians, planners and other stakeholders to identify, adopt and adapt to local circumstance the factors that have underpinned success elsewhere. The DfT (2013: 5.3.5) recognises that more evidence is needed here and the opportunity to carry out more, and more through analyses of HSR overseas should not be missed.

---

4   In Manchester's case HSR means 'low-speed high speed' running at a maximum of 200 kph / 125 mph over existing tracks.

Strategic Visions: A Missed Opportunity

So far this chapter has concentrated on how history might inform the debate over HS2 as a project framed by governments, the DfT and HS2 Ltd – as one designed to meet anticipated congestion on domestic transport networks and to stimulate long-term economic growth and regional regeneration. But these are not the only ways to think about HS2 or indeed whether more HSR should be built at all in the UK. MTPs are always inherently political projects in the sense that they embody choices between alternative futures – or at least between alternative *visions* of the future since, as we have seen, it is difficult to predict developments over tens of decades. Building HS2 would certainly have far-reaching consequences for the UK in the very long term and in this sense it is indeed reasonable to argue that uncertain BCRs are irrelevant 'bean counting': a slavish adherence to monetarised cost–benefit analysis does stifle our collective imagination about how transport might express a wider range of human values. But the key questions are: What kind of values? What kind of society? And hence what kind of transport networks and technologies do we want? The rest of the chapter argues that history has an important role in demonstrating the possibility and indeed the necessity of thinking more imaginatively about the future of transport in the UK.

The transformative power of some MTPs is so great that in retrospect it can be very difficult to imagine a world in which they had not been built – to stretch definitions a little, what would the UK have looked like had mainline railways not been constructed from the 1830s or the motorways from the late 1950s? We cannot tell other than in the broadest of terms (for example, Hawke 1970), but in both cases there were alternative visions about how transport might serve social and economic goals. Some of these were eventually realised, at least in part. For example, once the first trunk railways demonstrated a demand for long-distance travel the private companies extracted sizeable profits from carrying relatively small numbers of elite passengers in those parts of the country where the early lines ran. It is exaggerating only a little to characterise the rest of the nineteenth century as a struggle to obtain a measure of social and spatial equality of access to this 'railway speed' by means of excursion trains, third-class carriages on long-distance trains, 'workmen's tickets' and so on (Divall and Shin 2011). There are striking parallels here with the criticism that business travellers and the better-off in the metropolitan areas of the English central regions would benefit most from HS2. The DfT is sensitive to this issue, stressing how HS2 services would serve many destinations off the new line and suggesting that fares policy could facilitate travel by poorer people (DfT 2012: 16; DfT 2013: 56–67). Similar issues were addressed in debates about the French TGV network in the 1960s and 1970s (Meunier 2002). Here is another topic where more historical research is needed: it is arguable that our knowledge of the relationship between social disadvantage and rail usage over the last 50 years is weaker than that in the nineteenth century, with the consequence that the base against which HS2 might be judged in terms of social equity is far less firm that it could or should be (Hine 2011; Lucas 2011; Rajé 2004: 10–12).

But perhaps the most striking absence from official discourse about HS2 is any recognition of just how sharply total greenhouse-gas (GHG) emissions from land-based transport must be reduced by 2050 in order to meet the UK's legally mandated contribution to combating climate change (Goulden, Ryley and Dingwall 2014: 139). While concerns over the environmental impacts of transport infrastructure date back at least to improvements to river navigations in the early modern period, the kind of existential threat posed by climate change (at least to societies that are not as rich as the UK) amounts to a rupture with these earlier histories. Nevertheless, a long-term perspective drives home the point that the present scale and scope of the ways we move are highly dependent upon what the sociologist John Urry calls a historically 'momentary period of carbon hubris' (Urry 2011: 17). Urry thus questions whether societies like the UK are culturally, socially and politically prepared to make the transition to a post-carbon world with sufficient urgency to avoid a potentially catastrophic collapse in our high-carbon mobile lifestyles.

Because HSR can potentially be operated by electricity with low, or even very-low GHG emissions, it has been put forward as a partial solution to the conundrum of how we can become ever-more mobile without imposing huge ecological costs on future generations; modal shift from aviation and road has been a key environmental objective of HS2 (National Audit Office 2013: 5). There is an evolving debate about whether HSR can really be counted as 'low carbon', particularly once the large volumes of GHG emissions embedded in the infrastructure are reckoned. As with the modelling of transport and wider economic impacts, much depends on the assumptions that are made; on matters such as the rate at which electricity supplies are decarbonised, the proportion of the route in tunnels or on viaducts, the total volume of passenger-journeys, the level of generated traffic, the degree of modal shift and the period over which GHG emissions are calculated (Preston 2009: 16–18; Gourvish 2010: 29–30; Chester and Horvath 2010; International Union of Railways 2011; Westin and Kågeson 2012; Greengauge 21 2012). One life-cycle analysis suggests that under certain (very) favourable circumstances HS2 might by 2033 save 100,000 tonnes of CO_2 emissions annually on the Manchester–London route (Miyoshi and Givoni 2013). This is another subject where further research on existing HSR would be informative, to check the validity of new models and to provide more empirical information that could incorporated into them.

The most important (if necessarily provisional) conclusion from the little historical research that has been done is that even if HSR reduces GHG emissions on a per-journey basis, it does so under circumstances that are so restricted as to make a negligible contribution to reducing absolute volumes (Albalate and Bel 2014: 169–71, 178–9; Miyoshi and Givoni 2013: 120–24). An early report for HS2 Ltd admitted that CO_2 emissions might go up or down but '[w]hichever scenario takes place the contribution of HS2 would be insignificant when compared to other transport, especially conventional road vehicle emissions in the UK' (Booze & Co. and Temple Group Ltd 2011: 15). Not surprisingly the DfT's 2013 iteration of the strategic case only briefly mentions GHGs, claiming that over the project's assumed life cycle of 120 years (twice the usual appraisal period!) 'HS2 is expected to be carbon beneficial' (DfT 2013: 4.10.10–11).

All this suggests that the *symbolic* importance of HS2's claims to ecological sustainability is more important than any practical outcome before the critical date of 2050. Seen in the context of UK transport and environmental policy over the last few decades, HS2 appears as the latest chapter in a story of appeals to technology as a means of allowing us to keep moving without wrecking ourselves or the planet. But such technological fixes, for all the clever engineering that lies behind them, rarely deliver the promised environmental returns. Indeed, by concentrating on the real benefits that new technologies deliver in terms of carbon intensity and energy efficiency – less CO_2 per kilometre, more miles per gallon – the rhetoric of technological fixes can divert attention from continuing transport, land-use and economic policies that drive up the critical *total* volume of GHG. HS2 fits the dominant paradigm of UK transport policy since the Second World War, 'predict and provide': a policy that has generally boosted traffic levels across all modes and hence, with rare exceptions, GHG emissions. Of course it is possible that a massive modal shift to rail with HS2 at its core *might* produce lower absolute volumes of GHG than would otherwise be the case. On the other hand there might be alternatives ways of living and working – particularly those that reduce the need for personal mobility – that would produce still-lower volumes: in the rush to gain approval for HS2 these options have not been seriously addressed (Goulden, Ryley and Dingwall 2014; Divall 2012; Lyons 2011; Banister and Hickman 2009; Banister 2009; Vigar 2002). Moreover, unless we can be sure that the economic growth that HS2 is intended to spur will be carbon neutral, then a good case can be made for saying that far from being a symbol of the UK's environmental responsibility the project is a sign that we have yet to face up to the hard choices that will effect a decisive shift to a post-carbon world.

One does not have to agree with all this analysis to conclude that the brief history of HS2 suggests that far from being a bold, strategic initiative at risk of being derailed by short-term economic appraisals and NIMBYism, the project has become prematurely closed to thinking about radically different ways of moving and the kind of societies these might sustain and enable. This is a common characteristic of MTPs (OMEGA 2012; Priemus, Flyvbjerg and van Wee 2008). There is little sign that politicians, policy analysts or the DfT have undertaken the kind of scenario-building that has occasionally been used in other parts of government to develop distinctive and highly differentiated visions of what the UK might look like in 50 years' time (Banister and Hickman 2013). By comparison the DfT's 'sensitivity tests' of predicted travel demand amount to little more than tinkering with growth rates predicated upon more-of-the-same – a risky tactic in a complex, part-globalised economy where arguably the only long-term certainty is uncertainty.

The evidence is therefore mounting that the strategic case for HS2 has been 'not selected but shaped' (Priemus, Flyvbjerg and van Wee 2008: 6): shaped, that is, by a coalition of powerful actors that prefers the comparative certainties of continuing with the present project than running the 'risks' of pausing, engaging in open debate about the wider purposes of HSR in the UK, and fully considering alternatives. Eddington noted this danger in 2006:

> I have argued for policymaking that starts with the policy goal or problem, and then assesses a range of solutions that could be adopted in order to address the situation … It is evident … that, in transport debates across the world, the opposite process can occur. We see situations where the solution develops first – perhaps driven by the prospect of an exciting new technology, aspirations of transforming the economic fortunes of a region, or even simply because a competitor city or country 'has one'. The idea rapidly becomes a solution looking for a problem … The risk is that transport policy can become the pursuit of icons. (Eddington 2006: 47–8)

It might be that the HS2 project is now too far advanced for a full debate to take place, although Peter Hall – who believed that HS2 'will almost certainly prove necessary one day' – argued in 2013 that there was no urgent need for a decision to proceed and there 'could be no harm, and a great deal of merit, in waiting' so that more consideration could be given to the project's goals (2013: 352–3). And there are signs that important elements of the political class are uneasy about the policy vacuum within which HS2 is developing. In March 2015 the House of Lords Economic Affairs Committee (2015a) that had been hearing evidence since the autumn of 2014 concluded that the government had not yet made a robust economic case for HS2. Just two months earlier, in January, the influential House of Commons Public Accounts Committee had concluded that the DfT lacked a 'clear strategic vision' for the UK's railway network and so 'cannot provide a clear explanation for how it prioritises programmes in which it invests', including HS2 (House of Commons Committee of Public Accounts 2015: 7). It recommended that the DfT should develop a 30-year strategy for transport infrastructure (House of Commons Committee of Public Accounts 2015: 4).

The point is well made, because we have been here at least twice before. During the Railway Mania of the mid-1840s a predecessor of the DfT, the Board of Trade (BoT), reviewed the flood of privately promoted schemes coming before Parliament for approval. The BoT feared there was a danger of losing the advantages of connectivity and economy of construction and operation that a strategic national plan could deliver. Modern network theory suggests that the BoT was essentially right and its schemes for a set of inter-connected regional systems well thought through. Unfortunately the BoT's ambitions were defeated by the powerful influence of MPs, who were too often prepared to sacrifice the long-term advantages of national planning for the more obvious – and less risky – advantages that came from supporting schemes in their own localities. Thus the network that covered much of the UK by 1914 was at least 50 per cent larger than it needed to be and provided much weaker connections between provincial cities and regions than was ideal (Casson 2009). It is unfortunate that the DfT now seeks to justify HS2 as a partial solution to the lack of inter-regional connectivity brought about by the unwillingness of Victorian politicians to plan strategically while failing to learn from the attempts at good practice by its predecessor.

The rationalisation of the nationalised railways in the mid-1960s is also instructive. As head of British Railways Richard Beeching attempted to align the network more closely with anticipated traffic flows over a 20-year period. However, his radical cuts to passenger services were largely driven by an urgent short-term political imperative to reduce the railways' capital spending and operational losses. Line closures were therefore carried out piecemeal with only cursory consideration being given within the Ministry of Transport to their possible impact on other aspects of government policy such as regional development in the shape of New Towns, even though some local authorities took a more strategic view. Not surprisingly given the widespread assumption that mass-motoring was taking over, no thought was given within Whitehall to the possibility of maintaining or upgrading lines or even building new links in order to enhance connectivity (Loft 2006; Gourvish 1986: 401–68). Thus in the mid-twentieth century a perception in the national corridors of power that railways had no long-term future beyond niche markets blocked any serious consideration of alternative arrangements of the network, with consequences that are all too apparent today in the form of road congestion in several conurbations that might otherwise still be rail-served.

Conclusion

This chapter has argued that HS2 is – or will be, if it is built – a Mega Transport Project. Like many such projects it shows signs of being prematurely closed to systematic consideration of alternative ways of structuring personal mobility in the UK. This does not mean that, if completed, HS2 would be an outright failure when judged against the 'strategic case' that is being used to justify it, as long as the underlying assumptions about economic growth and people's propensity to travel over the next couple of decades turn out to be broadly correct. Once an expensive piece of transport infrastructure has been built, it is not particularly difficult in a rich, densely populated country with crowded roads like the UK to persuade people to use it. Moreover, if stringent measures are taken to integrate HS2 with the rest of the national rail and regional public-transport networks, the line could help to correct some of the legacies of short-term infrastructure planning in the nineteenth and twentieth centuries. But the history of HSR in Europe and elsewhere – or at least our rather scanty understanding of that history – suggests that even over 20 years or more, traffic volumes will probably be lower than predicted, that the impact on wider economic growth will be more limited than suggested, and that regional regeneration, while not impossible, will also be restricted in scope and scale. The UK can afford to spend £50 billion on a new trunk railway and it is understandable that many people are excited by the prospect of doing so. The question is whether even in narrow transport terms this i the best way to spend the money – the BCRs still do not compare at all favourabl with the kind of small-scale improvements to, say, facilities for urban walking an cycling that the Eddington report favoured and that in aggregate could make a rea difference to the way we live and move.

And in the still longer term, who knows? A high-speed railway networl would almost certainly eventually help to transform many aspects of urba life in the UK – but would it do so in ways that meet the main challenge o the early twenty-first century, to develop ways of living that do not blight th prospects of future generations by causing runaway climate change? HSR wa not conceived half a century ago to tackle this problem, and recent attempt to frame HS2 as the backbone of low-carbon transport system for the UK ar not convincing. Whether HSR in general and HS2 in particular are truly par of the solution is impossible to say at the moment because the question is no being properly asked. HSR is often hailed as a symbol of modernity and eve of national virility (Guigueno 2008; Hood 2006), and that is currently part o the problem – politicians and civil servants frame HS2 as a symbol of the UK commitment to the highly-mobile, carbon-intense lifestyles of global consume capitalism. So for the time being the response to those who argue that its eithe £50 billion on HS2 or nothing should probably be – no thanks.

References

Albalate, D. and Bel, G. (2012). High-Speed Rail: Lessons for Policy Makers fron Experience Abroad. *Public Administration Review* 72(3), pp. 336–49.
————— (2014). *The Economics and Politics of High-Speed Rail: Lessons fron Experiences Abroad.* Plymouth: Lexington Books.
Anguera, R. (2006). The Channel Tunnel – An Ex Post Economic Evaluation *Transportation Research Part A* 40(4), pp. 291–315.
Banister, D. (2009). The Sustainable Mobility Paradigm. *Transport Policy* 15(2) pp. 73–80.
Banister, D. and Givoni, M. (2013). High-Speed Rail in the EU27: Trends, Time Accessibility and Principles. *Built Environment* 39(3), pp. 324–38.
Banister, D. and Hickman, R. (2009). Techno-Optimism: Progress Towards CO Reduction Targets in Transport – A UK and London Perspective. *Internationa Journal of Sustainable Development* 12(1), pp. 24–47.
Booze & Co. and Temple Group Ltd (2011). *HS2 London to the West Midlands Appraisal of Sustainability: Non-Technical Summary: A Report for HS2 Ltd* London: DfT.
de Bruijn, H. and Leijten, M. (2008). Mega-Projects and Contested Informatior In *Decision-Making on Mega-Projects: Cost–Benefit Analysis, Planning an Innovation*, ed. H. Priemus, B. Flyvbjerg and B. van Wee. Cheltenham: Edwar Elgar, pp. 84–101.

Casson, M. (2009). *The World's First Railway System: Enterprise, Competition and Regulation on the Railway Network in Victorian Britain*. Oxford: Oxford University Press.

Chen, C.-L. and Hall, P. (2013). Using High Speed Two to Irrigate the Regions. *Built Environment* 39(3), pp. 355–68.

Chester, M. and Horvath, A. (2010). Life-Cycle Assessment of High-Speed Rail: The Case of California. *Environmental Research Letters* 5, pp. 1–8.

DfT (2011). *High Speed Rail: Investing in Britain's Future: Consultation Summary February 2011*. London: DfT.

——— (2012). *Economic Case for HS2: Updated Appraisal of Transport User Benefits and Wider Economic Benefits*. London: DfT.

——— (2013). *The Strategic Case for HS2*. London: DfT Publications.

Divall, C. (2012). Business History, Global Networks and the Future of Mobility. *Business History* 54(4), pp. 542–55.

Divall, C. and Shin, H. (2011). Cultures of Speed and Conservative Modernity: Representations of Speed in Britain's Railway Marketing. In *Trains, Culture, and Modernity: Riding the Rails*, ed. B. Fraser and S. Spalding. Plymouth: Lexington Books, pp. 3–26.

Eddington, R. (2006). *The Eddington Transport Study: The Case for Action: Sir Rod Eddington's Advice to Government*. London: HMSO.

Flyvbjerg, B. (2004). *The British Department for Transport: Procedures for Dealing with Optimism Bias in Transport Planning: Guidance Document*. London: DfT.

——— (2008). Public Planning of Mega-Projects: Overestimation of Demand and Underestimation of Costs. In *Decision-Making on Mega-Projects: Cost–Benefit Analysis, Planning and Innovation*, ed. H. Priemus, B. Flyvbjerg and B. van Wee. Cheltenham: Edward Elgar, pp. 120–44.

——— (2009). Survival of the Unfittest: Why the Worst Infrastructure Gets Built – And What We Can Do About It. *Oxford Review of Economic Policy* 25(3), pp. 344–67.

Goulden, M., Ryley, T. and Dingwall, R. (2014). Beyond 'Predict and Provide': UK Transport, the Growth Paradigm and Climate Change. *Transport Policy* 32, pp. 139–47.

Gourvish, T. (1986). *British Railways 1948–73: A Business History*. Cambridge: Cambridge University Press.

——— (2006). *The Official History of Britain and the Channel Tunnel*. London: Routledge.

——— (2010). *The High Speed Rail Revolution: History and Prospects*. London: HS2 Ltd.

Graham, D. and Venables, T. (2014). Professor Dan Graham and Professor Tony Venables – Oral Evidence. In House of Lords Committee on Economic Affairs (2015b), pp. 311–22.

Greengauge 21 (2012). *The Carbon Impacts of High Speed 2*. Kingston-upon-Thames: Greengauge 21.

Guigueno, V. (2008). 'Building a high-speed society': France and the Aérotrain, 1962–1974. *Technology and Culture* 49(1), pp. 21–40.

Hall, P. (2013). High Speed Two: The Great Divide. *Built Environment* 39(3), pp. 339–54.

Hawke, G. (1970). *Railways and Economic Growth in England and Wales 1840–1870*. Oxford: Clarendon Press.

Hay, A., Meredith, K. and Vickerman, R. (2004). *The Impact of the Channel Tunnel on Kent and Relationships with Nord-Pas de Calais*. Canterbury: Centre for European Regional and Transport Economics. Available at: https://duckduckgo.com/l/?kh=-1&uddg=http%3A%2F%2Fwww.kent.ac.uk%2Feconomics%2Fdocuments%2Fresearch%2Fseminars%2Farchive%2FSummaryReport.pdf (accessed 17 February 2015).

Hine, J. (2011). Mobility and Transport Disadvantage. In *Mobilities: New Perspectives on Transport and Society*, ed. M. Grieco and J. Urry. Farnham: Ashgate, pp. 21–39.

Hood, C.P. (2006). *Shinkansen: From Bullet Train to Symbol of Modern Japan*. London: Routledge.

House of Commons Committee of Public Accounts (2015). *Lessons from Major Rail Infrastructure Programmes*, HC 709. London: The Stationery Office.

House of Lords Committee on Economic Affairs (2015a). *The Economics of High Speed 2*, HL 134. London: The Stationery Office. Available at: http://www.publications.parliament.uk/pa/ld201415/ldselect/ldeconaf/134/134.pdf (accessed 29 March 2015).

———(2015b). *The Economic Case for HS2: Oral and Written Evidence*. Available at: http://www.parliament.uk/documents/lords-committees/economic-affairs/Economic-case-for-HS2/hs2-final-ev-vol.pdf (accessed 29 March 2015).

International Union of Railways (2011). *Carbon Footprint of High Speed Rail*. Paris: UIC.

Loft, C. (2006). *Government, the Railways and the Modernization of Britain: Beeching's Last Trains*. London: Routledge.

Lucas, K. (2011). Transport and Social Exclusion: Where Are We Now? In *Mobilities: New Perspectives on Transport and Society*, ed. M. Grieco and J. Urry. Farnham: Ashgate, pp. 207–22.

Lyons, G. (2011). Technology Fix versus Behaviour Change. In *Mobilities: New Perspectives on Transport and Society*, ed. M. Grieco and J. Urry. Farnham: Ashgate, pp. 159–77.

Mackie, P., Niblett, M. and Vickerman, R. (2014). Professor Peter Mackie, Dr Matthew Niblett and Professor Roger Vickerman – Oral Evidence. In House of Lords Select Committee on Economic Affairs (2015b), pp. 662–76.

Merriman, P. (2007). *Driving Spaces: A Cultural–Historical Geography of England's M1 Motorway*. Oxford: Blackwell.

Meunier, J. (2002). *On the Fast Track: French Railway Modernization and the Origins of the TGV, 1944–1983*. Westport, CT: Praeger.

Miyoshi, C. and Givoni, M. (2013). The Environmental Case for the High-Speed Train in the UK: Examining the London–Manchester Route. *International Journal for Sustainable Transportation* 8(2), pp. 107–26.

Mom, G. (2005). Roads Without Rails: European Highway-Network Building and the Desire for Long-Range Motorized Mobility. *Technology and Culture* 46(4), pp. 745–72.

Nash, C., Wardman, M., Button, K. and Nijkamp, P., eds (2002). *Railways.* Cheltenham: Edward Elgar.

National Audit Office (2013). *High Speed 2: A Review of Early Programme Preparation.* Report by the Comptroller and Auditor General HC 124 Session 2013–14, 16 May 2013. Available at: http://www.nao.org.uk/report/high-speed-2-a-review-of-early-programme-preparation/ (accessed 14 May 2015).

Olsson, N., Økland A. and Halvorsen, S. (2012). Consequences of Differences in Cost–Benefit Methodology in Railway Infrastructure Appraisal – A Comparison of Selected Countries. *Transport Policy* 22, pp. 29–35.

OMEGA Centre (2008) *Channel Tunnel Rail Link Case Study: Project Profile.* London: OMEGA Centre, UCL. Available at: http://www.omegacentre.bartlett.ucl.ac.uk/wp-content/uploads/2014/12/UK_CTRL_PROFILE.pdf (accessed 29 March 2015).

——— (2012). *Mega Projects: Executive Summary: Lessons for Decision-Makers: An Analysis of Selected Large-Scale Transport Infrastructure Projects.* London: OMEGA Centre, UCL. Available at: http://www.omegacentre.bartlett.ucl.ac.uk/publications/reports/mega-project-executive-summary/ (accessed 20 March 2015).

Overman, P. (2014). Professor Henry Overman – Oral Evidence. In House of Lords Committee on Economic Affairs (2015b), pp. 767–82.

Preston, J. (2009). *The Case for High Speed Rail: A Review of Recent Evidence.* London: RAC Foundation.

Priemus, H., Flyvbjerg, B. and van Wee, B. (2008). Introduction: Scope of the Book. In *Decision-Making on Mega-Projects: Cost–Benefit Analysis, Planning and Innovation*, ed. H. Priemus, B. Flyvbjerg and B. van Wee. Cheltenham: Edward Elgar, pp. 1–20.

Rajé, F. (2004). *Transport, Demand Management and Social Inclusion: The Need for Ethnic Perspectives.* Aldershot: Ashgate.

Smith, R. (2014). The Economic Benefits of High Speed Rail: Introduction. Conference paper delivered at 1964–2064 High Speed Rail: Celebrating Ambition. University of Birmingham.

Tomaney, J. (2011). The Local and Regional Impacts of High Speed Rail in the UK: a Review of the Evidence. Written evidence to the House of Commons Select Committee on Transport, Session 2010–12. Available at: http://www.publications.parliament.uk/pa/cm201012/cmselect/cmtran/writev/rail/m14.htm (accessed 17 February 2015).

Urry, J. (2011). Does Mobility Have a Future? In *Mobilities: New Perspectives on Transport and Society*, ed. M. Grieco and J. Urry. Farnham: Ashgate, pp. 3–19.

Vickerman, R. (2014). Professor Roger Vickerman – Written Evidence. In House of Lords Committee on Economic Affairs (2015b), pp. 697–98.

———— (2008). Cost–Benefit Analysis and the Wider Economic Benefits from Mega-Projects. In *Decision-Making on Mega-Projects: Cost–Benefit Analysis, Planning and Innovation*, ed. H. Priemus, B. Flyvbjerg and B. van Wee. Cheltenham: Edward Elgar: pp. 66–83.

Vigar, G. (2002). *The Politics of Mobility: Transport, the Environment and Public Policy*. London: Spon Press.

van Wee, B. and Tavasszt, L. (2008). *Ex-ante* Evaluation of Mega-Projects: Methodological Issues and Cost–Benefit Analysis. In *Decision-Making on Mega-Projects: Cost–Benefit Analysis, Planning and Innovation*, ed. H. Priemus, B. Flyvbjerg and B. van Wee. Cheltenham: Edward Elgar, pp. 40–65.

Westin, J. and Kågeson, P. (2012). Can High Speed Rail Offset Its Embedded Emissions? *Transportation Research Part D* 17: pp. 1–7.

Chapter 7

'Interminably Delaying What Needs to Be Done': Drink-Driving Control in Britain 1970–1985

Bill Luckin

Between the 1890s and the late 1950s a handful of government initiatives failed to make an impact on British attitudes towards drink driving. Throughout this 50-year period most offenders escaped with a routine warning or minimal punishment. When cases were referred to higher courts, well-to-do private motorists frequently drew on the expertise of solicitors or barristers versed in the intricacies and contradictions of road-traffic law. Working-class drivers of vans, buses and trams usually pleaded guilty in a magistrate's court and paid a fine. In exceptionally serious cases offenders from both groups could be charged with manslaughter. Throughout the period, libertarian pro-motorism ruled supreme, with drink driving occupying a no-man's land between misdemeanour and quasi-criminality. Judged by early twenty-first-century standards, punishments were lenient to a degree (Willett 1965; Luckin 2010b: 365–8).

In the mid-1950s and early 1960s Graham Page, Conservative member for Crosby near Liverpool and chairman of the Pedestrians' Association, kick-started a parliamentary reform campaign. This prepared the way for Harold Macmillan's Minister of Transport, Ernest Marples, to make the first move towards rewriting Britain's drink-driving laws. Marples insisted that senior officials gain in-depth knowledge of recent scientific research on the impact of relatively small amounts of alcohol on driver performance (Drew 1959; Borkenstein 1964). He sent delegations on fact-finding tours, mainly to Scandinavia. Officials prepared reports on legislative systems that had long relied on scientific criteria – notably measurement of blood alcohol concentration (BAC) by means of blood tests (Ministry of Transport 1960; Ross 1975). Marples bequeathed Castle the expertise and legal building blocks to prepare her controversial breathalyser bill, which passed into law in 1967 (Ross 1973; Baggott 1990: 139–41; Greenaway 2003: 166–74; Luckin 2010a). This was the first British measure of its kind. Earlier attempts to reduce road accidents had been tacked, almost as an afterthought, on to traffic or criminal justice bills.

This chapter focuses on the decade and half following the Castle act. These years witnessed a falling-off in commitment to reform. In the immediate aftermath of the introduction of the new law, large numbers of motorists appear to have made an effort to drink less before setting off on their journeys The very existence of the new 'device' – the breathalyser – exercised a deterrent effect, and numbers of alcohol-related deaths and injuries declined (Ross 1973). But this proved transitory: drivers who were almost certainly over the limit of 80 mg of alcohol per 100 ml of blood rapidly realised that they were no more likely to be stopped by the police than in the pre-Castle era. The new device – the Alcotest 80 – failed to inspire confidence and the law was less rigorously applied than it should have been. National alcohol consumption increased. With ever-larger numbers of vehicles on the roads, the proportion of drivers minimally but – as was now more widely acknowledged – significantly impaired, moved upwards.

This chapter seeks to throw light on the role that the immediate past plays in the policy-making process. Memoranda and draft bills produced at the Ministry of Transport provide a bird's-eye view of the ways in which senior officials learnt from the small number of successes (and numerous failures) in the quarter century between the beginning of Graham Page's campaign and Norman Fowler' Transport Act in 1981. Second, analysis of relationships between civil servant responsible for road safety, on the one hand, and policing and law enforcement on the other, allows the historian to assess the effectiveness of inter-departmental cooperation. The Ministry of Transport (MoT) and the Home Office (HO) had rarely seen eye-to-eye (Luckin 2010a, 2010b). Did relations deteriorate between 1970 and 1985?

The chain of events in this 15-year period also illuminates the extent to which Edward Heath's experiments in administrative reorganisation between 1970 and 1974 adversely affected the already insecure status of the MoT. This in turn is linked to the issue of whether ministers and senior officials in the 1970s and early 1980s found themselves confronted by similar or different sets of problems to those faced by their predecessors in the 1960s. The underlying though at times semi-hidden, rationale of the Castle act had been ideological - to strengthen opposition among the driving and non-driving public to the kind of motoring libertarianism that had long dominated the social relation of mobility in twentieth-century Britain. Perhaps the 1970s and early 1980 simply witnessed a laborious and halting attempt to strengthen Castle' technically flawed measure? For historians seeking to identify a usable past, this sub-theme clearly introduces the problem of commensurability. It is impossible to argue with Pat Thane's statement that 'we can save ourselves a lot of time and a lot of mistakes by taking the past more seriously' (Thane 2009: 145 Divall 2010; Hirsh 2011). But which past, and which problems and policies in that past?

The Castle act generated lengthy (and at times savage) interchanges in Parliament, at political meetings, in the press and on television and radio. All interested parties, from curmudgeonly members of the anti-car Pedestrians Association (PA) to fervent libertarians, voiced their views about a measure designed finally to render drink driving a fully criminal act rather than a breach of the traditional 'courtesies' of the road that might sometimes end in tragedy. All this continued to be widely discussed among road safety reformers, in the media and by the general public in the 1970s and 1980s. Legislation induced cultural change, and cultural change may have played a major role in belatedly persuading politicians that they must draw on and reinforce growing popular animosity towards those who flouted the anti-drink-driving laws. To paraphrase John Braithwaite, did this period witness a process of 'shaming, criminalization and reintegration' (Braithwaite 1989)?

One might assume that the coordinated television road safety campaigns that began in the early 1960s had a much more telling effect than earlier efforts on the part of the Royal Society for the Prevention of Accidents (RoSPA), the PA and the MoT to persuade the British population to 'adjust' to an age of incipient mass-motorisation (Moran 2006). However, between the early 1970s and the mid-1980s many experts in the field, notably John Havard, secretary of the British Medical Association, who played a major networking role in persuading ministers to take road safety more seriously, insisted that the media had made little impact on the problem (Waymark 1978). The same position was taken up at the very end of our period by the authors of an inter-departmental report, who claimed that it was impossible to evaluate the effect of television campaigns on the incidence of dangerous and alcoholically impaired driving (Department of Transport 1987). Nevertheless, and for whatever reason, by the early 1990s awareness of the dangers associated with a now more widely criminalised form of behaviour had clearly penetrated much more deeply into popular consciousness. A road user in 1990 was 50 per cent less likely to be killed or suffer serious injury as a result of the actions of an alcoholically impaired driver than 10 years earlier. By the beginning of the new millennium that figure had been reduced by a further 30 per cent (Institute of Alcohol Studies 2010: 10).

Belatedly 'discovered' in Britain in the 1960s, alcoholic impairment and methods of reducing its incidence were subject to recurring political, legal, scientific and cultural construction and reconstruction. What does this say to road safety reformers in the early twenty-first century who are determined to bring fatalities associated with every form of dangerous driving closer to a now widely disseminated 'target zero' (Whitelegg and Haq 2006)? To move closer to an answer to this question a concluding section engages with the unknown history of road safety; the centrality of anti-drink-driving reform to that still semi-hidden narrative; and the role of science, both as 'causal' story and 'real' objective presence in the shaping of anti-accident legislation (Stone 1989). Towards the end of the period discussed in this contribution, drug-impaired driving entered a preliminary phase of political, social and cultural construction and reconstruction. Similar in many respects to the alcohol issue, in others it radically differed and requires separate consideration.

'Revolution', Crisis, Inertia

By the early 1970s Barbara Castle's Road Safety Act had lost its cutting-edge. The breathalyser selected by the Home Office, the Alcotest 80, lacked reliability and lagged behind a new generation of breathalysers routinely used for evidential purposes in other countries, notably in Scandinavia (Medico-Legal Correspondent 1976: 766). The weaknesses of the British device reduced police confidence, and inhibited effective policing and enforcement. By the early 1970s critics were complaining that the Castle measure had failed and become no more than an 'artificial ritual' (BMJ 1976: 1103). In Lord Hailsham's phrase, the measure had lost its 'therapeutic value' (Hailsham 1974). Writing in the *The Observer* in 1976, the acerbic Adam Raphael condemned the legal working of the act as a 'jurisprudential disgrace' (Raphael 1976a). Three years later *The Times* scathingly parodied 'a complicated procedure which must [still] be carried out as flawlessly as a sacrifice in ancient Rome if it is to be blessed with success' (The Times 1979). The legislation left the police with one foot in the future and the other in the past. To ensure that drivers would be treated fairly, the law stated that initial screening must be confirmed at a station by a police surgeon administering a blood or urine test. From the vantage-point of the mid-1970s, an expert in the *British Medical Journal* glumly concluded that this 'procedurally cumbersome system' had been introduced primarily 'to *permit*' the police to undertake their legislatively sanctioned duties (Medico-Legal Correspondent 1976: 766). The implication here was that Castle's anti-drink-driving revolution had degenerated into an amending clause to ensure that a larger proportion of potentially offending drivers would cooperate with the police and obey the law in its traditional pre-breathalyser form.

That the deterrent effect of the measure had declined was demonstrated by research undertaken by Laurence Ross, an American sociologist with a pioneering interest in the effectiveness of different kinds of national legal instruments designed to reduce the incidence of drink driving (Ross 1973, 1992). Ross's findings were confirmed by the Home Office. During the first full year's operation of the act, only 15 per cent of post-mortems of drivers involved in a fatal accident revealed blood-alcohol concentrations above the legal limit. This had risen to 35 per cent in 1974. Among drivers in their twenties the figure increased to 40 per cent in 1971 and 45 per cent in 1974 (BMJ 1976: 1103). The position had become critical. Consumption of alcohol was rising rapidly, particularly among the young who had abandoned respectable interwar notions of the desirability of 'social drinking'.

As Virginia Berridge and her co-authors have emphasised, moral panics about alcohol have been a recurrent feature of British life (Berridge, Herring and Thom 2009). Nevertheless, the data for the period between the 1970s and the early 1980s suggest a radical shift in drinking habits. In terms of annual litres per head of 100 per cent alcohol the figure climbed throughout the 1960s and reached 5.3 by 1970. Ten years later it had leapt to 7.3. From the early 1960s spirits and wine had been replacing steadily declining volumes of beer, and mixing drinks had become more widely accepted (van der Vat 1981). Refuting twenty-first-century fears about unprecedented levels of binge drinking, by 1990 the rate of increase in per capita consumption had begun to level off and the years between 2000 and 2010 registered levels almost identical to those recorded 20 years earlier. Meanwhile vehicle ownership spiralled upwards. Licence data confirms figures of just under 9.5 million in 1960, 15 million in 1970, just over 19 million in 1980 and an astounding 25 million in 1990 (Light 1994: 166).

In the early 1970s both parties acknowledged that new legislation was urgently required. In 1974 the transport minister, Fred Mulley (who once dropped asleep next to the Queen during an air display), announced the establishment of a departmental investigation, to be chaired by a judge, Frank Blennerhassett. The committee confirmed that 'proof of the offence [of drink driving] has become inextricably bound up with proof that the procedure has been rigidly followed', and added that the 'proliferation of case law' had become an 'absurdity' (Department of the Environment 1976: 3). Horse-trading during the savage debates leading up to the final version of the Castle bill had led to the creation of a flawed measure. The central procedural problem was that the great majority of British drivers insisted on a urine rather than blood test – the taken-for-granted and socially accepted method used in many countries, and pioneered in Scandinavia in the interwar years (Ross 1975).

In Britain, following roadside breathalyser screening, a suspect was taken to a police station and had to provide two samples within an hour of one another, with 50 per cent of each being assessed by analysts for the prosecution and defence respectively. The Blennerhassett Committee concluded that screening had led to a 10 per cent inaccuracy rate, rising by a further fifth following urine testing at a police station. Little wonder that over 90 per cent of crown court proceedings were heard at the request of the defence. Barristers and solicitors specialising in road traffic law capitalised on disputes over police procedure and disparate findings produced by analysts: the translation of breath into blood concentration indicators took up many hours of court and jury time. The committee concluded that a new and simpler law must be introduced. This would bypass the pitfalls of the urine test: 'A breath test should normally be used to determine a driver's blood alcohol concentration ... but with a fall-back option of providing blood if the breath analysis is over the limit'; the latter proviso would become known as the 'statutory option' (Department of Environment 1976: 6). If accepted Blennerhassett's recommendations would bestow *primary* evidential status on a mechanical measuring device rather than blood or urine analysis supported by the often impressionistic testimony of a policeman and/or another witness or witnesses. As a Home Office circular later put it, the new method envisaged the '... introduction in evidence of a breath testing machine' (Home Office 1983).

The Blennerhassett Committee also proposed that the police should finally be given a right to stop and test any motorist on any road at any time of day or night. The logic was clear. The Road Safety Act had left the police in a difficult position. An officer could stop a driver if his or her control over a vehicle seemed erratic or dangerous. He could also request a breath test if, during the process of issuing a warning about a non-drink-related problem – a punctured tyre or broken indicator – face-to-face contact suggested the presence of alcohol on the breath. Finally a policeman could screen a driver in the aftermath of an accident or an incident resulting in the death of a passenger or another road user. However, none of these options significantly increased an officer's preventative powers. In this respect the Castle measure had something in common with the late nineteenth-century Licensing Act. That law had been designed to prosecute grossly inebriated carters or omnibus and tram drivers whose wobbling and swerving vehicles self-evidently indicated that they were likely to be 'drunk in charge' (Hansard 1924).

Many 'obvious' recidivist offenders of this kind continued to endanger road users in the later twentieth century. But Scandinavian approaches to control had sought to cast the net as widely as possible, thereby hammering home the message that even very small amounts of alcohol could adversely affect perception and reaction – and the fact that driving and drinking were (and are) mutually incompatible activities. Moreover, path-breaking research undertaken in the United States and Britain in the 1950s and 1960s, which had underwritten the Castle measure, focused on motorists who were convinced that they were able to drive effectively but who nevertheless displayed dangerously impaired responses as a result of consuming a relatively small amount of alcohol (Drew 1959; Borkenstein 1964). From a preventative perspective, in other words, large numbers of drinking though not necessarily drunk drivers needed to be brought within the full purview of the law.

Within a British context the Blennerhassett Committee concluded that the government must stringently control the behaviour of both recidivist and low-consumption offenders who drank before setting off on a journey; consolidate the legal and cultural process of publicly endorsed criminalisation initiated by the Castle act; and deploy road traffic law to unequivocally underline the point that driving is always a danger-fraught activity. However, and finally, the Blennerhassett Committee decided that the existing blood alcohol concentration level – 80 mg per 100 ml – should remain unchanged. This had profound and long-lasting repercussions. It was based on the assumption that a lowering of the limit to 50 mg would adversely affect relations between the police and public and lead to no more than a small increase in numbers of convictions.

Edging Uneasily towards New Legislation

Like earlier investigations into road safety, publication of the Blennerhassett recommendations met with long delays. The proposals were announced in the Commons in April 1976. The Automobile Association (AA) immediately went on to the offensive. A.C. Durie, the organisation's director, complained that random testing constituted an assault on the 'inviolable' rights of the citizen and an 'affront to individual liberty'. Police man-power would be stretched beyond breaking-point and relations with the public seriously damaged, with diversions of resources providing many a field-day for thieves and murderers. Assuming that random testing would be accepted, Durie painted a lurid picture of innocent drivers being forced to prepare themselves for large-scale Saturday car park swoops – what the media were already beginning to call 'pub door testing'. Surely this exceeded the powers that should be granted to a police force in a democracy (Durie 1976)?

In *The Observer* Adam Raphael hinted that behind-the-scenes pressure had been applied by the AA and RAC in the hope of moving the nation back towards the 'golden age of motoring'. Raphael argued that a heavy price had been paid in 1966 when the Labour Cabinet had failed to force through an upper limit of 50 mg rather 80 mg per 100 ml. Motoring interests, he said, remained unconcerned by the fact that 'more than a 1,000 lives are lost each year through drink and driving [with the chief victims being] young men in their twenties ... or that a third of all drivers on the roads are found to have drunk more than the legal limit ...'. The cost of alcohol-related road fatalities had reached £100 million per year. The time had surely come to stop giving ground to lobbying groups skilfully organised by the majoring motoring organisations (Raphael 1976b).

Lord Widgery, the lord chief justice, located the problem within the context of the upcoming findings of the James Committee on the distribution of business in the judicial system which was about to recommend that a chronic log-jam be cleared by restricting all offences except those carrying a sentence of more than two years to magistrates' courts (Interdepartmental Committee 1976). Widgery was concerned that in some areas this would mean that the 'right to trial [might] be on its way out'. However he had few complaints about the Blennerhassett proposals. If legislation were effectively to enshrine its main findings, unscrupulous barristers would find it increasingly difficult to 'force acquittals'. Castle's law had failed to deliver. According to Widgery the courts remained unconvinced that road safety was a major social problem and had made a virtue out of acquitting drivers charged on the basis of roadside breath tests. The object had been to 'acquit suspects as soon as possible'. The government must make it increasingly difficult for offenders to escape via legal loop-holes (Kershaw 1976). Adding his voice to the chorus of attacks on the AA, *The Times'* motoring correspondent Peter Waymark reminded his readers that 'liberty' could also mean liberty to 'maim and kill innocent people' (Waymark 1976). *The Guardian* agreed: a 'breath sample should be sufficient to measure] blood alcohol concentration' and gain more convictions (Durie 1976). The *Daily Mirror* reiterated the ubiquitous slogan that 'drink driving kills': legal and technical complexities were avoided – they made for clumsy headlines (Daily Mirror 1976).

The publication of the report generated a torrent of parliamentary questions. Dr John Gilbert, the Labour minister of transport, warned the Commons that nothing could be done before the government had access to the findings of an investigation by the Advisory Committee on Alcoholism into how education and training might reduce the dangers associated with spiralling national consumption of liquor (Advisory Committee on Alcoholism 1979). In December of the same year John Horam, Labour's parliamentary secretary at the MoT, told the House that the complexity of the recommendations made it unlikely that legislation could be debated, let alone drafted into a bill for the foreseeable future. The MoT made a tentative move, but then immediately retreated: legal problems, the use of the breathalyser as a primary form of evidence, random testing and the shibboleth of self-incrimination halted progress. These were issues for the Home Office and senior police officers who provided advice on enforcement. Officials in that department were convinced that new drink-driving proposals could only be transformed into the hard currency of legislation if the police were provided with reliable breath-measuring equipment. This technical issue dominated departmental thinking for more than a decade (Cobb and Dabbs 1985).

A year after the publication of the report Peter Waymark in *The Times* launched an attack on Bill Rodgers, who had taken over at the MoT in the recently elected Callaghan administration. Waymark complained that action on the road-safety front had been indefinitely delayed and that some kind of action must now be taken both in relation to seat-belts and drink driving. Rodgers entered the predictable plea of an over-crowded legislative agenda. However, Waymark knew that Blennerhassett himself had privately dismissed Rodgers' explanation as a 'feeble excuse' (Waymark 1977). *The Guardian* went further. The road safety lobby had urged Rodgers to take action on three fronts: speeding, compulsory use of seat-belts and drink driving: 'To fail one test is human; to fail two forgivable; but to fail three looks worse than careless' (The Guardian 1977). To be fair to Rodgers, he had taken over at the MoT during a time of institutional convalescence. In 1970 the ministry had been engulfed by governmental reorganisation. Edward Heath, the modernising Conservative premier, decided to create a massive experimental super ministry, the Department of the Environment (DoE), comprising housing and local government, transport, and building and public works. Administratively diffuse, the success of the new department depended on a senior minister's ability to manage a large team of six or seven senior colleagues, delegating responsibility but formulating coherent inter-ministry policies. Experience soon confirmed that the experiment had been a mistake – only Peter Walker and Michael Heseltine possessed the political skill and energy to hold the new colossus together. The DoE lacked cohesion and was too big to be run by single minister (Campbell 1993: 314–15; Holmes 1997: 11).

Between 1970 and 1976, then, the MoT, a politically weak department, had been relegated to the status of a sub-ministry. This led to or coalesced with another problem – a lack of dynamic leadership. John Peyton, minister between 1970 and 1974, had been a friend of Heath's at Oxford in the 1930s, and amicable relations were revived in the early 1950s (Biffen 2006). But he was the opposite of a moderniser. A member of the Monday Club and obsessive opponent of anything smacking of Labourism or socialism, Peyton espoused a hyper-traditional variant of backwoods Conservatism. However, he hankered after office. When the great moment arrived, his spirits sank: the 'department would at a time uncertain b sucked into a huge and hideous pile [at what] was to be the home of the new Department of the Environment' (Peyton 1997: 137). Peyton had little interest in transport and none at all in road safety. He simply hoped that, one day, the nation's railways, docks and roads would be transferred to private control.

As we have seen, in 1976, following a multi-minister interregnum over the two preceding years, James Callaghan dismantled the DoE and asked Bill Rodgers to take over at the MoT. Rodgers stayed until 1979 and later revealingly recalled that the job had not been 'particularly onerous' (Rodgers 2000: 171). Rodgers had a long-standing interest in the role that an integrated transport system should play in an advanced industrial society but, as Patrick Waymark's attack indicated, he had little time for the legal and technical complexities of the road-safety problem. Rodgers had though inherited a stray compulsory seat-belt bill and, to rebut his critics, he decided to try and push ahead with it. He put his case to Callaghan, and came away with the unnerving impression that the prime minister may not have been entirely sure what seat-belts were meant to do: the prime minister simply asked whether the measure had any 'electoral advantage'. There was more than a hint that Callaghan thought road-safety reform might be a vote loser (Light 1994: 101). Rodgers did not know how to respond to Callaghan's unexpected questions, but he secured a place on the parliamentary timetable and the bill went through on a free vote. Then, with rashes of strikes threatening to paralyse the transport sector, his diary began to fill up with emergency meetings with trade-union leaders. Policy and planning sessions with senior advisors at the MoT went by the board (Rodgers 2000: 175–6).

Norman Fowler was a different proposition. A former shadow minister, he knew a lot about transport. He was also intensely ambitious. By the end of 1979 he was beginning to come round to the view that action must be taken on the Blennerhassett recommendations. Like Marples and Castle, Fowler well understood that decisive ministerial action in a minor ministry could lead to promotion and a place in the Cabinet. However the way in which he implemented the recommendations harked back to the bad old days – he inserted his safety clauses into a miscellaneous Transport Bill. As we have seen, from the beginning of the motoring age until the passing of Castle's measure in 1967, legislation designed to reduce road accidents had been tagged on to general traffic and criminal justice bills. Fowler's measure was mainly concerned with the privatisation of subsidiary companies owned and administered by the British Railways Board – the road safety clauses came just before a miscellaneous section dealing with humps in the road. All Fowler had to say in his memoirs was that the measure had 'enabled private investment to be introduced into the subsidiary companies of British Rail and effectively denationalized the British Transport Docks Board' (Fowler 1991: 131).

Fowler accepted all the proposals with the exception of random testing. Debate was intense and witnessed a brief re-emergence of pro-libertarianism. The long-running seat-belt controversy dragged on for two decades (Irwin 1985). It provided an opportunity for backbenchers to revisit radical anti-statist positions remarkably similar to those that had gained prominence in the earliest days of drink-driving reform in the mid-1950s. 'Personal liberty' – yet again – seemed to be at stake. Hardly surprisingly, the most articulate proponent of this line of thinking was Enoch Powell, now a semi-detached Unionist member for South Down. During a seat-belt debate in 1979 he turned the clock back to the Blennerhassett proposals. Claiming that quantitative data could not logically be deployed to predict whether a driver would be more or less likely to become involved in an accident, Powell denied the existence of a relationship between interventionist forms of road-safety legislation and a reduction in fatalities: no such effect could be attributed to the years in the immediate aftermath of Castle's act. Informing the Commons that he had read every line – and every footnote – in the Blennerhassett Report, he used the tables in the long-shelved document to bolster his case for a return to radical libertarianism. At a more fundamental level, he told his fellow MPs that there must be limits to the powers the state could or should take unto itself to protect its own citizens, whether in relation to drink-driving controls, seat-belts or anything else (Powell 1979a). A few months later, Powell told a meeting of magistrates that Fowler's act, now at the drafting stage, would 'defile the statute book ... with a law which is contrary to natural justice'. No citizen should be required actively to volunteer his or her own self-incrimination (Powell 1979b). However, by this juncture, 'natural justice' opposition to measures to reduce death on the road smacked of anachronism. Had the world finally moved on? It seemed so: Powell gained only minimal backbench support.

Fowler's act came down heavily on heavy-drinking recidivists: individuals found guilty in a 10-year period of two offences at more than double the officially sanctioned blood alcohol concentration. Offenders of this type would be disqualified from holding a licence until the Medical Adviser to the Secretary of State decided that they were fit and safe enough to drive (Light 1994: 108). But on two other issues – 'random testing' and the 80 mg per 100 ml blood alcohol concentration limit – the act left the law unchanged. On the first point, Fowler sympathised with the conservatism of powerful motoring and drinks-industry lobby groups. 'Random testing' elicited the usual legal-cum-semantic wrangling over meaning and intent. Would it allow the police (like their Swedish counterparts) to set up road blocks to test every passing driver? Or did it simply imply that officers would be given increased room for operational manoeuvre? Several Labour MPs, notably Barry Sheerman, member for Huddersfield East, and an ardent young road-safety activist, told the minister that now was the time to grasp the preventative nettle and make a decisive move away from the kinds of 'rituals' that had undermined the police in the immediate post-Castle era. Officers must finally be given power to make the law work (Sheerman 1981). Fowler held firm, not least since those who opposed him were unable to provide a clear working definition of how the powers would be defined in a court of law, and the legal and constitutional difficulties that they might bring in their wake (Fowler 1981).

Following yet more field trials the new law came into operation in May 1983 (Cobb and Dabbs 1985). It immediately fell foul of public opinion and the law. In December of that year a solicitor at Basingstoke demanded to know whether a breathalyser computer print-out could be accepted as a valid form of evidence: his question passed to a higher court (Witherow 1983). Then in spring 1984 the libertarian *Daily Express* launched an anti-breath-test campaign. Readers were asked to send in their experiences of the Fowler act. Some claimed that the new device had yielded wildly wayward readings. Others, who insisted that they suffered from a chronic chest or lung condition which prevented them from providing a sample, had nevertheless been charged with refusing to cooperate with the police. Others reiterated the kinds of complaints that had been levelled at anti-drink-driving legislation for nearly 25 years: the new device provided readings that revealed significant differences between prosecution and defence versions of equivalent blood concentrations; punishments had been harsh and ignored the fact that motorists depended on cars for their livelihood; arresting officers had been unforgivably arrogant. The campaign made a splash: the *Daily Express* claimed that it represented a 'triumph for justice'. Emphasising that the paper had always 'emphatically [opposed] drink driving', editorial writers asserted that it was the great British public that had won a famous libertarian victory (Daily Express 1984).

An unlikely fellow-campaigner, *The Times*, now joined the fray. How could any government have allowed itself to adopt a device that had been inadequately tested? The Conservatives had displayed 'blind faith' in their new toy, 'even when it began behaving badly' (The Times 1984). Pressure-groups added their voices to the anti-breathalyser chorus. The AA, the Association of Police Surgeons, and the Magistrates' Association urged compromise. The law clearly stated that drivers whose breath-test registered a value of up to 15 mg above the limit of 35 mg per 100 ml of breath could ask for a blood or urine test, with the proviso that a police surgeon would decide which option would be offered in each individual case. A spokesman for the Magistrates' Association stated that 'at the moment it must be admitted we don't know in a situation which gives rise to doubt whether the machine is working or not'. 'Working or not!' A savage criticism: the 'statutory option' should be restored (Evans 1989).

The courts made the final, adverse decision and Leon Brittan at the Home Office opted for cautious compromise. The *status quo ante* would be restored: every driver suspected of alcoholic impairment would be allowed to have a blood test, regardless of the level indicated by the new breathalyser. Only in 1988, eight years after the passing of Fowler's act, thirteen after the publication of the Blennerhassett Report, and twenty-two after Barbara Castle (side-lining the contributions of Graham Page and Ernest Marples implied that she had single-handedly transformed road safety policy in Britain), did a predominantly but still not exclusively breathalyser-based method of further reducing the incidence of drink driving finally struggle on to the statute book.

Historicising Death on the Road

In 1987 the government published an interdepartmental report, the first survey of its kind for 20 years (Department of Transport 1987). During that period the Commons had largely ignored a subject that, in the Marples and Castle era, had gained a more prominent public profile than at any other time in the twentieth century: the first full-scale parliamentary debate for 20 years had been held in November 1985. The interdepartmental report concluded that compared with other economically highly developed nations the British performance was 'average', and considerably worse than that of world pace-setters like Norway, Sweden and Japan. Fatalities in the 10–14 age group was a national disgrace, with twice as many children dying annually on Britain's roads than in a majority of European nations (Ministry of Transport 1987: 6).

The report identified structural, institutional and financial failings. Very few backbenchers had an interest in the topic, which had never appeared in a party manifesto. Road-safety pressure groups lacked expertise and were repeatedly outmanoeuvred by motoring organisations, and by the car and drinks industries. Neither the CBI nor the TUC had ever held a debate on the issue. Media coverage was poor. Celebrities attracted heavy coverage. So, for a day or two, did pile-ups on motorways and coach crashes involving the death of schoolchildren. But newspaper and television editors had never found or attempted to find a way of communicating the unimaginable tragedy following large numbers of individual, spatially widely separated, and in media terms anonymously similar, events. Finally, and dispiritingly, the precise impact of television campaigns on road safety remained obscure. The report read like a study in failure and only contained two positive proposals: fully enforceable methods of deterrence and commitment to internationally agreed targets, in this case the reduction of fatalities to two-thirds their 1987 level by 2000 (Department of Transport 1987: 27).

Many things had gone wrong in the 1970s. Destabilised by Heath's creation of the Department of the Environment, the MoT entered a period of institutional confusion. Under Marples's and Castle's leaderships, the 1960s had seen the emergence of a cumulative anti-drink-driving agenda, with clearly articulated and publicised legislative-cum-administrative objectives – the process as a whole fits well into the now forgotten but still revealing 'growth of government' model (MacDonagh 1977; MacLeod 1988).

During the Heath and Callaghan years – and in Wilson's brief premiership between 1974 and 1976 – inertia and indecision prevailed. Did seat-belt reform divert attention from the need to complete the job that Marples and Castle had started? Probably not, but with the exception of a section in Norman Fowler's Transport Bill in 1981, successive governments stood aside from a now widely perceived need routinely to belt up. Reform was left to private-members motions, and Lords-based and voluntaristic initiatives, with RoSPA playing a prominent role. Absence of firm governmental commitment to legislate on either the drink-driving or seat-belt issues threatened to precipitate a regression to an era in which road safety had been the province of less than a handful of politically powerless backbenchers (Luckin 2010b).

Had the problem been pushed on to the back-burner by the financial, economic and industrial relations crises that plagued the Heath and Callaghan governments? To accept that explanation requires giving credence to Bill Rodgers' response to media criticism in 1977: more pressing issues had crowded road safety off the parliamentary agenda. But this turns a blind eye to the fact that in the mid- and late 1960s the Wilson administration found itself repeatedly enmeshed in major balance of payment and industrial relations crises. These had not prevented Barbara Castle from pushing ahead with her bill. The difference, surely, lay in the tenacity (and political drive and ambition) of ministers responsible for running a low-profile department. Castle knew what she wanted and was willing to fight for it: John Peyton and Bill Rodgers lacked that kind of tenacity and self-belief.

Between 1979 and 1981 Norman Fowler restored a degree of confidence. But he also encountered testing legal and scientific problems. There was no serious falling-out with the Home Office. But the publication of the Blennerhassett Report intensified the need to concentrate on enforcement. Hence the commitment to breathalyser field-tests; research into the equivalence between blood- and breath-derived levels of blood alcohol concentration; and clearly defining the investigative powers of officers on traffic duty. Fingers had been badly burned at the Home Office in the early 1970s: there must be no repetition. In the event, however, history nearly repeated itself. The death-knell may have sounded for Enoch Powell's anti-statist brand of philosophical libertarianism. But in 1984 Leon Britain succumbed to a well-organised pro-motorist newspaper campaign. As a result Fowler's technically revamped measure only came into full operation at the end of the 1980s. Even then it included yet another version of the 'statutory option' – anyone with a breathalyser reading as low as 50 mg per 100 ml would be allowed to request a confirmatory blood or urine test.

The interdepartmental report, published in 1987, seems to confirm that early twenty-first-century road-safety reformers and policy makers have little to gain from spending too much time sorting out the complex narrative that has lain at the heart of this chapter. Little can be learnt from a saga dominated by indecision, inertia and administrative confusion. Nevertheless, even a narrative dominated by missed opportunities has something to reveal about creative uses of the past. In a pioneering article, John Urry identified what he called an extraordinarily powerful twentieth-century automotive 'machinic complex', involving innumerable feedback and multiplier relationships with an ever-expanding range of economic, industrial, financial, medical and service-based sectors and agencies (Urry 2004). In complementary vein, Steffen Bohm has delineated contradictions between economically highly developed – or developing – nations actively encouraging an extension of mass motorisation but failing to devote sufficient attention to the regulation of harmful consequences (Bohm 2006).

Why, given these penetrating sociological schema, has so little been written about the history of traffic accidents – by far the most important negative impact associated with a twentieth-century economic, social and cultural infatuation with the car? Routine reference is now made in general texts to military metaphors that point to the magnitude and horror of death on the road over the last 130 years. Writing about interwar Britain Martin Pugh has noted that 'the [nation] experienced 122,000 fatalities and 1.5 million injuries, making motoring comparable to fighting a war' (Pugh 2008: 246). But analogy and metaphor are no substitute for analysis and interpretation. Precisely why, with a handful of exceptions, this seismic transformation of the social relations of mobility and quality of life in Britain and many other countries is now only belatedly attracting scholarly attention is too large a subject to be tackled in this contribution (Ladd 2008; Norton 2008; Luckin 2012). Suffice it to say, Pat Thane's dictum that politicians and policy makers will make fewer errors if they know something about earlier developments and problems in the area with which they are concerned is based on the assumption that there actually is a relevant historical literature to be consulted (Thane 2009: 145).

Why start with the incidence and control of drink driving? Writing about the seminal North Report of 2010, which dug more deeply into the problem than any previous governmental investigation, Sally Cunningham offers compelling reasons (North 2010). She argues that the long-term reduction in drink driving demonstrates that the law in this area 'has succeeded where other regulatory driving offences seeking to reduce risk-taking, such as speeding, or even careless driving have failed' (Cunningham 2011: 26). Measures against those who venture on to the road following one or more drinks too many have '… set down [the] simple rule that you must not drive with a BAC of more than 80mg/100 ml [and this has become] acceptable to the majority …' (Cunningham 2011: 26). This mode of thinking can clearly be related to the events of 1965 and 1966 when Barbara Castle and her senior officials realised that the introduction of law directed against drink drivers might, if all went to plan, constitute the first step on the long road towards automotive self-discipline *in all areas of road safety* while at the same time hastening the death-knell of the traditional verities of libertarian pro-motorism.

Second, and crucially, the longer-term success of laws to control alcoholic impairment depended on what seemed to most people to be objective – that is to say, scientific – criteria. As Deborah Stone has pointed out in an important article, reformers in every field depend heavily on the acceptance of credible 'causal stories'. In the case of drink driving, this had less to do with detailed understanding of the minutiae of cutting-edge research among parliamentarians and the public than the construction, popularisation and dissemination of a plausible narrative that might convert social and ethical disapproval into fully fledged criminalisation (Stone 1989).

Finally, there is the issue of 'real' science and the transmission of scientific knowledge. The credibility of Britain's post-1960s adhesion to a limit of 80 mg per 100 ml – a ratio now only shared in Europe by Ireland and Malta – had begun to be undermined before the outbreak of the Second World War. Already, by that juncture, a Scandinavian–American research axis had confirmed the progressively deleterious impact of different levels of alcohol on the physiological, neurological and psychological variables that determine performance levels in relation to a wide range of repetitive and fine motor skill-based activities. These findings were embedded in road traffic law in the Scandinavian nations at a remarkably early date: by the mid-1960s Norway had acknowledged that very large numbers of accidents attributable to reckless behaviour on the part of drivers in the 80 mg per 100 ml range could have been avoided if maximum permissible blood alcohol concentration level had been fixed at 50 mg per 100 ml. In Britain in the late 1950s, G.C. Drew at University College London had come to the same conclusions in a government-commissioned report (Drew 1958). In 1964 Robert Borkenstein coordinated the massive Grand Rapids project and used detailed epidemiological material to confirm laboratory-based findings that had set the regulatory ball rolling – particularly in Scandinavia – between the 1920s and the 1950s. In the run-up to the enactment of the Road Safety Act Barbara Castle endowed the Borkenstein data with mantra-like status to convert a still scientifically ill-informed Commons to the general 'causal story' that underpinned her measure (Borkenstein 1964). To many MPs the fine detail of impairment theory remained incomprehensible. But the general narrative carried massive confirmatory and conversionary power.

In 2010 the North Report advised David Cameron's coalition government that it could save more lives – and educate more drivers in the central tenets of road safety – by lowering the limit to 50 mg per 100 ml (North 2010). As we might expect, little happened. Then it was announced that Britain was awaiting the publication of an EU directive to bring every nation in the 80 mg category down to 50 mg or a lower figure. Road-safety activists now hoped that – pressure-group power allowing – the scientifically authenticated lessons of the preceding half century would finally be absorbed.

References

Advisory Committee on Alcoholism (1979). *Report on Education and Training.* London: HMSO.

Biffen, J. (2006). Lord Peyton of Yeovil. *The Guardian*, 27 November.

BMJ (1976). Editorial: Drinking Drivers and the Law. *British Medical Journal*, 8 May, p. 1103.

Bohm, S. (2006). Introduction to 'Against Automobility'. *Sociological Review* 54(1), pp. 1–16.

Borkenstein, R.F. (1964). *The Role of the Drinking Driver in Traffic Accidents 7.* Indianapolis: Indiana University. Department of Police Adminstration.

Braithwaite, J. (1989). *Crime, Shame and Reintegration.* Cambridge: Cambridge University Press.

Callaghan, J. (1987). *Time and Change*. London: Collins.

Campbell, J. (1993). *Heath: A Biography*. London: Pimlico.

Cobb, P. and Dabbs, M. (1985). *Report on the Performance of the Lion Intoximeter 3000 and the Camic Breath Analyser*. London: HMSO.

Cunningham, S. (2011). The North Review of Drink Driving: Some Sobering Proposals. *Criminal Law Review* 4, pp. 296–310.

Daily Express (1984). *Daily Express*, 16 March, pp. 1, 5.

Daily Mirror (1976). *Daily Mirror*, 19 April, p. 2.

Department of the Environment (1976). *Drinking and Driving: Report of the Departmental Committee*. London: HMSO.

Department of Transport (1987). *Road Safety: The Next Steps*. London: Department of Transport.

———— (1991). *Road Accidents Great Britain*. London: HMSO.

Department of Transport and Home Office (1988). *Road Traffic Law Review Report*. London. HMSO.

Divall, C. (2010). Mobilizing the History of Technology. *Technology and Culture* 51(4), pp. 938–60.

Drew, G. (1959). *Effect of Small Doses of Alcohol on a Skill Resembling Driving*. London: Medical Research Council.

Durie, A. (1976). *The Guardian*, 19 July, p. 14.

Evans, R. (1989). Home Office Urged to Dispel Doubts About Test Intoximeter. *The Times*, 10 March, p. 3.

Fowler, N. (1981). *Hansard* 996, 13 August, col. 861.

———— (1991). *Ministers Decide: A Personal Memoir of the Thatcher Years*. London: Chapman.

Hailsham, Lord (1974). *Hansard* 352, 11 June, col. 448.

Hansard (1924). *Hansard* 56, 19 February, col. 191.

Hirsh, R. (2011). Historians of Technology in the Real World: Reflections on the Pursuit of Policy-Oriented History. *Technology and Culture* 52(1), pp. 6–20.

Holmes, M. (1997). *The Failure of the Heath Government*. Basingstoke: Macmillan.

Home Office (1983). Home Office Circular no. 46/1983.

Institute of Alcohol Studies (2010). *Drinking and Driving: IAS Factsheet*. St Ives, Cambridgeshire: IAS.

Interdepartmental Committee (1976). *Report of the Interdepartmental Committee on the Distribution of Criminal Business between the Crown Court and Magistrates' Courts*. London: HMSO.

Irwin, A. (1985). *Risk and the Control of Technology: Public Policies for Road Traffic Safety in Britain and the United States*. Manchester: Manchester University Press.

Kershaw, R. (1976). Breath Testing at Random is 'Coming'. *The Times*, 2 July, p. 4.

Ladd, B. (2008). *Autophobia: Love and Hate in the Automotive Age*. Chicago, IL: University of Chicago Press.

Light, R. (1994). *Criminalizing the Drinking Driver*. Aldershot: Dartmouth Co.

Luckin, B. (2010a). A Degree of Consensus On the Roads: Drink Driving Policy in Britain 1945–70. *Twentieth Century British History* 21, pp. 350–74.

——— (2010b). A Never-Ending Passing of the Buck? The Failure of Drink Driving Reform in Interwar Britain. *Contemporary British History* 24, pp. 363–84.

——— (2012). Motorists, Non-Drivers and Traffic Accidents Between the Wars: A Provisional Survey. *Transfers: Interdisciplinary Journal of Mobility Studies* 2, pp. 4–21.

MacDonagh, O. (1977). *Early Victorian Government 1830–1870*. London: Weidenfeld and Nicolson.

MacLeod, R., ed. (1988). *Government and Expertise: Specialists, Administrators and Professionals*. Cambridge: Cambridge University Press.

Medico-Legal Correspondent (1976). Drink Driving Offences. *British Medical Journal*, 29 September, pp. 765–6.

Ministry of Transport (1960). Report on the Methods Employed in Denmark, Norway and Sweden to Combat Driving under the Influence of Drink, July 1960. The National Archives, MT 92/122.

Moran, J. (2006). Crossing the Road in Britain, 1931–1976. *Historical Journal* 49, pp. 477–96.

North, P. (2010). *Report of the Review of the Report of Drink and Drug-Driving Law*. Available at: http://northreview.independent.gov.uk/docs/NorthReview-Report.pdf (accessed 10 May 2015).

Norton, P. (2008). *Fighting Traffic: The Dawn of the Motor Age in the American City*. Cambridge, MA: MIT Press.

Peyton J. (1997). *Without Benefit of Laundry*. London: Bloomsbury.

Powell, E. (1979a). *Hansard* 964, 22 March, col. 1737.

——— (1979b). *The Times*, 3 December, p. 4.

Pugh, M. (2008). *'We Danced All Night': A Social History of Britain between the Wars*. London: Bodley Head.

Raphael, A. (1976a). Tougher Laws for Drinking Drivers. *The Observer*, 18 April, p. 1.

——— (1976b). None for the Road, *The Observer*, 2 May, p. 12.

Rodgers, B. (2000). *Fourth Among Equals*. London: Politicos.

Ross, H.L. (1973). Law, Science and Accidents: The British Road Safety Act of 1967. *Journal of Legal Studies* 2, pp. 1–78.

——— (1975). The Scandinavian Myth: The Effectiveness of Drinking and Driving Legislation in Sweden and Norway. *Journal of Legal Studies* 4, pp. 285–310.

——— (1992). *Confronting Drunk Driving: Social Policy for Saving Lives*. New Haven: Yale University Press.

Sheerman, B. (1981). *Hansard* 996, 13 August, col. 920.

Stone, D. (1989). Causal Stories and the Formation of Policy Agendas. *Political Science Quarterly* 104, pp. 283–301.

Thane, P. (2009). History and Policy. *History Workshop Journal* 67, pp. 140–45.

The Guardian (1977). *The Guardian*, 3 May, p. 12.

The Times (1979). *The Times*, 22 December.

———— (1984). *The Times*, 28 March, p. 15.

Urry, J. (2004). The 'System' of Automobility. *Theory, Culture and Society* 21, pp. 25–39.

van der Vat, D. (1981). Sobering Statistics On Drinkers. *The Times*, 18 August, p. 4.

Waymark, P. (1976). A Wider Look At Blennerhassett. *The Times*, 29 April, p. 21.

———— (1977). Political Qualms Holding Back Road Safety Laws. *The Times*, 22 June, p. 35.

Whitelegg, J. and Haq, G. (2006). *Vision Zero: Adopting a Target of Zero for Road Traffic Fatalities and Serious Injuries*. Stockholm: Swedish Environmental Institute.

Willett, T. (1965). *Criminal on the Road: A Study of Serious Motoring Offences and Those Who Commit Them*. London: Tavistock.

Witherow, J. (1983). Thirty Seven Per Cent Rise in Drink-Driving Prosecutions. *The Times*, 8 December, p. 1.

Zeliser, J. (2000). Clio's Lost Tribe: Public Policy History Since 1978. *Journal of Policy History* 52, pp. 369–94.

PART II
Marketing Im/Mobility

Chapter 8

Marketing and Branding for Modal Shift in Urban Transport

Nicola Forsdike

This chapter explores the extent to which history is relevant to contemporary transport and marketing practitioners. In particular it considers whether and how knowledge from the past is applied in day-to-day practice. It also debates whether the lessons of history are used to full advantage, or whether learning is being missed that would, if applied, enable practitioners to derive better value for stakeholders, shareholders and taxpayers.

Issues are explored from the practitioner's standpoint with particular reference to how marketing and branding theories can and have been used to deliver modal shift in urban transport. Beginning with a discussion of those much abused terms of 'marketing' and 'branding', the theoretical context – how contemporary business marketing and branding theory can be applied to a transport context to deliver modal shift – is examined. Case studies are then developed to demonstrate whether historical evidence can show if and how theory has worked in practice. The first study relates to Network SouthEast, a brand applied to rail commuting services serving London during the 1980s and early 1990s; the second refers to Metro, the brand used by the Passenger Transport Authority and Passenger Transport Executive in West Yorkshire to encompass their regional transport services.

In delivering a practitioner's response academic references are largely absent from the text. The transport and market theory comes from my own working knowledge, albeit based on years of study and regularly updated to maintain chartered status. No academic texts are referred to directly in the chapter; however, when I took my professional exams in the 1990s the syllabus drew heavily on the work of Drucker, Levitt, Kotler, McDonald and other academics. What follows is therefore based on a working knowledge of market and transport theory: the former based on professional study refreshed and extended through formal professional development over many years; the latter on over 25 years' practical experience of applying that knowledge within transport and infrastructure businesses. For the case studies I have drawn heavily on the public domain for evidence using two specific websites in particular. The first covers the development of Network SouthEast and contains material written by Richard Sharp, the advertising manager for London & South East/ Network SouthEast between 1984 and 1987. The second is that for West Yorkshire PTE (2015). Again, the material from these sites is interpreted and augmented from my own experience of working for over two decades in the rail industry.

What is Marketing?

The term marketing is possibly one of the most abused in modern business. I often begin talks and lectures by asking the audience how they themselves would define the term. Typical answers range from 'spin' to 'selling people things they don't want'. The situation is not helped by the explosion in marketing techniques that has occurred as a result of the technological revolution of the late twentieth century. The availability of courses in, for example, 'digital marketing', 'relationship marketing', 'search engine marketing', 'mobile marketing' and 'social media marketing' serve to reinforce perceptions that marketing is about channel rather than strategy, about spin rather than substance. This is a pity: marketing encompasses some powerful concepts that if embraced can deliver real strategic change both for businesses and society.

In the analysis that follows I shall use the term 'marketing' in accordance with the definition first developed by the Chartered Institute of Marketing (CIM) in 1976: that marketing is 'The management process responsible for identifying, anticipating and satisfying customer requirements profitably' (CIM 2009). There has been considerable soul searching since then as to whether the concept of a management process is still relevant, or whether modern trends to specialise in a narrow field make an over-arching definition redundant. Indeed, the evolution of marketing as a discipline is worthy of a discussion in its own right. In particular, new media have facilitated a world where old mass forms of communication and commercial transactions have been replaced by what some have described as a 'new ecosystem' where 'millions and billions of unstructured one to one and peer to peer conversations' take place (Fetherstonhaugh 2009). In this brave new world, products are customised in real time and change constantly.

However, whilst real-time customisation may be the mantra in some industries it is difficult to conceive of a real-time customised transport industry outside of the private car. The concept of timetables which change on an instantaneous basis (deliverable by taxis, but hardly by buses and metro systems, and even less so by trains) is difficult to apply. New vehicles take months, if not years, to develop and produce, whilst infrastructure schemes can take decades from first thoughts to final commissioning. At a strategic level then the 1976 CIM definition continues to be relevant and provides a robust starting point for analysing whether marketing and branding can help to deliver modal shift. This is not, of course, to overlook the changes that new technologies are bringing, particularly in the field of customer information and ticketing. The definition's requirement for 'profit' is arguably not relevant to all sectors. In practice I often add a caveat such as 'satisfying customer requirements within a defined budget' or 'satisfying customer requirements whilst delivering a specified Return on Investment (ROI)', reflecting the reality that not-for-profit organisations also can and do use marketing to achieve their goals.

Taking this revised definition as a starting point, it is possible to apply it at several distinct levels of an organisation. First, it can be applied on a philosophical or conceptual basis – anticipating and satisfying customer requirements requires the plans and policies of that organisation to be 'customer-led' and predicates an externally focussed approach. Thus it influences the strategic approach taken at a leadership level. Second, the term 'process' suggests that the marketing approach can be used to help a firm or organisation organise its resources to meet marketing needs. Marketing planning processes as defined by McDonald and others provide frameworks within which decisions on investment in new product development, advertising spend, distribution channels and so on can be taken.

Finally, it delivers a toolkit for commercial teams (however named – typically they might have a marketing, communications, or other designation) around three distinct functions. Firstly, research tools whether conventional market surveys or analytics from relational and other databases help fulfil marketing's role of anticipating customer needs. Second, new product development (not always seen as a marketing function in the transport sector) helps to ensure that those needs are satisfied. Third, a range of tools from market segmentation to branding help to answer the profit or return on investment objectives by ensuring the organisation's resources are targeted in an appropriate way, that is, at those elements of the market or population that will deliver the highest return and/or are most in need of the benefits being delivered.

Note that marketing is not, therefore (or not just), advertising, sales promotion, sales campaigns or branding, although all of those are tools within the marketer's toolkit. Interestingly, the articles from the UK transport planning world that I have reviewed in developing this text have all used the terms marketing and advertising as interchangeable – although, curiously, the same was not true for some of the overseas case studies in my background reading.

In summary, marketing enables organisations to anticipate and satisfy the needs of their customers or users and provides a framework within which resources can be allocated to ensure other objectives – including financial ones (whether profit, ROI or budgets) – can be met. As a marketer working in the field of transport and engineering, I am constantly frustrated that the general view of marketing is that it is advertising, spin, public relations (PR). In fact its basic building blocks – product design (think timetable, vehicle type, the end-to-end customer journey), price, promotion (advertising), and place (how the product is accessed – ticket distribution, station location, bus stops and transport interchanges) – are all typically planks of public-transport service provision. Whether an organisation is aiming to make a profit or to provide the maximum benefit to the greatest number of people at the lowest cost, a thorough understanding of the market/public and its needs is the starting point. Public-transport providers and planners, therefore, whether they like it or not, are in the business of marketing.

What is Branding?

Marketers tend to agree that branding is one of the most useful tools that they have, enabling them to defend market share, pricing and value. Classic definitions include 'a name, term, sign, symbol, design or a combination of these that identifies the maker or seller of the product or service' (Kotler et al. 2005).

Classic this definition might be, but it fails to capture what many regard as the key essence of branding – namely that it speaks as strongly to the emotions as it does to reason. Brands (or the symbols associated with them) act as triggers that bring specific associations to the mind of an individual. Thus, they act as shorthand devices conveying a particular standard of quality, specific product features and benefits, and at their best a specific personality of their own. Most importantly they build trust in the mind of the individual consumer so that a transaction (that is, a purchase of a service or product) takes place. Thus for a certain generation, the Heinz brand, as linked to sub-brands such as 'Heinz Baked Beans' or 'Heinz Tomato Soup', speaks not only of a particular colour, texture and taste, but also of family, comfort and security. In some cases brands are worth a premium with users prepared to pay a price considerably above simple production costs or that of competitor products. Thus 'first class' denotes status as much as leg room.

These emotional associations are understood by commercial marketers who develop and extend them using advertising and other means. Brands and their identities (the physical application of the brand to tangible features) are based on careful analysis and research of existing and potential markets. Brand values are identified that will set a product apart from that of another producer.

Whilst the producer tries to influence the associations through promotional campaigns the consumer creates their own vision of the brand, based on their experience of it. For transport operators this presents a challenge, particularly when a single brand is delivered by a range of operators (as in the Metro case study which follows). Delivering consistency within any service industry is a challenge. Unlike consumer goods, services are consumed in real time by users. Consistency of experience is always at risk from a failure of service which could range from buses or trains not running to time (perhaps as a result of traffic congestion or mechanical failure) to poor quality exchanges with operator staff or inconsistencies in information given from different sources. Moreover, the visual manifestations of the brand – including vehicle liveries, access points such as rail stations, staff uniforms, print and electronic communications – may lie outside the span of control of the organisation wishing to apply a brand on a network-wide basis. In this case delivery of the brand may rely in part or even in whole on the specification and delivery of detailed contractual clauses.

How Can Theory Be Applied in Practice?

How then can the theory of marketing and branding, largely derived from the world of commercial business (and indeed initially largely from the world of fast-moving consumer goods, although latterly there has been substantial research in the area of marketing services), be applied to help public-transport providers deliver their objectives?

Typically in the commercial world, marketers use the tools of marketing to fill the gap between their current business position in relation to the markets they serve and their corporate aspirations, pulling the levers of product, price, promotion and place (distribution) to, for example, improve their sales, create new markets, improve their return on investment, and to achieve their corporate goals, whether those be related to market domination and/or improved profitability. In contrast to this proactive activity of influencing, anticipating, and supplying human needs it has sometimes seemed that transport planners can all too often be interested only in reacting to forecast demand, planning services on a predict-and-provide basis, to meet the baseline demand that they predict will occur in the market place. In doing so, they miss the aspiration gap that marketers would seek to close.

Much of our transport planning appears to be all too often reverse engineered out of what has gone before; as one econometrics expert described their work to me, they drive 'using only the rear view mirror'. Transport models, which are firmly bounded within economic theory, typically model transport-user behaviour using today's behaviours to predict tomorrow's. Whilst this could be said to represent a usable past, or at least, a usable present, in practice it draws on only a very narrow interpretation of data – typically limited years of usage statistics, along with generalised data on GDP, population, car ownership and other factors that are held (through research) to influence travel patterns. Granularity and richness of data is, of necessity, lost. Although adjustments can and are made for notable factors such as rail strikes, other factors that can affect transport patterns, including variations in the competitive environment, weather patterns and the impact of advertising and branding are lost in the overall picture. One result of this is that when major discontinuities occur (for example, recessions such as that of 2008–11) models may fail to predict and explain actual results. Without contextual history there is no understanding of the past; without that, it is difficult to predict accurately the results of future activity.

There are, of course, good reasons why planners may approach the marketing toolkit with something akin to hesitation. These could include the desire to avoid accusations of social engineering, as well as one of timescales. Whilst marketers tend to work in one- to five-year timeframes, planners must grapple with a much wider scope ranging from months for small-scale, low-investment schemes, to decades for major infrastructure changes. However, this does beg the question as to how well economic models can predict the future. In particular, by predicating future development on a very narrow view of the past, today's patterns are reinforced. Today's successful city is also tomorrow's successful city as success draws investment under current appraisal methods.

One wonders whether today's appraisal methodologies would have allowed the London suburban railways, built partly before the suburbs they now serve to have come into being? And how useful are the methodologies in answering contemporary debates in relation to the planning of new high-speed rail routes such as the proposed link between London and Birmingham and ultimately the North (see Chapter 6)? It is possible that if, as we are seeing, econometric models cannot wholly answer the issue of how we want our world to be then moving our paradigm from one of predict-and-provide to one of closing the gap against a vision of the future may offer a way forwards. In changing paradigms, history offers an anchor, suggesting parallels (for example, the springing up of new economic communities around new railway lines) from the past that can guide us to better decision making in the future if we are willing to learn.

Many decisions in relation to transport planning are however much shorter term and there are already some notable examples of transport practitioners moving beyond predict-and-provide to using marketing tools to change the way in which people think about and use transport. How useful are such tools in making operational policies such as modal – or temporal – shift in travel patterns?

Any robust marketing plan begins with a study of two aspects – first, an audit of the market, and second an 'internal' review that looks at the strengths and weaknesses of the enterprise concerned.

The market audit seeks to understand the external environment and particularly those aspects that present opportunities or threats that will influence the success of achieving a particular set of objectives. Typically an audit begins with desk research which seeks to answer questions affecting the macro-environment in which a product or service operates. Within a transport context these might typically cover the political, economic, social, legal and environmental factors that influence the journeys people make. Transport demand models have tried and tested methods for incorporating known demand drivers such as GDP, journey times (including between competing modes), housing and other development plans. Marketing tools offer a complementary approach by bringing consideration of more nuanced changes or more in-depth field research of the market. This may include a quantitative study or studies to measure the size of a particular segment or qualitative work to explore in depth more intangible aspects such as people's attitudes to a particular mode. Marketing seeks to understand what type of people are travelling now and in the future. Why do they travel, and how might that change in the future? What is the current market structure and what are the strengths of weaknesses of different modes in relation to each other?

In parallel, the 'internal' audit looks at the current resources available to an organisation or institution to support the delivery of its objectives. For transport this will include availability of vehicles and infrastructure capacity (with the added nuance that there may be an extended supply chain required to deliver a service to an end user). However, whilst resource gaps in such physical resource are generally explicit in traditional cost–benefit analyses, it is important to recognise also the requirement for and availability of professional knowledge to deliver schemes. Similarly, the potential availability or otherwise of funding for investment is also a critical – and potentially limiting – factor.

By understanding these issues and by beginning to formulate answers to the questions, planners and policy makers can begin to arrive at policies and plans to bring about the situations they desire. For example, in thinking about people's future needs, and the strengths and weaknesses of one mode over another, it is possible to arrive at a plan to improve the product for public transport – perhaps by increasing train-service frequencies to stimulate demand for rail over road at certain times of the day, by improving reliability of public-transport services and branding them consistently to help the public gain confidence in the transport system; they can then be tempted to use that system using price or other promotional mechanisms; successful use can then lead to repeat purchase – and effect modal shift.

Of course, transport planners do pick up many of these elements already, but I argue that in the recent past too much of our system has been focussed on measurement and too little on a qualitative understanding of the people that will need and use services (although the Department for Transport is beginning to give leadership in this area) or on the localised competitive context of different modes. Whilst planners tend to measure the current usage of different modes, the differences in journey time and so on, less attention is paid to the wider competitive context of the different modes. I have seen many models that build in end-to-end journey times, public-transport-fares elasticities and so on – but few that consider the wider context, including the level of city-centre car-parking charges and the availability of that parking. Moreover, the concentration on current usage as a base for modelling tends to reinforce existing patterns of development rather than open the possibility for a different kind of future. Only by thinking strategically, by thinking like a marketer trying to place a product in relation to those of their competitors, can the tools of marketing achieve their full potential in relation to the delivery of modal shift. And only by understanding history – what tools have achieved what effect in what context – can planners and marketers begin to predict a range of possible outcomes.

It may help to consider a theoretical example. Sam is the newly appointed marketing officer for a new transport authority for an English city/city region. Her organisation has been remitted to effect modal shift from private car for both peak and off-peak journeys to alleviate the negative effects of road-traffic congestion, both in improving average journey times (regardless of modes) and reducing carbon emissions. As a classically trained marketer, she seeks first to understand the market situation, as outlined above. In particular, she wants to know what kinds of journey people are making and the length of their journeys so that she can do an initial segmentation to identify the best modal alternatives for each segment. She also wants to understand better the relative strengths and weaknesses of the different transport modes and to identify the barriers to change. To do this, she uses market research techniques, both quantitative (for example, number and types of journeys made by time of day/day of week) and qualitative (for example, to identify not only what are the factors that lock people into different travel patterns and modes, but also people's attitudes to public transport). She also looks at social and other trends – for example, will patterns of living and working remain the same? Will technological changes, such as internet-enabled patterns of working reduce the overall demand for travel? What will be the effect of changes to employment patterns, and an increasing trend towards freelance, agency and self-employment? Do people need to get to work on Sundays and if so, what hours do they work? And what is the most cost-effective way of meeting this need whilst providing access to work and other opportunities for the greatest number of people?

Having used research to identify the current situation, future potential and barriers to change, she looks at the data she has collected and begins to build up a picture of the different market segments within her transport region by trying to group people together according to shared characteristics. In doing so she identifies different groups of people who through reasons of demographics (age, gender, work type, for example) and social outlook are more inclined to use public transport. Having done that, she has a number of different marketing tools; the extent to which she will use each tool depends on the relative strengths of the modes whose use she wants to promote and the market segments she is trying to reach. These fall into a number of different types, based on the 4Ps of marketing, namely:

- **Product**
  Does the core product meet customer needs, or will investing in timetable changes/different routes/increased frequencies/more comfortable or accessible vehicles/better walking routes/better cycle provision help to fill spare capacity or move people away from crowded modes?

- **Price**
  Are fares levels set at a rate people are prepared to pay? Do they reflect the strengths/weaknesses of the public-transport services against the comparative position of the private car (theory argues that where roads are heavily congested you can afford to price high)? Do they exacerbate over-crowding at certain times of the day or help to spread the load more evenly?

- **Promotion**
  Are people aware of the services on offer, their quality, strengths over the car? Are services consistently badged and presented to them (branded) promising a consistent quality of experience (and is that quality delivered)?

- **Place**
  How easy is it for people to change their travel habits? Is it easy for them to get to the station or the bus stop when compared with using the car? Is the information they need to be able to use the service readily available?

The 4Ps offer a framework around which to build a comprehensive – and market-based – plan. This framework allows for the evaluation and comparison of different approaches (investment in product, increased prices, versus no investment and lower prices, for example) helping to identify the optimum way in which available (and future) resources. Other models based on research in service industries add further Ps including one standing for People – which covers customer service and face-to-face interactions between service providers and their users. This can be a useful enhancement for a transport provider, helping to identify how a passenger's interface with a transport mode (how easy it is to buy a ticket, whether the bus driver smiles) and future attitudes to and patterns of travel can be influenced by what have traditionally been regarded as 'softer' elements.

Is There Any Historical Evidence that Marketing Has Delivered Results in Practice?

Theory is interesting, but can historical evidence show what has happened in the past, and provide lessons that will improve future practice? Reviewing what has happened in the past, using the lens not only of econometrics but also the historical context of particular interventions offers a potential method for this and can be tested through case studies. Given that a market-led approach is more often associated in the mind of the public with commercial business than the public sector it is perhaps ironic that it is public-sector organisations that spring to my mind when looking for role models of what can be achieved in terms of shifting travel patterns by using the tools of marketing.

Network SouthEast

The first case study is drawn from British Rail (BR), the nationalised provider of rail infrastructure and services in Britain from 1948 to 1997 and specifically from Network SouthEast. For readers who are not steeped in the recent history of the rail network in Britain, a short explanation may be helpful. In 1982 British Rail introduced a major restructuring of its operations into market-focussed business sectors, supported by a series of headquarters and functional organisations. The concept, introduced by British Rail Chief Executive Robert Reid, followed a lengthy period of government criticism of the lack of efficiency within the company and was a direct attempt by British Rail managers to get clarity on and control over the costs of the organisation. In a radical departure from the previous production and engineering-led structure, a new organisation was designed and implemented to facilitate the development and implementation of business strategy around distinct market sectors. Three passenger sectors were established; Intercity, London & South East and 'other provincial services' (later known as Provincial and then Regional Railways).

Each in turn had small subsector teams located within geographical regions to ensure the presence of local business-sector managers close to regional operating and engineering managers.

London & South East brought together the management of the passenger commuter railways into London; its market and hence operation was thus largely, though not wholly, homogenous. Information available in the public domain suggests that at its inception, London & South East carried 37 per cent of the London commuter market. Initially subsidised to the tune of £322 million, over the next three years it reduced its subsidy to £205 million, a reduction of 36 per cent (Hillman 2012).

Having done what it could to reduce its cost base, and with money required for future investment, the business began to look at what it could do improve revenue. It therefore set about improving the reliability of its product, ensuring delivery was of a consistent quality (one of the core ingredients of building a successful brand). Much management effort went into improving train-service performance and other measures to enhance customer satisfaction.

Six months after the launch of the quality drive, the Network SouthEast (NSE) brand was launched. Trains and stations were painted (Chris Green, the director of NSE, reportedly told another BR manager that it was better to have no benches at all on a station than non-corporate benches), and the distinctive identity based on a palette of red, white and blue rigorously applied to all physical manifestations of the brand, including not only trains and stations but also all advertising material, staff uniforms (ties and badges), timetables and stationery. The new brand was heavily supported by advertising, including high-profile television campaigns and rapidly achieved recognition amongst users of 84 per cent (note the British Rail brand had an unprompted recognition score amongst the general public that was in the high 90s). New tickets were launched – including the Network Card giving commuters discount on weekend leisure journeys, which survives to this day. During the 12 months to March 1986, prior to the drive to improve product quality, its commuting market grew by 4 per cent: over the three years to March 1988, the commuting market grew by 15 per cent.

So to what extent did the marketing and branding effort contribute to the growth in peak-time use, and was modal shift delivered? Answering these questions lies at the nub of this chapter, but conclusions are at best flimsy. Given that business grew by 4 per cent to March 1986, before the marketing and branding endeavours really got underway, does the further 9 per cent achieved to March 1988 really reflect marketing efforts, or is it more to do with external effects, such as GDP growth and increasingly weak competition (in the form of ever worsening road congestion)? And to what extent was rush-hour growth on the railway constrained by capacity? – leisure journeys increased significantly over the same period. Would the unconstrained growth have been even higher? Detailed analysis may provide the answer, but I suspect that much of the quantifiable data required to answer the question is lost – if indeed, it was ever captured.

Moreover, one of the things that is fascinating about this case study is that I knew about it only from my own experience. As a practitioner, rather than an academic, I had no awareness of the historical sources available. My key source initially was an internet posting that was entirely the result of an initiative by individuals. This was supplemented by a recent book co-authored by a former director of Network SouthEast (Green and Vincent 2014). Without these uncoordinated efforts of individuals, valuable knowledge might have remained buried in archives, retrievable in useful form only by combing a variety of sources, or indeed have been lost all together. We appear to have no formal mechanisms for recording our collective history and risk losing the knowledge this holds.

Metro (West Yorkshire PTE)

Building a brand 1974–1986

Metro is an umbrella brand, used by the West Yorkshire Passenger Transport Executive (WYPTE) to connect public-transport services within their county. A little history may be useful here in understanding the context before a discussion on the application of the brand is introduced.

The institutional framework that facilitated the creation of Passenger Transport Executives (PTEs) was introduced in the 1968 Transport Act. The Act gave authority to the minister of transport to designate Passenger Transport Areas for those parts of Great Britain (outside of Greater London) where he/she deemed it expedient to secure 'the provision of a properly integrated and efficient system of public passenger transport to meet the needs of that area' (Ministry of Transport 1968). The Act allowed for the establishment of Passenger Transport Authorities (PTAs) to run the Areas with members of each PTA being appointed by the local authorities falling within (or partly within) that Transport Area. Passenger Transport Executives (PTEs) were effectively to be the executive arms of PTAs, and were to be responsible for operating services, as well as planning, coordinating and financing them. As originally envisaged, then, PTEs were to operate all local road passenger transport services (specifically buses). The Act also made provision for PTEs to enter into agreements with the British Railways Board for the provision of local rail passenger services in return for an appropriate financial contribution.

The Local Government Act in 1972 led to the establishment of six Metropolitan Counties in 1974 as administrative districts based around England's largest cities. These in turn established PTEs to deliver integrated local transport systems. Established in 1974, WYPTE took on responsibilities for transport provision from local boroughs, merging the individual bus fleets of Bradford, Leeds City Transport, Huddersfield and Halifax and Calderdale into a single fleet providing services across West Yorkshire (West Yorkshire Buses 2015). The Metrobus branding was introduced early on. Advantage was taken of the central government bus grant being used to part-fund new vehicles across the country with the new vehicles representing a significant improvement in product quality. A new livery of green and cream was gradually applied across the entire bus fleet, presenting a consistent identity. Investment was also made into transport interchanges, such as that at Bradford. Ticketing was also standardised, with the launch of a countywide concessionary fares scheme and of the Metrocard (a multi-operator ticket) By 1981 a consolidated fares scale had been achieved across the county and in 1983 saver-strip tickets were introduced offering savings to users who were prepared to buy in advance. The result was that 'By late 1985 a truly integrated system of ticketing and bus networks had led to rising usage in contrast to the trends of previous years' (West Yorkshire PTA 1999).

Looking back we can therefore see a clear use of the marketing toolkit to improve both physical public transport and its image in order to increase usage First, significant investment was made in product improvements including new vehicles and new passenger waiting facilities. Second, fares and ticketing were standardised county-wide, making pricing easier for users to understand (and to choose the ticket best suited to their needs). Third, countywide travel on both rail and bus was promoted consistently, with the use of a clear and unified identity for bus services signalling the integration of services, in line with the PTE' objective of delivering integrated transport services. This was combined with the development of strong route identities, making network maps easier to read (in the style of London Underground) whilst providing a localised feel for residents Unfortunately, whilst the qualitative components of the early WYPTE usage o marketing can be retrieved from documents and the memory of those involved a the time, there are no quantitative data to give us an exact measure of marketing' effect; we have to rely on qualitative data such as the quote above on 'rising usage'

Moreover, the study of marketing in public transport cannot be separated from its political and institutional context. By the 1980s the political mood had changed Encouraged by the Chicago school of economists, the mantra was the rolling back of the suffocating hand of centralised state control to allow market force to deliver greater efficiency and better services for users. The 1985 Transport Act deregulated and privatised bus services. The PTEs lost not only their role as service providers but also control of the services themselves. In order to meet social needs, PTAs (along with county councils) were given powers to supplement commercial services with additional subsidised services (typically running evenings and weekends). Moreover, controls over subsidised services in terms o fare levels, type of bus and so on, could be retained by the PTAs. Nevertheless, b 1986 the major part of the bus network in West Yorkshire was operated by privat operators on a commercial basis. New operator specific tickets and fares bega to appear alongside the PTE's multi-operator and multi-modal offers. Moreover individual operators promoted their own liveries, unpicking the careful integration of the previous decade.

It is now generally recognised that the changes did bring some benefits – and i particular, smaller bills to councils for transport provision. However, the 1985 Ac failed to address a principal objective – the decline in bus usage. With the exceptio of London (which retained an over-arching brand and livery regardless of operato bus usage fell across Britain. Analysis of the reasons tends to concentrate o macro- and micro-economic issues, including the impact of regulatory structure. To the best of my knowledge there has been no formal, systematic assessment of softer issues including customer confidence in the system, although some years ago Paul Kelvill did rhetorically raise the issue of the importance of marketing in the bus industry (Kelvill 2005).

Within West Yorkshire the PTE retained a coordinating role including the delivery of integrated passenger information system, providing a one-stop shop for those seeking bus or rail journey information. Moreover, they continued to run bus stations and to provide stops and shelters. A new 'Metro' brand and identity were introduced and applied consistently on physical passenger infrastructure across the bus and rail networks. And the bold decision was taken to combat potential passenger confusion arising from bus deregulation with an advertising campaign, reassuring users that their usual bus services would still be available together with the integrated and multi-modal ticketing to which users had become accustomed. Once again, quantitative evidence is lacking – for example, detailed price comparisons are not readily available – but a 1999 publication suggested that whilst bus patronage did decline within West Yorkshire following deregulation it 'did not bite with the severity seen in other parts of the country thanks to the on-going coordinating role played by the PTE' (West Yorkshire PTE 1999).

In 2005–06, the House of Commons Select Committee on Transport investigated the state of bus services across the UK, leading to a report in 2006. Evidence was sought from a range of witnesses in the attempt to understand whether the 1985 Act had exacerbated the decline in bus patronage. The committee's final conclusion was that:

> We commend those cities and counties that have made the deregulated bus system work for them, we rather suspect that they have done so in spite of the arrangements they work within, not because of them. It is clear, however, that for many areas, including all of our major metropolitan areas outside London, the current regime is not working. It has been over twenty years since deregulation, six years since the Transport Act 2000. This leads us to conclude that the current arrangements cannot be made to work. (House of Commons Select Committee on Transport 2006)

Much of the committee's findings were based on the realisation that the institutional and regulatory structure within which bus companies were operating and providing services were making it more – not less – difficult to meet market-led needs, such as the delivery of a consistent and appropriate quality of service (including quality vehicles), an integrated bus network including coordination of services and provision of through ticketing. The committee also recommended pricing initiatives targeted at specific segments of the population; for example, offering cheaper fares to those still in full-time education to cut down on the number of 17- to 25-year-olds driving (something that the public-sector railway had been doing for many years through its Young Person's Railcard).

Investment in the rail network: 1982–present

Although in early years much management attention had perforce been focussed on running and improving bus services, the PTE increasingly began to work with local British Rail managers to invest in and improve rail passenger services across the West Yorkshire County. In 1982 Fitzwilliam station opened; over the next decade 18 new stations were brought into use across the county. The work of the PTE in this area was arguably facilitated by changes to British Rail's own structure – changes that were of themselves designed to make that organisation more business, and market, focussed.

As described above, in 1982 British Rail made major changes to its operation in an attempt to become both cost-efficient and market-led. West Yorkshire fell geographically within British Rail's Provincial Eastern region, which had its offices in York, a short train ride from Metro's own team in Leeds. Gradually the two management teams learned to work together. Whilst the objectives of the individual organisations (including cost objectives) did not always align, common purpose was built around the desire to create a network that was easy to use and met the needs of the public. The result was significant improvements to rail passenger services during the 1980s and early 1990s including the purchase of new rolling stock. The organisations worked together to promote rail travel through sharing the costs of promotional campaigns and collaborating on their content (including a winter fares promotion on the Leeds–Settle–Carlisle line for West Yorkshire residents that is still being used as a tool to increase winter ridership some 15 years later). In the mid-1990s the electrification of services between Leeds and conurbations to the north-west of the city (including Bradford and Skipton) brought significant benefits in terms of journey times, timetables and journey quality although legal and contractual issues around privatisation led to some interesting institutional problems, particularly around the introduction of new electric trains. Whilst privatisation might potentially have caused a hiatus in partnership working the local rail management team remained largely intact, at least in the early years, providing a consistency that bridged the initial change and maintaining inter-organisational relationships. When Metro (by now the public name for WYPTE) published Railplan 6, outlining its plans and strategies for the five years from 2006 to 2011 it was able to reflect on many years of improvements (West Yorkshire PTE 2006). This demonstrated clearly how WYPTE invested in product improvement – new rail services, investment in infrastructure to improve journey times, accessibility and interchange together with investment in rolling stock – and distribution (new stations) to achieve above-average passenger growth in the period 2000–04.

Again, much of the evidence is qualitative, but the plan does contain some hints of the value of these changes. Over the years 2000–04 rail patronage in West Yorkshire was reported to have risen by 26 per cent – twice the national average. Moreover, rail's modal share of peak journeys increased by 25 per cent over the years 1991–2004 at a time when the overall market grew, suggesting that rail in the county was attracting both new ridership and ridership that had switched from competing modes (including the private car). Modal share varied from corridor to corridor, depending on many things including local demographics and the relative competitive position of rail in relation to road borne transport. The plan suggests that at its strongest, rail held a 75 per cent market share for journeys on the Skipton–Shipley corridor into Leeds during the peak. Based on such evidence, the argument for using marketing and branding techniques to deliver modal shift appears to be unequivocal. Railplan 6 also reported that 'the average distance travelled to work increased by 25% between 1991 and 2002. It is now over 10km. Rail is well placed to serve the needs of longer distance commuting with its fast inter urban network' (West Yorkshire PTE 2006).

Thus improving the rail network had potentially changed patterns of living and working, allowing people to live further from their place of work. Rail had not only delivered modal shift, a sustainable objective, but had stimulated new, longer distance journeys, much as those London commuter railways did over a century ago. But the benefits delivered were not without cost. Whilst the railway provided access to work for a greater number of people and allowed businesses to expand, it facilitated the concentration of jobs in certain geographical localities. Transport is truly an instrument for social and economic change.

The Future

In 2015 Metro was still being used as the brand and identity for the West Yorkshire Integrated Transport Authority and Passenger Executive. It continued to specify and fund socially necessary bus services (that is, those without a commercial operator), promote improvements, act as the integrating authority for ticketing and promote the use of public transport. It was also actively working on the future introduction of smart-media ticketing, a technology that has huge potential in the area of public-transport marketing. Much is being written on the potential of smartcards to deliver a wide range of data on transport usage and users. Initially much of the focus was on transport-usage data and the benefits to transport planners of having specific and comprehensive journey information on which to base future-demand models. This includes not only journeys made (origin and destination) but the time of travel, data operators and planners have traditionally found it difficult to collect although legal restrictions on data usage may place restrictions around this. Additional benefits include more efficient mechanisms for sharing revenue from multi-modal products (by capturing journeys to specific operators) replacing current reliance on diary and other surveys.

Whilst the benefits of smart-media ticketing in relation to improving demand models and hence decision-making on investment in product improvements have been self-evident, recent discussions have considered how data can be used for more focussed marketing. By requiring users to register for smartcards operators can request and gather profiling data such as age, family status and even household income. This can be used to target advertising and promotional campaigns both to attract new, similar users or persuade existing users to make specific types of journeys (at a basic level, for example, by extolling the benefits of travelling at off-peak rather than peak times, including those of cheaper fares). Meanwhile social media offers both an opportunity to those who would build great brands, holding the potential to create (for example, through a consistently defined presence on social networks) as well as to destroy (with negative stories going instantly viral).

As a classically trained marketer I find the wealth of opportunities from new technologies exciting. Yet at the same time I fear that the view of the wood will be obscured by the trees: detail will replace vision, short-term replace long-term. As the historical examples above illustrate there are benefits to be had from a consistent and sustained focus on the customer in transport, supporting their daily journeys from leaving home to arriving at their destination by providing consistent and reliable information, both before and during their journey, consistent and reliable services and a consistent and reliable brand presence. In chasing the new, there is still much to be said for a market-focussed and strategic approach. This combined with technology-enabled offers individually tailored for travellers opens up an exciting future for marketing in transport optimising short-term use and long-term development of services.

Conclusion

I make no apologies for being an un-reconstructed marketer, but hope I have demonstrated the potential power of the tools of marketing, when properly used, and based on a thorough understanding of 'the market' in improving the bottom-line performance of transport services and delivering changes in user behaviour. My plea is for planners not only to be familiar with those tools (they are already taught elements of marketing), but to have some exposure to the use of them in a commercial context, not just a public-policy context. It is particularly important to remember that economic models, whilst based on numbers and assumptions, purport to represent the behaviour of individual people. In developing transport solutions it is essential that the limitations of modelling and the characteristics of people are understood. When the science of modelling is brought together with an understanding of marketing tools and a marketing focus then the accuracy of forecasts can be increased. As the case studies above illustrate, marketing presents an option for those seeking to deliver modal – and social – change.

To return to this chapter's original question: is history relevant to contemporary transport and marketing practitioners, and is it used to full advantage? Transport professionals do draw on data from the past to predict the future. This can for example take the form of the numbers of journeys made between two points and even some of the characteristics of the people making those journeys. However, this data is rarely recorded within its historical context and specifically its social-history context. Knowledge on public attitudes to transport, the impact of branding and other marketing interventions on these and subsequent impact on travel habits are rarely recorded and hence are rarely used when attempts are made to the predict the future. Moreover, much of what practitioners know about the past is stored in their heads and on their individual hard drives. There is no formal process for establishing what is known by transport professionals and for recording our collective history in this area.

At present, there is little conscious seeking of answers from historians by transport professionals, who tend to concentrate on numbers, not the people behind them. Yet I know from my interaction with some academics that historians hold a resource that when combined with contemporary and quantitative data can give us new insights into finding solutions to transport problems (the transport planner's dilemma) and changing the way society behaves. By taking a joint approach we stand a better chance of truly understanding the cause and effect of changes to the transport system: only the historical context gives us the market one.

How then can we achieve crossover between the world of the planners and the world of the historians? Academic collaborations such as the project which has led to this book offer one powerful way forwards. Another could be the promotion of a research agenda that seeks to bring the methodologies of contemporary transport economics and planning together with transport history to investigate matters of common purpose, such as the value of branding in a transport context. Finally, as practitioners we should consider how our history is recorded. In the context of our daily working lives it can be difficult to make space for the future, yet, unless we can establish processes for capturing and re-using our knowledge that does not rely on our own memories or hard drives, that knowledge is at worst transient or unrealised and at best impermanent.

References

Chartered Institute of Marketing (CIM) (2009). *Marketing and the 7Ps.* Available at: http://www.cim.co.uk/files/7ps.pdf (accessed 9 May 2015).

Fetherstonhaugh, B. (2009). The 4 Ps Are Out, the 4 Es Are In. Available at: http://www.ogilvy.com/On-Our-Minds/Articles/the_4E_-are_in.aspx (accessed 9 May 2015).

Green, C. and Vincent M. (2014). *The Network SouthEast Story.* Hersham: Oxford Publishing Company.

Hillmann, A. (2012). *Network SouthEast Publicity.* Available at: http://www.srpublicity.co.uk/nse/history.htm (accessed 9 May 2015).

House of Commons Select Committee on Transport (2006). *Bus Services across the UK.* Available at: http://www.publications.parliament.uk/pa/cm200506/cmselect/cmtran/1317/1317.pdf (accessed 28 January 2013).

Kelvill, P. (2005). Marketing Awareness in the Bus Industry: Threats to Progress In J. Hibbs, E. Butler, G. Parkhurst, O. Knipping and P. Kelvill, *The Dangers of Bus Re-regulation and Other Perspectives on Markets in Transport.* London Institute of Economic Affairs, pp. 106–17.

Kotler, P., Wong, V., Saunders, J. and Armstrong G. (2005). *Principles of Marketing.* 4th edn. Harlow: Pearson Education.

McDonald, M. (1984). *Marketing Plans.* London: Heinemann.

Ministry of Transport (1968). *Transport Act 1968.* Available at: http://www legislation.gov.uk/ukpga/1968/73/pdfs/ukpga_19680073_en.pdf (accessed 28 January 2013).

West Yorkshire Buses (2015). *1974 to 1999 – 25 Years Metrobus to Firstbus* Available at: http://www.westyorkshirebuses.freeserve.co.uk/riderhistory1.htm (accessed 24 January 2013).

West Yorkshire PTE (1999). 25 Years of Metro. Available at: http://www.pteg.net system/files/general-docs/Metro25yrannualreview.pdf (accessed 9 May 2015)

——— (2006). Railplan 6. Available at: http://www.wyltp.com/NR rdonlyres/6ACA278F-95C7-4A5F-9729-4CAF266D4370/0/06033(Railplan6.pdf (accessed 24 January 2013).

——— (2015). West Yorkshire PTE. Available at: www.wypte.gov.uk (accessed 20 March 2015).

Chapter 9

Gaining Modal Share in Exogenously Driven Markets: Lessons from Urban Transport

Martin Higginson

This chapter explores how historically marketing has been used to effect modal shift in urban-transport sectors where the overall size of the market is largely outside an individual provider's control. These markets might include, for example, comparatively stable or mature ones such as commuting to work and education, where the geographical separation of home and place of work or education along with levels of (sub)urban congestion are of overwhelming importance; or expanding sectors driven partly by a some combination of wider policy initiatives and technological change – such as the extension of public transport into the suburbs as trams were replaced by buses before the Second World War – that threaten incumbent providers' market share. In such cases imaginative marketing (along with other measures) could help to protect or even grow the incumbents' share. This chapter therefore applies to the urban context the insight that the 'demand' for travel depends partly on commercial efforts to expand markets as providers and governments try to maximise returns on capital. It examines how historically various kinds of urban-transport providers have tried both to shape and to exploit public attitudes towards travel in and around towns and cities, helping to explain why 'demand' for personal mobility has reached today's levels and forms. This has implications for the long-standing debate between those who argue that future demand for urban mobility can only be forecast and then catered for ('predict and provide') and advocates of demand management: the steps taken in the past to influence modal split despite the existence of exogenous factors driving the overall size of the market might be applicable to the challenge of developing sustainable ways of moving around our conurbations.

The definition of 'urban' used in this chapter is a wide one, including suburban and even peri-urban areas beyond the continuously built-up zone (Gay et al. 2013). Understanding the lessons of the past raises the following questions:

- What defines urban mobility?
- What understanding do providers have of public attitudes to different ways of moving?
- Does demand modelling adequately capture these views?
- How important are brands in influencing modal choice for urban travellers?

Core Characteristics of Urban Mobility

Urban mobility prior to the industrial revolution was largely on foot, with towns and cities small enough for most residents' daily lives to proceed without recourse to vehicular or mounted transport. Some people worked at or adjacent to their homes: hand knitters and weavers (Hartley and Ingilby 1951, 1976), many shopkeepers, blacksmiths and publicans, for example; or from home: tinkers, hawkers and so on. Hartley and Ingilby (1976) suggest that industrial-scale homeworking largely originated in the eighteenth century but almost died out during the nineteenth: nevertheless, walking towns and cities lived on through the first industrial revolution and into the second, with mines, shipyards, railway depots, potteries and factories typically being associated with housing, often company-owned, close to the workplace. Nevertheless, change had begun to occur in the nineteenth century and by the early twentieth century Williams (1915), for example, noted the use of bicycles or group hire of a 'conveyance' by some of the more remotely situated railway workers. While the walking town survives to this day – for example, in the networks of pathways connecting residential areas to potteries in Stoke-on-Trent and around the railway areas of York – its importance is much reduced. As late at the mid-1970s 19 per cent of journeys to work were made on foot but by 2011 it was only 11 per cent. The critical factor is the distance from home to work: the higher proportion in the 1970s was linked to the fact that 68 per cent of journeys under one mile were on foot (Pooley, Turnball and Adams 2005: 51–82, 111–38; Hillman and Whalley 1979: 68; Office for National Statistics 2013).

The growth of urban mobility and its subsequent mechanisation stem substantially from the burgeoning need to travel greater distances from home to work as industrialisation created bigger, more concentrated workplaces. These involved (mostly male) employees in longer journeys as towns and cities became larger, with higher populations spread over wider geographical areas. Itinerant labour, traditionally associated with agriculture, evolved in the Victorian era to meet the needs of urban construction: schools, homes, public buildings and, as part of a self-perpetuating cycle of development, transport infrastructure (Samuel 1973). The conflicting needs of family life and remote employment were partly resolved by making it possible for the worker to travel daily to and from the workplace, and while there were significant differences in uptake between social classes, first horse-drawn and then mechanically-powered vehicles became more common (Lampard 1973).

Similar considerations apply to children and young adults' access to education, although attendance was only made compulsory, up to the age of 10, in 1880. Victorian schools would generally have been located within walking distance of where children lived. It was perhaps Balfour's Education Act of 1902, establishing secondary schools run by local authorities, and subsequent legislation requiring all children to attend them that gave rise to a significant demand for vehicular transport to and from school, a practice formally recognised in the provisions for free school travel under the Education Act 1944. In recent decades some journeys have also become longer and more complex, partly as parents exercise their right to send children to other than the local school (Pooley, Turnbull and Adams 2005: 83–110).

Shopping for essentials would also have been undertaken locally well into the twentieth century, mainly on foot at family-owned shops and latterly at multiple outlets such as the Co-operative, Sainsbury's or Home & Colonial on many high streets; deliveries to the home by retailers were also important for some families. But longer journeys to specialist retailers for discretionary purchases can be traced back to the eighteenth century and by the time department stores typically arrived in the larger British towns and cities in the last decades of the nineteenth century such trips would often have been made by early mechanised forms of transport such as horse buses and tramways (Stobart, Hann and Morgan 2007; Hosgood 1999: 97–102). By the 1970s many neighbourhood shops had disappeared, and shopping as a leisure activity increased as a proportion of all trips in the latter decades of the twentieth century; out-of-town shopping centres such as Brent Cross (opened in 1976), mainly accessed by car, became more important from the 1970s (Pooley, Turnbull and Adams 2005: 170–72). More recently some out-of-town centres have begun to develop into public-transport hubs (for example, Meadowhall, Sheffield, and Metro Centre, Gateshead); a phenomenon that may be expected to grow as land uses change and road congestion increases. Although access by car, via comprehensive road networks to almost unlimited free parking, will remain dominant for the foreseeable future, there are some signs that consumers are beginning to move away from large out-of-town superstores, at least for some kinds of shopping, and is renewing interest in historical forms of retailing such as local ('convenience') stores and home deliveries, as well as novel types of fulfilment such as 'click and collect' at public-transport hubs.

Providers' Understandings of Public Attitudes to Moving

Providers and policy makers have tended, and to a great extent continue, to pay greater attention to commercially exploitable modes of transport than to those with no market such as walking (Pooley 2013: 17–31; Hillman and Whalley 1979). While the differences between past and present urban mobility can be overstated, as outlined above the trend has been for journey lengths to increase and for a greater proportion to require the use of mechanised transport. While acknowledging that the relationship between transport provision and urban morphology in the UK is highly complex (Divall and Bond 2003), Table 9.1 summarises the fundamental relationships that need to be borne in mind when considering the historical role of marketing and branding in the urban context. The suggestion here is that such initiatives have tended to focus more on trying to effect modal shift than on growing the overall market: the latter has largely been due to exogenous factors such as

Table 9.1   The development of urban transport, morphology and mobility

Period	Transport technology	Urban form	Urban travel opportunities
To *c.*mid-nineteenth century	Pre-railway	Dense: all trips within walking distance	Walk
Second half of nineteenth century	Coarse urban rail networks	Dense: limited attempt to facilitate internal movement	Limited intra-urban rail
Late nineteenth century	Horse buses and tramways	Dense: start of encouragement to extend built-up area	Wider short-distance urban public transport opportunities
End of nineteenth to early twentieth century	Electric tramways Erosion of short-distance urban rail market	Mainly dense, but over more widespread area	Longer urban public transport trips on more intensive network
Late nineteenth to early twentieth century	Cycling	Encourages non-radial development	Unrestricted short/medium distance trips
Early to mid-twentieth century	Motor buses	Lower density, more widely dispersed suburban development, mainly orientated to radial travel	Extension of public transport to newer and less dense suburbs
Twentieth century	Car	Lower density, widely dispersed residential, commercial and employment developments requiring 360° access	Unrestricted trip geometry and lengths
Second half of twentieth to early twenty-first century	Congestion, environmental degradation	Encourages reversion to higher density, less dispersed developments and reduced car use	Limited reversion to tramways, increased rail commuting, bus priorities, attention to needs of pedestrians/cyclists; but continuing reluctance to take draconian measures
The future	Concern over and action on air quality and unpredictable journey times	Comprehensive non-car permeability and segregated public transport	Polarisation between motorised suburbs and car-free nodes/centres

public policy (especially in relations to health and social welfare) (Capuzzo 2003; Carr 2003) and shifts in economic geography, such as that which over the last decade or so has dramatically increased commuting into the more successful northern English cities as their economies have shifted towards the service sector. As concerns over air quality, carbon emissions and urban congestion become more serious, modal shift is likely to become a major spur for future policy development: while growing populations and changing patterns of employment mean that absolute reductions in urban traffic levels seem unlikely, at least in the short term, the principle of restricted market growth will endure.

Historically, urban-transport services in the UK have been provided by a mix of private- and public-sector operators and authorities, with the balance varying considerably over time and between places. Private enterprise dominated until the last decade of the nineteenth century, when modernised local governments started to take over and electrify tramways, although in some towns private enterprise either undertook the task or continued to provide bus services. With the exception of London – where in 1933 the new London Passenger Transport Board gained responsibility for all public transport apart from many suburban rail services – this mixed provision continued largely unaltered until the deregulation of bus services outside of London in the 1980s; although the creation from 1968 of passenger transport authorities (PTAs) and their executives (PTEs) in the provincial metropolitan regions (later, in England, counties) (Greater Manchester, Merseyside, Tyne and Wear and so on) provided opportunities for planning over more extended geographical regions. Whether privately or (after 1948) publicly owned, urban and suburban rail services were largely free from political direction at the local level until the PTAs were formed – and even so, there were one or two significant networks such as the South Wales valleys where devolved authority had to wait until the 1990s. The exception was again London, where the Metropolitan Railway became part of the LPTB, which in turn built new railways into the open countryside to encourage new development (Haywood 2009).

With this very mixed picture it is impossible to generalise about the degree to which over much of the twentieth century modal split was subject to political regulation, the dictates of oligopolistic bodies, or 'free' market forces. However, it is fairly safe to say that most providers often worked on the basis of predicting future demand and then providing infrastructure and services to cater for it. Since the 1960s policies have changed, firstly with the formalisation of subsidies for preferred modes (operational and capital grants for rail and bus services, public funding for infrastructure and rolling stock) and more recently with discriminatory schemes such as congestion charging (London, 2003) and workplace parking levies (Nottingham, 2012) intended to discourage car use and support public transport, walking and cycling. Such measures have become a double-edged instrument in transport planning; for instance, car-parking charges have evolved from a means of controlling the quantity and location of parking into a profitable commercial industry, with some local authorities unenthusiastic about funding bus services (a cost) and keen to generate parking income (revenue) (Buchanan 1958: 203–7, 1963: 19–22, 194–5).

Infrastructure was sometimes a severe constraint on providers' attempts to win market share. Even when railways dominated inland transport the challenge of constructing lines in the urban environment often trumped any other consideration. For instance the companies were sometimes forced to develop circuitous routes such as that between north London and Victoria station and those around Nottingham; these quickly succumbed when more direct competition developed. In many towns and cities intra-urban demand was hindered or precluded by the lack of stations serving the central business districts; the prime example being London, where the legacy was a ring of termini around the perimeter of the then built-up area, rather than a much smaller number of through stations closer to the centre (Haywood 2009; Simmons 1986: 26–170; Kellett 1969). The same issue has now arisen in relation to stations for the proposed London–Birmingham–Leeds and Manchester high-speed rail line, threatening the efficacy of intra-urban and regional connections. The historical 'fault', if that is the correct term, probably lies more with the planning system than with the railway companies; but the outcome was less satisfactory and less enduring suburb-to-centre links, offering fewer connectional opportunities, than might have been the case. Developments such as London's Crossrail and Manchester's Northern Hub are addressing this deficiency in the UK's urban rail network and advances were made in Glasgow Birmingham, Newcastle and Liverpool in the second half of the twentieth century (Haywood 2009).

In any case it was inevitable that the mainline railway's coarse networks of routes and stations would only meet the needs of a small proportion of potential urban flows. As improved technology from the 1900s, notably the introduction of mechanically powered trams and buses, enabled road transport to offer more comprehensive services covering longer routes, the mainline railways lost much of their (sub)urban market: with a very few exceptions there is little evidence that they were prepared to do anything about it by way of electrification, more frequent services and spirited marketing. However, with dedicated local operator for whom urban and suburban traffic was their bread and butter the picture could be different. These included the Liverpool Overhead ('thirteen mile round trip – see the docks'), Mersey Railway, North London ('Open Air Route Non-stop trains from Hampstead') and above all the Metropolitan Railway, whose Metroland campaign created a commuting brand that along with the company' extensive property development generated the necessary passenger demand Similarly a Great Eastern Railway advertisement of 1912 offered copies of *Home by London's Woodland*, detailing 'Convenient Residential Districts for London Business Men' in 'a selection of 20 charming outer suburbs' (GER 1912). The London Underground Electric Railways group (which included the London General Omnibus Company), developed the famous roundel logo in the early twentieth century, which became an internationally recognised marketing device and lives on under Transport for London (TfL) (Taylor 2001: 143).

We should not make too much of these instances from before the First World War: at least not until further research demonstrates whether they were truly more than the isolated examples they appear to be. Judging by the National Railway Museum's extensive collection, the principal pre-grouping (1923) companies or the later Big Four made little use of pictorial posters to market or brand (sub)urban services, although a search of the contemporary press might reveal other expenditure directed to this end. The overall pattern of spending by three of the Big Four strongly suggests that their advertising focused largely on long-distance discretionary travel, although this is not to say that none sought to build regular (sub)urban flows (Divall and Shin 2012; Divall 2011). Surviving material for local services mainly comprises of handbills and notices giving factual information on the likes of timetable changes, fog services, ticketing and so on rather than the kind of aspirational marketing that was developed to encourage long-distance travel by prestige express trains or to holiday and day-trip destinations (Medcalf 2012; Thompson 2011; Bennett 2001). Did the companies expect the image of the best trains to trickle down to the more mundane end of the business, or did they really not consider urban and suburban trains worth much marketing?

The one exception was the Southern Railway (SR), which electrified, marketed and branded suburban and inter-urban routes under the Southern Electric banner and experienced substantial increases in patronage. Passenger traffic accounted for almost three quarters of the Southern's revenue in the late 1920s, compared to under half for the other three Big Four companies. Electrification had been started before the First World War by two of the SR's constituent companies, the London Brighton & South Coast Railway (LBSCR) and London & South Western Railway (LSWR), which had introduced regular-interval timetables, faster journey times, more frequent train services and new fare scales (Klapper 1973: 161–96). In 1925 the SR under Sir Herbert Walker pioneered the appointment of a public-relations manager, journalist John Elliot, initially to enable the company to respond to a critical press rather than for overt marketing (Bonavia 1987: 62–72; Elliot 1982) and the company produced many often imaginative posters promoting its modernisation and electrification schemes (Hillman and Cole 1999). But how much of the patronage increase was down to marketing and branding as distinct from improved services requires further investigation; for example by comparing the results for electrified and non-electrified routes.

Another railway that is widely believed to have engaged in branding suburban services, the Great Eastern Railway (GER), in fact probably did not. In 1920 the company hugely improved its busiest commuter services out of Liverpool Street, and these quickly became known as the Jazz Services on account of the 'jazzy' coloured bands – white for first class, blue for second – above the carriage doors. But the service improvements were probably made for operational reasons and to relieve overcrowding (Allen 1920: 176–89; Anon. 1920; Cairns 1922) and the Jazz nomenclature appears to have been coined by a London newspaper rather than by the company. The GER canvassed passengers' opinions on the new services, but appears not specifically to have marketed them. Similarly, in 1921 the GER held a Directional Signs Competition to determine the location, general type and colour, including lettering of its signage: evidence perhaps of attention to branding. However, on balance the signage was probably conceived more as a means of providing clear information and thus improving operations since any correspondence had to be held with the company's architect or chief civil engineer (Anon. 1921). Nevertheless, it is significant that the GER and SR were both companies for which short- and intermediate-distance urban passenger traffic was more important than it was for most railway companies and thus had proportionately more to gain from this part of their businesses.

Did Demand Modelling Adequately Capture These Views?

Although econometric passenger-demand modelling was not developed in the UK until the 1960s, we should not assume that earlier urban-transport providers were ignorant of basic techniques of what we should now call market research. However further research is required to establish the extent to which railway companies and other operators sought to predict levels of demand before putting on services and to encourage their use. Reliable data on existing traffic flows was a necessity, but even this was apparently in short supply for much of the twentieth century. The North Eastern Railway (NER) was an exception before the First World War: it identified detailed catchment areas and populations for its stations, and in combination with patronage data calculated trip rates per head of population and trends therein. The NER's successor, the London and North Eastern Railway (LNER), continued the practice in the 1920s. Analysis of a sample of stations around York shows higher annual trip rates for small out-of-town stations (Copmanthorpe 11.5, Ulleskelf 15.7, Poppleton 21.1 and Pilmoor 29.5 in 1901), compared to 7.8 for York, where most local trips would be made on foot or by tram (NER 1913; LNER 1924). Did other railways do anything similar? In any case there is little or no evidence that the NER and LNER used this data to market particular groups of urban and suburban services: maybe the railway relied on its very presence in places where it was the only form of mechanised transport.

How then did the railways determine whether to electrify and set the priorities for implementing schemes? Pre-grouping inner-suburban schemes such as those of the NER, LSWR and LBSCR were a response to tramway electrification, but what sense did the companies have about how much of the lost traffic could be regained or whether the resultant business would be profitable? The decision to proceed with the NER's North Tyneside electrification scheme of 1902–04 was underpinned by a basic understanding that the more intensive and faster service would appeal to urban travellers, but despite that scheme's very considerable success the company never proceeded with the similar South Tyneside scheme when it was proposed in 1908 (Irving: 174–5, 257–61). Similarly, David Turner's study of the LSWR suggests that the information upon which decisions were made before 1914 was sketchy by modern standards even if it was by no means absent (Turner 2013). There is little doubt that generally electrification generated significantly greater increases in patronage than improved stream services (Moody 1979: 73–7). But the question remains what difference, if any, the marketing and branding of such services made. A more thorough comparison between, for instance, the outcomes for the GER's enhanced steam services and electrification south of the Thames would be instructive; the work should include an assessment of the levels of publicity and branding used by different companies.

How Important Are Brands in Influencing Modal Choice for Urban Travellers?

This chapter does not claim to offer more than a summary sketch of the history of marketing and branding urban transport in the UK. Nevertheless, it would be useful to have some sense of how providers' initiatives fitted with the broader sweep of developments. Although we should be sensitive to differences between North American and European approaches to marketing, Tedlow and Jones's (1993) periodisation of product marketing into four phases is a useful rough guide (Table 9.2).

Table 9.2   Phases of marketing after Tedlow and Jones (1993)

Phase	Characteristics	Period
I Fragmentation	High margin Low volume Restricted market size due to high transport costs and lack of timely information	To the 1880s
II Unification	High volume Low margin Incorporation of the whole nation in a mass market	1880s to 1950s
III Segmentation	High volume Value pricing Demographic and psychographic (behavioural) segmentation	1950s to present
IV Micromarketing	Information technology Just-in-time Customisation Personalised Consumer confusion	Present to future

Urban public transport experienced the market phases somewhat later than characterised by Tedlow and Jones. For example, independent tramway operators offered their own brands until around the turn of the twentieth century (when many of them were taken over by municipalities) and the independent bus industry was at its height in the 1920s. Both were examples of Phase I fragmented marketing, very locally based and often spearheaded by their founding entrepreneurs. When municipalities and area bus companies came to the fore, the need for 'buccaneering' local market development receded, ushering in Phase II unified marketing, arguably on a more 'respectable' – but lower profile – basis. (Sub)urban rail travel is not thought to have been extensively marketed except by the companies specialising in this market, as discussed above.

The apparent lack of branding by most urban-transport operators over the past century might suggest that they did not consider marketing to be important: that all three of the historical phases of marketing largely passed them by, perhaps in the belief that the presence of their hardware on the streets and of prominent railway stations sufficed to attract passengers. However, further research is required into this hypothesis, and it should be borne in mind that measures such as the application of distinctive liveries were a form of what we should now call corporate branding. Local councils were proud of their tramway and bus undertakings, a phenomenon that endures in the small number of locations where this form of ownership persists. The Southern Railway made extensive use of publicity and public relations to promote its largely suburban and regional passenger trains, for example through the circulation to its first-class season-ticket holders of the *Over the Points* magazine (Southern Railway 1929–40), but we have not established how and to what extent the GWR, LMS and LNER sought to promote their (sub)urban services. This was a version of Phase II (unified) marketing, in which municipal operators sought to distinguish themselves from other operators, but three of the four main line railways made little attempt to acknowledge different market sectors; for example, between the wars and with a very few exceptions Great Western chocolate-and-cream, LMS crimson and LNER varnished-teak vehicles served equally for long-distance express, local suburban and rural trains. On the other hand as we have delved more deeply into these railway companies' practices it is becoming clear that by the 1920s at the latest they *were* starting to segment their markets, at least when it came to long-distance travel: it is arguable that the railways were among the leaders in developing new approaches to Phase III segmented marketing in the UK. But as already noted for much of the twentieth century there was little systematic marketing of (sub)urban transport. Advertising was largely limited to posters at stations, on trains and on public hoardings, although extensive use was also made of the press: less dramatic but arguably just as effective. Increased competition with road operators between the world wars encouraged the railways to expand canvassing (as marketing was termed at the time) to passengers, although this was largely limited to efforts to boost group travel and so probably had little relevance for the strictly urban market (Pole and Milne 1925: 156–61).

But again we are coming up hard against the limits of our historical knowledge: an examination needs to be made of the extent to which public-transport providers advertised in the press and, in the second half of the twentieth century, on commercial television and radio. Locally based operators were disadvantaged by their inability to capitalise on national (newspapers) or major regional (television) media. Since around the start of the twenty-first century the rise of personal electronic communication has enabled smaller undertakings to participate in marketing and sales directly to consumers, exemplifying the arrival of Phase IV marketing and branding. Research needs to be undertaken to establish whether the apparent absence of branding and marketing in the past was real, and if so whether it was due to inertia and lack of entrepreneurial vision, or conscious decisions were taken that they were unnecessary.

Another area requiring investigation is the balance between the use of discounted pricing in the urban context as a way of maximising revenue and profits and that for social-policy reasons. The availability of workmen's tickets on some commuter routes had a mixed rationale; to spread peak loads by requiring journeys to work to be made before the main peak hour, but also to enable lower-paid workers to travel by train. In some situations cheap workmen's fares and train services were imposed, for example as a condition of planning consent to demolish tenement homes on the site of the new Liverpool Street station, London in the 1870s (Allen 1955: 63; Simmons 1986: 120–23). Other social motives are suggested by policies such as the local authority's requirement in Northampton in the 1970s that residents displaced from inner-urban clearances to outlying estates should not pay higher bus fares on the municipal buses (Higginson 1980: 29).

With the exception of Southern Electric none of the Big Four railway companies or their predecessors created separate brands to distinguish different parts of their passenger businesses. Phase II unified branding was apparently considered sufficient so far as sub(urban) transport was concerned. If these local services did indeed receive no specific marketing then, as already suggested, it is possible that the companies expected them to benefit from the corporate image projected by prestige trains and the marketing of longer-distance discretionary travel. Some companies were simply unenthusiastic about off-peak suburban flows; for example, in sharp contrast to the Metropolitan Railway's heavily promoted, frequent trains between London and Buckinghamshire the GWR and LMS provided sparse services, with gaps of up to two hours, to places at a comparable distance like Tring and Maidenhead. In the nationalised era Phase III segmented branding developed in the provincial conurbations, when the PTEs assumed responsibility for local passenger rail service planning in the 1970s; but the term Southern Electric faded from use with initially nothing to replace it except the very bland London & South East services. The Southern alone of the Big Four railways had practised Phase III market segmentation, which largely had to wait until the formation of the PTA/Es in the 1960s and 1970s and BR's split into quasi-autonomous business sectors, which led in 1986 to Network SouthEast. As outlined in Chapter 8 this effectively reintroduced the concept of the erstwhile 'Southern Electric' branding to cover all urban suburban and regional rail services in London and the south east (Green and Vincent 2014: 26).

Subsequently, specific branding has been introduced for many individual lines notably on designated Community Rail routes, some of which are wholly or partly (sub)urban in character. The extent to which the local branding has been exploited varies between routes, but the increased managerial, voluntary and marketing attention have typically led to increased patronage; for example, by 300 per cent (from 0.33 million in 2004 to 1.06 million in 2013) on the Severnside Line in Bristol (Severnside Community Rail Partnership 2014).

A recurring theme has been that of political or operational factors taking precedence over the marketing of urban transport. Where towns and cities ran their own buses and trams, municipal branding, often incorporating the authority's coat of arms, was usually applied, probably more for reasons of civic pride than to encourage patronage (Harrington 2003). In various localities both public and privately owned operators had route-based liveries, more for ease of identification by passengers than as a marketing tool. In Edinburgh colour coding was mandated by a bylaw of 1869 and the practice of colour-coding tram routes continued until the system closed in 1956 (Hunter 1992: 13; Grantonhistory 2012). In contrast, in London the privately owned Underground Group and Metropolitan Railway and then the publicly run London Transport Passenger Board and its successors were early adopters of strong branding for road and rail operations, despite public transport being much more of a captive mode in the capital than in other urban centres (Barman 1979). The Yerkes tube lines were probably the first to introduce strong branding to urban railways, with early twentieth-century stations exhibiting dark-red terracotta tiled fascias, many of which survive. Between the wars London Transport and the Southern Railway developed modern station designs, often built of concrete, which became central elements of the respective brands (Edwards 2003; Jackson 1991: 187–202). Similar initiatives in provincial conurbations had to await the PTEs in the 1970s, some of which introduced strong corporate identities that included rail and bus stations as well as buses and, in some cases, trains; for example, Merseytravel's grey and lemon and West Yorkshire's Metro (see Chapter 8). But bus deregulation and privatisation since 1986 has largely swept away these near-ubiquitous PTE brands. Now that business corporations deliver almost all urban bus and rail services, the desire for a uniform national branding often detracts from what were more focused and arguably stronger local identities: First Group's universal purple-and-grey 'barbie' bus livery (now given way to a slightly more localised branding); TfL's insistence on all-over red for every London bus; and Transport Scotland's reversion to mainly dark blue in place of the distinctive colour scheme in the Strathclyde Passenger Transport area. On the other hand branding bus routes in order to promote business (Hill 2012) is product of the post-deregulation era and embraces operators in the public sector such as Reading Buses as well as private companies such as the Go-Ahead subsidiary Go North East. Such developments may be characterised as being at the crossover between Phase III segmented and Phase IV customised marketing.

These examples are helpful but it would be instructive to carry out further investigations to distinguish the historical weight of the distinctive role of branding as a corporate identifier from that as an element of marketing campaigns and thus to gain a deeper perspective on current practice. Does, for example, the extension of the long-established London Transport bar-and-wheel logo to identify TfL's streets division detract from its value in marketing the capital's public transport? Can the history of the varied branding practices of the National Bus Company in the 1970s and 1980s cast light on the comparative effectiveness of the contrasting approaches to corporate identities adopted by the like of First Group and Stagecoach (uniform), Arriva (partial standardisation) and Go-Ahead and Transdev (devolved)?

It would also be useful to understand more about the historical significance of branding and marketing in helping to shape public perceptions of collective forms of urban mobility. Over the past century road-based public-transport's failure to maintain an up-to-date image has contributed to its decline, especially compared to the car. Firstly, tramways. Despite being regarded as the epitome of modernity when electrified in the early twentieth century, these largely failed to modernise and in the opinion of the 1931 Royal Commission on Transport had become obsolescent (Higginson and Green 1993: 8–12). Despite the creation of some reserved tracks, Britain's first-generation tramways never succeeded in re-inventing themselves as 'light rail': the new image had to await the arrival of second-generation tramways such as Manchester Metrolink, from 1992. The light-rail image has largely been a success, to the point that the description 'tram', initially suppressed by Metrolink's operator for fear of negative connotations, is again widely used both officially and by the public. In turn, the bus has struggled to retain a role as a transport mode of choice. Whether or not Margaret Thatcher ever really said 'if you are 26 or over and travelling on public transport, you are a failure', the expression has become part of the nation's psyche, which the bus industry's mainly low-key marketing and image creation has still not entirely shaken off. British public transport has yet to inspire sufficient confidence to enable the UK car industry to adopt the stance of Germany's, where Mercedes portrayed the intelligent driver knowing when to leave the car in the garage and take public transport. The image of even (sub)urban motoring as a form of freedom and independence is so deeply grounded that despite increasing congestion and other costs and constraints it is difficult to imagine a radical shift in attitudes in the short-term.

For much of the period after 1945 politicians, policy makers and planners have continued to create conurbations based largely upon unbridled car access, as evidenced by out-of-town shopping and employment centres and despite some, such as Sheffield's Meadowhall, being well connected by public transport (Vigar 2002). City-centre pedestrianisation schemes have seldom capitalised on the benefits they afford of freeing shoppers, workers and visitors from the tyranny of traffic; and local authorities have often resisted the 'cafe culture' that keeps traffic-free city centres alive at night. But the evidence from the limited instances where strong marketing and branding were adopted by public-transport providers in the twentieth century suggests that it is possible to shift attitudes and then modal choice, as long as marketing works with the grain of broader social trends. This is most strongly seen with rail commuting: the interwar successes of Metroland, Southern Electric and the extension of London Underground northwards were repeated from the 1950s as electrification and service improvements spread the capital's suburbs further out into Home Counties such as Essex, Hertfordshire and Berkshire, and beyond, deeper into Hampshire for example. While to some degree the new electric trains to Clacton, Northampton, Bournemouth and so on in effect sold themselves, British Rail(ways) nevertheless made sure that the advantages of the new services were kept well before the public eye: but now the basic techniques were no longer novel (the format of Terence Cuneo's poster for the 1960 opening of Glasgow's electrified Blue Trains would not have looked out of place 25 years earlier) and this period of marketing has largely been overlooked by historians. Opportunities for step-changes are perhaps fewer in urban areas, although new or heavily modernised rail systems such as London's Docklands Light Railway, the Tyne & Wear Metro and to some extent the light-rail schemes in cities including Manchester and Nottingham have been more heavily and effectively marketed than most urban services on the national network outside London and in some of the PTE areas. In 2014 the benefits of new homes or offices near London Crossrail stations were being canvassed – but by property developers rather than by public-transport providers – despite the line not being due to open until 2018.

The evidence from the three decades of the deregulated bus industry also suggests that when operators make a concerted effort to capitalise on improvements by bolstering their image and really go all-out to brand and market their services they often meet with surprising success. Examples include Brighton & Hove Buses' long-standing marketing campaigns (French 2010) and the increased patronage enjoyed by Harrogate & District as a result of its strong marketing of buses with leather seats on the Ripon to Leeds route 36 (Transdev Harrogate & District 2015). The growth in bus travel in cities such as London, Edinburgh and Oxford also suggest it is possible for buses to lose their image as a mode of last resort, in economic terminology an inferior good, and once again become a mode of choice: with signs that some younger people are delaying the purchase of a car and prefer to use buses, trams and trains partly because of the opportunities these offer to maintain on-line connectivity, the more dynamic urban operators are starting to market public transport as the perfect marriage of physical and virtual mobility.

Conclusion

In the past many passenger transport providers have given the impression that the urban market is a problem to be coped with rather than an opportunity from which to generate higher demand and generate surpluses or earn profits. They might have been right, as highly peaked demand requires heavy investment in infrastructure and rolling stock to provide capacity that is only used for a few hours each day. However, railway operators often reacted strongly when rivals such as the newly electrified tramways of the early twentieth century begin to erode their carryings: market share seemed to matter. Reacting to such competition often involved long-term, expensive investment like electrification. Perhaps the railways' coarse-grained (sub)urban networks could never have succeeded in winning back all of the traffic lost to a tramway product offering frequent, direct and cheap travel. A generation later the trams started to succumb to bus competition; and buses then lost much of their market to the car. None of these transitions seems at the time to have prompted incumbent operators to try quicker, cheaper forms of competition based upon marketing and branding. Of course it is possible that we have simply not found the evidence so far: further systematic research is needed to ascertain whether there were really no marketing campaigns, special fare offers or image creation to encourage, say, Edwardian rail users to stay riding the trains. And if they did exist, what impact did they have?

If the hypothesis that urban-transport providers do not seek to increase the size of their market was ever sustainable, it is likely to be less and less so as the commercial ethic spreads, aided and abetted by strengthened environmental considerations, the current political pressure for cuts in subsidies and services notwithstanding. It may be that the arrival of personalised public relations and information through mobile access to the internet will at last afford a breakthrough in the challenge of how to market local public transport services, for which national or regional campaigns may be inappropriate or unaffordable. As well as enabling customers to receive service information and to pay for travel on their mobile phones, transport operators are discovering the value of keeping in touch with users via social networks. There are doubtless many more surprise increases in urban public transport use waiting in the wings, if the providers and their partner urban planners and politicians choose to make them happen.

References

Allen, C. (1920). The Last Word in Steam Operated Suburban Train Services. *Great Eastern Railway Magazine* 10, pp. 218–19.

———— (1955). *The Great Eastern Railway*. London: Ian Allan.

Anon. (1920). What the New GER Suburban Service Reveals. *Railway Gazette*, p. 420.

———— (1921). Liverpool Street Station Directional Signs Competition. *Great Eastern Railway Magazine* 11, p. 30.

———— (1970). London Transport's Bar and Circle. *Journal of the Railway & Canal Historical Society* 16, p. 87.

Armstrong, J. (2000). From Shillibeer to Buchanan: Transport and the Urban Environment. In *The Cambridge Urban History of Britain. Volume III 1840– 1950*, ed. M. Daunton. Cambridge: Cambridge University Press, pp. 229–60.

Barker, T. and Robbins, R. (1963, 1974). *A History of London Transport*. 2 vols. London: George Allen & Unwin.

Barman, C. (1979). *The Man Who Built London Transport: A Biography of Frank Pick*. Newton Abbot: David & Charles.

Bennett, A. (2001). The Great Western Railway and the Celebration of Englishness. Unpublished DPhil thesis, University of York.

Bonavia, M. (1987). *History of the Southern Railway*. London: Unwin Hyman.

Buchanan, C. (1958). *Mixed Blessing: The Motor in Britain*. London: Leonard Hill.

——— (1963). *Traffic in Towns: A Study of the Long-Term Problems of Traffic in Urban Areas*. London: HMSO.

Carr, T. (2003). Changing Patterns of Travel, Transport and Land Ownership in a Victorian New Town: Middlesbrough to 1939. In *Suburbanizing the Masses: Public Transport and Urban Development in Historical Perspective*, ed. C. Divall and W. Bond. Aldershot: Ashgate, pp. 123–46.

Capuzzo, P. (2003). Between Politics and Technology: Transport As a Factor of Mass Suburbanization in Europe, 1890–1939. In *Suburbanizing the Masses: Public Transport and Urban Development in Historical Perspective*, ed. C. Divall and W. Bond. Aldershot: Ashgate, pp. 23–48.

Divall, C. (2011). Civilising Velocity: Masculinity and the Marketing of Britain's Passenger Trains, 1921–39. *Journal of Transport History* Series 3, 32(2), pp. 164–91.

Divall, C. and Bond, W., eds (2003). *Suburbanizing the Masses: Public Transport and Urban Development in Historical Perspective*. Aldershot: Ashgate.

Divall, C. and Shin, H. (2012). Cultures of Speed and Conservative Modernity: Representations of Speed in Britain's Railway Marketing. In *Trains, Culture, and Mobility*, ed. B. Fraser and S. Spalding. Lanham, MD: Lexington Books, pp. 3–26.

Edwards. D. (2003). *London's Underground Suburbs*. Harrow Weald: Capital Transport Publishing.

Elliot, J. (1982). *On and Off the Rails*. London: Allen & Unwin.

French, R. (2010). *Pride & Joy*. London: Best Impressions.

Gay, C., Landrième, S., Lefranc-Morin, A. and Nicolas, C., eds (2013). *Rehabilitating the Peri-Urban: How to Live and Move Sustainably in these Areas?* Paris: Éditions-Loco.

GER (1912). Advertisement. *Railway Magazine* 3(177), p. v.

Glover, J. (2013). *Principles of Railway Operations*. Shepperton: Ian Allan.

Goodwin, P. (1977). Habit and Hysteresis in Mode Choice. *Urban Studies* 14(1), pp. 95–8.

Grantonhistory (2012). Grantonhistory.org (accessed 11 May 2015).

Green, C. and Vincent, M. (2014). *The Network SouthEast Story*. Hersham: OPC.

Harrington, R. (2003). Civic Pride: Urban Identity and Public Transport in Britain, 1880–1980. In *Suburbanizing the Masses: Public Transport and Urban Development in Historical Perspective*, ed. C. Divall and W. Bond. Aldershot: Ashgate, pp. 251–67.

Hartley, M. and Ingilby, J. (1978 [1951]). *The Old Hand Knitters of the Dales*. Clapham: Dalesman.

———— (1990 [1976]). *Life and Tradition in West Yorkshire*. Otley: Smith Settle.

Haywood, R. (2009). *Railways, Urban Development and Town Planning in Britain, 1948–2008*. Farnham: Ashgate.

Higginson, M. (1980). *On the Buses: Municipal Bus Operation Under Contrasting Policies*. Polytechnic of Central London, Transport Studies Group Discussion Paper 9.

Higginson, M. and Green, O. (1993). London's Tramways in the Years of Decline. In *Tramway London: Background to the Abandonment of London's Trams 1931–1952*, ed. M. Higginson. London: LRTA, pp. 6–16.

Hill, G. (2012). Route Branding Versus Corporate Livery: A Comparative Study of Effectiveness in Bus Service Marketing: The Case of Veolia Transdev. Unpublished MSc dissertation, Newcastle University.

Hillman, M. and Whalley, A. (1979). *Walking is Transport*. London: Policy Studies Institute.

Hillman, T. and Cole, B. (1999). *South for Sunshine: Southern Railway Publicity and Posters, 1923 to 1947*. Harrow Weald: Capital Transport.

Hosgood, C. (1999). 'Doing the Shops' at Christmas: women, Men and the Department Store in England *c.*1880–1914. In *Cathedrals of Consumption: The European Department Store 1850–1939*, ed. G. Crossick and S. Jaumain. Aldershot: Ashgate, pp. 97–115.

Hunter, D.L.G. (1992). *Edinburgh's Transport: The Early Years*. Edinburgh: James Thin.

Intermodal Passenger Transport in Europe (2010). *The European Forum on Intermodal Passenger Travel: Final Report*. Available at: www.fgm.at/ linkforum/docs/214/LINK_final_report.pdf (accessed 11 May 2015).

Jackson, A. (1991 [1973]). *Semi-Detached London: Suburban Development, Life and Transport, 1900–1939*. Didcot: Wild Swan.

Kellett, J.R. (1969). *Railways and Victorian Cities*. London: Routledge and Keagan Paul.

Klapper, C. (1973). *Sir Herbert Walker's Southern Railway*. London: Ian Allan.

Lampard, E. (1973). The Urbanizing World. In *The Victorian City*, ed. H. Dyos and M. Wolff. London: Routledge, pp. 3–57.

London & North Eastern Railway (1924). Booklet on Traffic Statistics (NE Area). Held at the National Railway Museum, F1B/30.

Medcalf, A. (2012). 'What to Wear and Where to Go': Picturing the Modern Consumer on the Great Western Railway, 1921–1939. In *Trains, Culture, and Mobility*, ed. B. Fraser and S. Spalding. Lanham, MD: Lexington Books, pp. 61–89.

Moody, G. (1979 [1957]). *Southern Electric 1909–1979: The History of the World's Largest Suburban Electrified System*. London: Ian Allan.

North Eastern Railway (1913). Booklet on Traffic Statistics. Held at the National Railway Museum, F1B/30.

Office for National Statistics (2013). *2011 Census Analysis – Method of Travel to Work in England and Wales Report*. London: Office for National Statistics.

Pole, F. and Milne, J. (1925). The Economics of Passenger Traffic. In *Modern Railway Administration: A Practical Treatise by Leading Railway Experts* 2 Vols. London: Gresham Publishing, pp. 85–161.

Pooley, C. (2013). *Promoting Walking and Cycling: New Perspectives on Sustainable Travel*. Bristol: Policy Press.

Pooley, C., Turnbull, J. and Adams, M. (2005). *A Mobile Century? Changes in Everyday Mobility in Britain in the Twentieth Century*. Aldershot: Ashgate.

Royal Commission on Transport (1931). *Final Report*. Cmd 375. London: HMSO

Samuel, R. (1973). Comers and Goers. In *The Victorian City*, ed. H. Dyos and M Wolff. London: Routledge, pp. 123–60.

Severnside Community Rail Partnership (2014). *Progress Report*. Bristol: SCRP.

Simmons, J. (1986). *The Railway in Town and Country 1830–1914*. Newton Abbot: David & Charles.

Southern Railway (1929–40). *Over the Points*. London: Southern Railway.

Stobart, J., Hann, A. and Morgan, V. (2007). *Spaces of Consumption: Leisure and Shopping in the English town, c.1680–1830*. London: Routledge.

Taylor, S., ed. (2001). *The Moving Metropolis: A History of London's Transport since 1800*. London: Laurence King Publishing.

Tedlow, R. and Jones, G. (1993). *The Rise and Fall of Mass Marketing*. London Routledge.

Thompson, M. (2011). 'A Master Whose Heart is in the Land': Picturing the Tourist Utopia of the Great Western Railway, 1897–1947. Unpublished PhD thesis, University of York.

Transdev Harrogate & District (2015). http://www.harrogatebus.co.uk/36.htm (accessed 11 May 2015).

Turner, D. (2013). Managing the 'Royal Road': The London & South Western Railway, 1870–1911. Unpublished PhD thesis, University of York.

Vigar, G. (2002). *The Politics of Mobility: Transport, the Environment and Public Policy*. London: Spon Press.

Williams, A. (1915). *Life in a Railway Factory*. London: Duckworth.

Chapter 10

Plane Crazy Brits: Aeromobility, Climate Change and the British Traveller

Peter Lyth

Climate change ... is the greatest and widest-ranging market failure ever seen.

Stern 2006a

We live in an age of non-stop movement in which the demand for individual mobility seems to be insatiable. It is obvious in motor car use and the reluctance of many Britons to get out of their cars and onto public transport; but it also applies to flying. By 2005, a century after the Wright Brothers made the first powered flight, the British appeared to have become as addicted to the international mobility afforded by cheap air transport as they were to the flexibility offered by the car. But this 'aeromobility' has come at a price: incontrovertible evidence now exists to show that jet-engine emissions at high altitude are contributing to global warming and climate change.

This chapter looks at the rise in flying, particularly short-haul flying, by British tourists and travellers, and the charter and low-cost airlines which have helped to bring this about since 1950. It considers the particular appeal of flying to the British, and seeks to contextualise it within the history of aeromobility, which has been shaped by the history of civil aviation since the end of the Second World War. It concludes with a brief look at the question of how Britons might be persuaded to fly less over short-to-medium distances where environmentally cleaner surface-transport alternatives exist, in the interests of reducing carbon emissions and other types of atmospheric pollution associated with jet-aircraft operation. In his contribution to the 2009 volume *Mobility in History*, Tom McCarthy remarks that 'in powered flight environmentalists and environmental historians have struggled to find environmental stories worth exploring' (McCarthy 2009: 74). Writing six years later, it is hard to think of a more pressing 'environmental story' than global climate change; this chapter represents a small gesture in the direction of historical contextualisation.

Aviation and Climate Change

When the British government economist Nicholas Stern presented his report on the economic cost of climate change in 2006 he prefaced his remarks with an ominous message: from now on no one can say they did not know how much damage they were doing to the earth (Stern 2006b). With this in mind it is probably unnecessary to spell out in detail the evidence for global warming and climate change, although in an age of economic recession it may be necessary to remind ourselves of its danger. It was thought that it would take hundreds of years for the effects of rising CO_2 levels to be seen, but the extreme speed at which CO_2 is now rising – perhaps 75 times faster than in preindustrial times – has never been seen in geological records and is likely to be implicated in the increased frequency of extreme weather events such as heat waves, flooding and droughts. The former Intergovernmental Panel on Climate Change (IPCC) chairman and UK government chief scientific adviser Bob Watson noted in 2013 that:

> Passing 400 ppm of CO_2 in the atmosphere is indeed a landmark and the rate of increase is faster than ever and shows no sign of abating due to lack of political commitment to address the urgent issue of climate change – *the world is now most likely committed to an increase in surface temperature of 3–5 °C compared to preindustrial times.* (Watson 2013)

The latest data confirm the trend that was predicted in 2013. 2014 was the year with the highest average temperature since records began in 1880 and 14 out of 15 of the warmest years on record have occurred since the beginning of the twenty-first century. Since the first international protocol for climate-change limitation was agreed at Kyoto in 1997, frequent conferences have been convened to enable politicians to hear the latest findings from the IPCC and attempt to address the problem. But the results of these meetings have been meagre; at the 2009 Copenhagen meeting the sole achievement was an agreement that the figure by which global warming should be limited was a rise of two degrees Celsius above the average temperature at the beginning of the Industrial Revolution. As a result of the failure at Copenhagen, Yvo de Boer, the executive secretary of the United Nations Framework Convention in Climate Change (UNFCCC) resigned in disgust and in an interview at the time said that the only way the next meeting (in Paris in 2015) could get international agreement to stick to the two-degrees target, was for 'the entire world economy to grind to a halt' (de Boer 2015). Either that, or follow the Canadian polemicist Naomi Klein and dump capitalism in favour of an entirely new global economic order based on non-capitalist and environmentally sustainable principles (Klein 2014).

  With global warming almost a certainty and some degree of climate change unavoidable, the question arises as to the possibilities for mitigation in the coming years. And while technological solutions to the problem of carbon emissions from industry, power generation and motorised surface transport modes can be said to be well advanced, for air transport the picture is more troubling. While the world's scheduled airline industry enjoyed an impressive growth rate in traffic from 31 million in 1929 to 1,160 million in 1990, advances in technology during that time were much less even (ICAO 1971: 3, 1978: 19). Up until the 1970s, breakthroughs in the design and construction of airframes and aero-engines were indeed spectacular but since then they have been more modest. New light airframe materials such as those used on the Airbus A380 and Boeing 787 Dreamliner have been introduced and new airframe designs are certainly on the drawing board. But these new designs are a long way from introduction into airline service and if one was able to inspect a Boeing 787 from 2010 alongside a Boeing 707 from 1960, one would be hard put to find much difference in their shape or aerodynamic profile. More progress towards economy and silence has been made in the development of jet engines, particularly since the innovation of high-ratio by-pass engines in the 1970s, and the latest turbofans hanging beneath the wings of our holiday jets are undoubtedly more efficient that the noisy and thirsty straight-through engines of the 1960s. But commercial aircraft still rely on burning a fossil fuel (kerosene) to fly and, despite a whole range of experiments with biofuels and liquid hydrogen, no genuinely alternative, carbon-zero fuel is in sight. One cannot help drawing the conclusion that after half a century (1930–80) during which aeronautical engineering represented the fastest-developing and most path-breaking of technologies, progress in commercial aircraft technology has now slowed to a walking pace.[1]

Although aviation creates less than 10 per cent of global CO_2 emissions, there has been a steadily growing public perception in the western world that flying is a cause of global warming.[2] The traditional image of the airline industry, widely held up until the 1990s, of pretty air hostesses, romantic destinations, amazing technology and speed, is giving way to a more circumspect and utilitarian picture of flying. Accordingly jet planes are little more than buses with wings and flying in them has real environmental costs, even if the ticket is remarkably cheap. In Britain there has been rising concern in environmentalist quarters over these costs and the fact that 'aviation is the *fastest growing* contribution to climate change' (Sewill 2005: 8). Environmentalists generally despair of international action since attempts to limit flying for the sake of the natural environment have been characterised by almost universal failure. Starting with the exclusion of aviation from the 1997 Kyoto Protocol under which 140 nations agreed to cut greenhouse emissions below 1990 levels, and continuing in Britain with the watering down of the Royal Commission on Environmental Pollution's target of a 60 per cent cut by 2050, British governments have found themselves unable to balance the interests of the airline industry with environmental sustainability (Sewill 2005: 13).

---

1   For a general introduction to commercial air transport history see Heppenheimer (1995). For engines see Constant III (1980) and Lyth (2003a).

2   In addition to carbon dioxide, jet engines also emit nitrogen dioxide, sulphur dioxide and water. One estimate in 2007 held that aviation contributed 4.6 per cent of total anthropogenic greenhouse gases (Gössling and Peeters 2007).

Aviation's confrontation with the natural environment has two fronts: firstly, as noted above, although its total contribution to carbon emissions is modest by comparison with terrestrial polluters, it is the only one which in the British context is growing, and secondly, because of the high altitude at which jet aircraft operate, aviation damages the climate significantly more, per ton of CO_2 emitted, than all other modes of transport. Moreover the social inequity of aircraft carbon pollution is clear: while demand from airline passengers is the cause of the problem, it is not they who pay its cost, but rather other people who do not fly; for example, the farmer living in Bangladesh who must pay the environmental price of a British tourist flying to Thailand. For an economist the simple solution to this social inequity is to internalise the external costs of carbon pollution and use the market mechanism to 'punish' transport users through taxation 'for the external costs they cause' (Gerike 2007: 210). However, short of creating a government composed entirely of independently minded economists, the tax option is never likely to be imposed with any significant effect. In Britain there is no tradition and little experience of using taxation to effect behavioural change among consumers. Instead the long-standing and centralising power of the Treasury ensures that taxation largely remains a strictly fiscal matter of revenue collection rather than a potential vehicle of social engineering.

Beyond new technology and taxing flying, other mitigating strategies of carbon reduction do not seem to have been very effective. Carbon 'offsetting', by which airline passengers make a small contribution to some ecologically beneficial project is problematic because, according to one authority, it has 'arisen not from attempts by environmentalists and climate scientists to design an appropriate response to climate change, but from politicians and business executives trying to meet demands for action while preserving the commercial status quo' (Omega 2008). And likewise so-called carbon trading, according to the Friends of the Earth (FoE), simply threatens another 'sub-prime fiasco'. For the author of a 2009 FoE report, cap-and-trade carbon markets have done little to reduce emissions and are plagued by inefficiency and corruption.[3]

It is likely that the only effective way to reduce aviation's impact on the atmosphere is to seriously reduce demand. And given that the British government, indeed governments everywhere, are unwilling to use taxation as a means to achieve this, encouraging fundamental behaviour change seems to be the only way to do it. Some reduction in demand could probably be achieved by simply allowing the trying experience of getting through a twenty-first-century airport to take its toll. But essentially, British travellers have to be persuaded either to cut back on certain kinds of leisure activities or use surface transport like rail for short-haul journeys. The remainder of the chapter attempts to explain why this will be difficult, by looking at the history of the British traveller's love affair with cheap flights.

---

3   Sarah-Jayne Clifton (2009) reported, 'Carbon trading is useless'. The British government had concluded some years before that 'the best way of ensuring that aviation contributes towards the goal of climate change stabilisation' was 'through a well-designed emissions trading regime' (Department for Transport 2003: 3.39).

Fast Tourism and Cheap Fares

Before the Second World War few people in Britain owned private cars and even fewer had had any experience of flying. Mass transport was public transport and the widespread use of bicycles, and it was universally perceived as a communitarian exercise, in the sense that it was a function of the connection between the individual and a local community of people with common interests and a common history (Avineri and de-Shalit 1992). Although the Second World War itself can be regarded as a communitarian effort by the British people, the post-war years saw an erosion of this spirit and its replacement by a greater prioritisation of individual rights and needs within a burgeoning consumer society. By 1960 Britain had achieved the status of a 'car-owning democracy'; the Mini, the great British motor car for the masses, had been launched and the first British motorway, the M1, had been opened for use by the new British motorist. By 1970 bicycle and public-transport use were generally associated with social and economic failure: if you did not have a car you were 'left behind' in the consumer society. And the treatment of the state-owned British railways in the 1970s and particularly in the 1980s reflected this new automobility and the association of public transport with a communitarian past which was no longer attractive to a society driven by market forces. By 2000 automobility had become the normal social and cultural position of the individual, to the point where many were hostile to any kind of regulation of motor transport, whether it was priority for cyclists and public transport, restrictions on car use, road tolls, or any serious form of environmentalist transport planning (Sheller and Urry 2000: Urry 2004).

Mobility is a crucial element of modernity, and automobility is surely emblematic of modernity in the Britain of the 1950s and 1960s. Mobility reflects the ethos of the modern consumer society because it always seems to carry connotations of freedom and individuality. For the sociologist John Urry the all-pervasiveness of individual mobility suggests that henceforth society should be described in terms of 'mobilities rather than societies', since mobile networks had transformed all social life (Urry 2000: 210, 2007). By the 1960s fast, flexible and even furious mobility had become the ultimate expression of consumer dedication, and the word 'freedom' was becoming common in the advertising of both car manufacturers and airlines, in the same way that the new contraceptive pill promised sexual freedom. Consider, for example, the following short extract from a script for a 1950s film commercial for the Italian scooter manufacturer Innocenti:

Sound – 'The air hostess can become the pilot herself …'
Image – Air hostess sprints across runway from plane to Lambretta
Sound – '… and there's plenty of room on that pillion for a friend!'
Image – Man in pilot's uniform leaps on behind her.
(Hebdige 2000: 98)

At the same time as Britain was becoming a society of car owners, the urge to mobility was extending into the air, into leisure. Post-war Britain was hungry for holidays and any kind of hedonistic 'escape', and a generation of young air-tourism entrepreneurs stood ready to help fly people of modest means to their first holiday abroad. This group included Vladimir Raitz, Ted Langton and Freddie Laker. Raitz was an energetic Russian émigré living in London whose company Horizon Holidays, began charter flight tours to Corsica in May 1950. For £32 10s (£32.50) Horizon offered an all-in package which included a six-hour flight to Calvi on a war-surplus Douglas DC-3, two weeks under canvas on a Corsican beach, meals 'with meat' twice a day and as much local wine as the holidaymakers could drink – a shrewd marketing ploy aimed at young people bored and frustrated by life in ration-book Britain (Bray and Raitz 2001: 9–14) The era of cheap flights, what we can call British aeromobility, had begun.

Horizon went from strength to strength and by the mid-1950s was taking young and impecunious Brits to a string of resorts across the Mediterranean on rickety piston-engined aircraft like the DC–3. Raitz's success inspired other newcomers to tourism, offering the adventure and excitement of first-time foreign travel to British holiday-makers, at a price and speed which placed it within the reach of people for whom foreign travel had previously been impossible. A more price-sensitive air travel market was emerging; as 'promotional' fares became an important marketing tool for scheduled carriers like British European Airways (BEA) demand for the cheaper product of the non-scheduled charter airlines grew apace (Lyth and Dierikx 1994).

It is hard to exaggerate the importance of the jet engine to twentieth-century tourism; it was certainly as important as the steam engine to Thomas Cook & Son. Not only did jets allow airlines to reduce the cost of flying significantly they also made it possible to transport British tourists so swiftly to Mediterranean beaches that holiday-makers did not have to 'acclimatise' in any way to foreigners or the whole intimidating business of 'travelling abroad'. The story of Britannia Airways exemplifies the British 'jet age'. It begins with the tour operator Ted Langton and charter carrier Euravia, which he used to fly inclusive tourists from Luton airport to Palma de Majorca for a £53 week's holiday. In 1964 Euravia replaced its ageing Lockheed Constellations with turbo-prop Bristol Britannia and changed its name to Britannia Airways. Harnessing the vision of aviation consultant J.E.D. Williams, Britannia set about creating a 'system-designed' charter inclusive tour operation (Williams 1968: 372). This meant the use of the previously little-used Luton Airport and the concentration on low-cost Spain as a holiday destination. Luton airport had minimal terminal facilities but was far cheaper to use than Heathrow and ideally situated within a couple of miles of the M1 motorway, which linked it to the major holiday markets of the Midlands and south Yorkshire. By connecting the low-price resorts of Franco Spain's Mediterranean coast to the low-earnings holiday catchment areas of northern England, Langton and Williams broadened and 'democratised' the British leisure air market and created one of the first mobility networks of the jet age.

When Britannia was acquired by the press baron Roy Thomson in 1965 it received a major capital injection and Williams placed orders with Boeing for the new 737-200 twin-jet, buying them practically off the drawing board. Britannia took delivery of its first 737 in 1968 and by 1975 it had 13 of them (Lyth 2003b; Cuthbert 1987: 11–45).

In the 1970s further developments in the scheduled international airline industry set in motion a series of events which were to have lasting effects on British tourism and aeromobility. In 1977, after years of battling against the entrenched interests of hostile flag-carriers like British Airways, Freddie Laker received permission to launch Skytrain, the first low-cost transatlantic scheduled airline. And the impetus towards cheaper scheduled air fares, which would match and eventually surpass the appeal of charter carriers like Horizon and Britannia, was continued with the passing of landmark legislation in the United States Congress in 1978 to deregulate the American domestic airline industry. The spirit (some would say virus) of deregulation spread to Britain and Europe in the 1980s, culminating in 1993 in a final deregulatory package within the European Union that removed all remaining restrictions on airline operations (Odoni 2009).

To what extent can we say that the group tours of Horizon, Britannia and even Skytrain were, broadly speaking, continuations of communitarian mass transport in Britain? They were clearly not public transport in the sense of trams and bicycles, but they did retain the critical aspect of *group* mobility: a standardised product delivered to a largely homogeneous market on the basis of low or affordable price. And for this reason it is possible to see them as within the stream of modern mobility that stretches back to the railways. In the 1970s, however, events occurred to herald the beginnings of significant if disorganised change. As the homogeneous markets of modernity began to segment and dissolve into what the tourism industry calls 'niche operations', a growing environmental consciousness began to take hold of the Western world, led by organisations such as Greenpeace and Friends of the Earth, and the first Green political parties. Modernity was passing, largely unobserved by all but a few philosophers and sociologists, into postmodernity.[4] In tourism, a more 'liquid' approach was manifesting itself. People wanted more varied and heterogeneous holiday experiences and they wanted them fast. For Zygmunt Bauman this 'liquid life' is characterised by a fast fluidity and the feeling that 'if only one moves quickly enough and does not stop to look back and count the gains and losses, one can go on squeezing into the timespan of mortal life ever more lives …' (Bauman 2005: 8). Aeromobility is a function of this 'liquid life' and, thanks to the jet engine and the rapid growth of cheap air fares described above, seems to have had a particular effect on British holidaymakers. Once he or she could fly, to go any slower than a jet plane was to somehow 'lose out', with

---

4   The term is used here in the sense adopted by Anthony Giddens (1990), as a form of life, specifically the experience of time and space, 'beyond modernity'. Jean-François Lyotard (1986: xxiii) suggests that the transition to postmodernity had been 'under way since at least the end of the 1950s'.

the smallest delay provoking fury in otherwise ordinary and peaceful people. For one commentator the age of speed had become the age of rage, as 'our hurry-up culture teaches that reaching the destination is more important than the journey itself' (Honoré 2004: 146). For critics like David Harvey, who sees postmodernity in terms of time compression and a loss of a sense of place, aeromobility and the tourist gaze is all part of an intensification of 'instantaneity' (Harvey 1989: 286). Wherever we are going, we have to be there now.

Aeromobility and Ryanair

The discussion so far has followed the story of how the motor car created automobility as a transport norm in Britain after 1950, and the jet engine and airline deregulation drove the British traveller further towards aeromobility after 1970. Before the jet travel was seen as a genuine part of the holiday, after the jet it was the inconvenient prelude to a foreign holiday, a sort of tiresome foreplay. Aeromobility was a sign that holidays and individual mobility were changing within the context of a broad social and cultural shift from modernity to postmodernity, from a traditional or communitarian lifestyle to individualistic and 'liquid lives'.

The pace of this change accelerated with the gathering storm of airline deregulation in the 1980s and reached its climax in Europe with the appearance of brash new low-cost carriers like EasyJet and Ryanair in the 1990s. By the end of the century it was possible for British tourists to fly around Europe for the price of a train or even a bus ticket. Moreover as the price elasticity of demand for air travel rose in the new era of deregulation, so price, rather than the intrinsic qualities of the holiday destination, increasingly determined where the British would go on holiday.

The extraordinary growth rate in foreign trips made by British residents in the 1990s suggests that the combination of 'no-frills' airlines and growing access to the internet had a major impact on British holiday-making habits. Between 1991 and 2000 the number of British residents making visits abroad rose from 30.8 million to 56.8 million (ONS 2013). The explanations for this revolution in mobility must include new travel patterns, especially the trend to more, but shorter trips taken by British holidaymakers. But at the centre of the storm was an overriding factor on the supply side: low-cost airlines (LCA) and in particular Ryanair.

Ryanair and its low-cost rival EasyJet followed a business model pioneered by the American regional carrier Southwest Airlines in the 1970s. They offered very low fares but no 'frills', which included onboard meals. It was a winning formula for the simple reason that over short journeys (two to three hours) people can do without meals and tolerate cramped seating. The Irish Ryanair had been operating for some years as a conventional airline before it was relaunched as an LCA, but EasyJet was brand new; launched in 1995 at Luton Airport by its founder Stelios Haji-Ioannou in a splash of high-visibility orange paint. At the time Stelios said he wanted to offer air fares for the price of a pair of jeans. Travel agents were bypassed and instead customers were booked onto their flights on the telephone by a team of EasyJet staff. In case anyone forgot the telephone number, it was painted in giant letters along the side of the aircraft fuselage (Skapinker 1997). Nobody in the European airline business had seen anything like it.

All LCAs share a number of common features – single-class seating, minimum service and catering, high utilisation of a single aircraft type, use of secondary airports, point-to-point rather than hub-and-spoke networks, flexible yield-management systems, internet booking and, of course, high labour productivity – but Ryanair has taken these operational criteria and turned them into something approaching a corporate culture.[5] Indeed, Ryanair's greatest achievement is arguably the creation of a very well-defined brand in an industry where most companies, for example, British Airways, have poorly articulated brand images, distinguishable from each other only by their vaguely perceived national origins. For Ryanair ruthless and relentless cost cutting was more than just the basis of a business model, it was a public image in civil aviation – 'flying Ryanair' became a brand in itself.

At the turn of the new century Ryanair was in full flight. Like other European LCAs it was untouched by the setback to international aviation caused by the 9/11 bombings in September 2001. By 2004 it was the third largest carrier in the European international schedule airline market, carrying 28 million passengers that year, and not far behind Air France/KLM at 45 million and Lufthansa at 30 million (Barrett 2004: 89). Ryanair seemed to be creating a sort of social revolution, an idea not surprisingly encouraged by the airline's marketing department. It happily fostered the notion that 'flying Ryanair' was 'democratising' what had hitherto been an elite form of transport. And this proposition got considerable support from commentators who saw the airline as a force for social equality, bringing air travel within the reach of low-income families and, by the same token, dismissing opponents of LCAs as snobs who would deny the British working-classes the chance to fly abroad on holiday while concealing their contempt for poor people behind a mask of sanctimonious environmentalism (O'Neill 2006).

Whether or not the market for flying in Britain has been widened by Ryanair and EasyJet since the 1990s, Britons are certainly flying more often over *short-haul* European routes. And here the very high aircraft utilisation rates and short turn-around times incorporated in the LCA business model have blended seamlessly with underlying 'liquid life' changes in tourist behaviour. Britons may not have worked fewer hours in 2010 than they did in 1950, but they certainly took more frequent 'breaks' from that work. Whether it was a party in Ibiza, a ski weekend in Switzerland, a stag night in Prague, a shopping tour in Barcelona, or a football match in Rome, Ryanair or EasyJet would get you there for the price of a British train ticket.

---

5   For an introduction to low-cost airlines see Groß and Schröder (2007), especially chapters 1 and 2. Also helpful is Calder (2008), which includes a section on Freddie Laker and Skytrain.

The sharp growth in the short-break market suggested a deeper change in tourism behaviour: the British holiday-maker appeared 'to prefer multiple holidays to the more traditional two-week break' (Johnson and Cottingham 2008: 19). Thanks to the LCAs, the British holiday was being reduced ('liquified'?) from an annual institution into a constant diversion. Moreover, short breaks are by their nature for 'fast' tourists, people who decide to go away at short notice, choosing their destination by the price of an airline ticket, rather than the intrinsic qualities of the destination itself. They represent a sort of 'ants-in-the pants' way of living, partly the result of the development since the 1980s of what has been termedthe 'experience economy' but also the 'liquid life' tourism unleashed by low-cost airlines.[6]

Conclusion

From an environmentalist perspective, short breaks, by driving a new carbon-rich mobility, have been a disaster. In fact the whole expansion of air transport and the extraordinary growth of British aeromobility since airline deregulation in the 1990s has come at a high cost to the environment. By 2006, when the Stern Report was issued, the link between aviation and global warming and climate change was incontestable. In the influential Tyndall Report, published the year before, the authors had lamented the confusion in British government policy on aviation and carbon emissions, concluding that 'the aviation industry is in the unenviable position of seeing the demand for its services grow at unprecedented rates, whilst at the same time being unable to achieve substantial levels of decarbonisation'. Meanwhile, the government had lost its way, showing 'a singular inability to seriously recognise and adequately respond to the rapidly escalating emissions from aviation' (Anderson, Shackley, Mander and Bows 2005: 50). And the 2006 study *Predict and Decide* shared Tyndall's concerns and felt that 'whilst aviation may be a poor candidate for emissions reduction through technological efficiency, it is a very good candidate for demand restraint' (Cairns and Newsome 2006: 36).

But despite the strength of the scientific evidence many Britons remained unconvinced that climate change has been caused by human beings, with others thinking that scientists have exaggerated the problem. The last survey before the 2008 banking crash of British tourists' attitude towards the environmental damage caused by tourism indicated that people did not think much about the natural environment when planning their holidays and had little sense of any personal responsibility for global warming. There was a general feeling instead that people should be able to do what they want; for people who had not been able to go abroad before the appearance of low-cost airlines, it was delightful 'after a childhood of yearning for overseas travel' to finally be able to 'hop on a plane. And I'm thinking "oh I can see the world". Then suddenly it's 'hold on, what about the environment?' (Miller, Rathouse, Scarles, Holmes and Tribe 2007: 51–2).

---

6   The classic text on the experience economy is Pine II and Gilmore (1999).

In 2006 the publisher of the *Rough Guide* travel books called on people not to fly in Europe but 'take the train' instead. 'Flying produces so much more CO_2 than any other area of our lives. There is an immorality in our generation flying casually and leaving the next with the consequences', said Mark Ellingham (2006). He compared the overindulgence in short-break flying with the British weakness for 'binge drinking', thus coining the unfortunate term 'binge flying'. The debate over flying and global warming was degenerating into an ill-tempered quarrel, with strong political overtones. As Michael O'Leary, the rumbustious chief executive of Ryanair, attempted to ridicule climate-change science, ageing rock star and fundraiser Sir Bob Geldof, before the 2008 banking crash, celebrated Ryanair's absurdly low fares with the comment, 'If I can get a £7 flight to somewhere within two hundred miles of Venice, well I'll fucking take it. Seven quid, I don't care where I fucking go!' (Calder 2008: 73).

After the onset of the economic recession at the beginning of 2009 the debate began to lose its idealistic power; people were no longer interested in the saving the planet, they were worried about keeping their jobs. In 2009 in Britain fewer than one in five people claimed to be trying to reduce the number of flights they took for the sake of the natural environment, it was cost not environmental consequences 'that deterred people from flying more often' (Ryley 2009: 14). Politicians followed their instinct for the popular mood. Ed Miliband, the Labour government's minister with responsibility for climate change, would not bring himself to curb flying in any way which might make it unaffordable 'for ordinary people'. The Labour Party would 'protect air travel for the masses'. No politician wants to be seen stopping people going on holiday, he said, and 'if you did 80 per cent [emission] cuts across the board [by 2050], as some people have called for on aviation, you would go back to 1974 levels of flying ... I don't want to have a situation where only rich people can afford to fly' (Miliband 2009).

In the years since the beginning of the global economic recession the debate over global warming and climate change has receded. There is a sense that concern for the environment is a luxury which can only be afforded when the economy is booming. The fact that this is dangerously misguided is irrelevant; most people have more pressing and immediate concerns in their lives than whether or not there is too much carbon in the atmosphere. It is the people, specifically British short-break tourists, who must be moved on the issue, the question is how? History suggests that taxation, for example to restrain demand, is rarely an effective tool by which to achieve a change in social habits. As we have seen above it is clear that the British are hostile to regulation and fiscal control in matters concerning their individual mobility. However, it is also true that history has few examples of socially or environmentally undesirable externalities being eliminated in a market economy without state intervention; there has to be a law, such as the ones that created the penny-a-mile parliamentary train in 1844, urban smokeless zones in 1956, and more recently eliminated tobacco advertising and outlawed smoking in pubs. To take a historical analogy from water pollution, in the nineteenth century it was assumed that rivers and seas would absorb whatever sewage and industrial effluent was poured into them, and in any case industry's profits mattered more than clean water. But after a hundred years of legislative initiatives Britain has cleaned up its rivers and beaches: can we do it with the atmosphere?

Legislation and government action is clearly important but they need to be supported by what we can call a cultural 'nudge' approach; generally speaking in market economies choice is likely to be more effective than coercion or prohibition (Beck and Beck-Gernsheim 2002: 4). Could British people be nudged towards a more environmentally responsible approach towards flying? Could they be moved to see short-haul flying, when there is an acceptable rail transport alternative, as abnormal and socially unacceptable, in the same manner that smoking or wearing fur animal skins became abnormal and socially unacceptable towards the end of the twentieth century? Plane Stupid, an activist group that specialises in airport occupations and aims to 'bring the aviation industry back down to earth', is probably no more than an annoyance to most of the airline industry, but their stress on the importance of achieving change in social perception is suggestive of how change might be nudged into reality, for example, by equating short-haul flying to binge drinking and thus making it … 'uncool'.

References

Anderson, K., Shackley, S., Mander, S. and Bows, A. (2005). Decarbonising the UK: Energy for a Climate Conscious Future. Working paper, Tyndall Centre for Climate Change Research, University of Manchester.

Avineri, S. and de-Shalit, A., eds (1992). *Communitarianism and Individualism* Oxford: Oxford University Press.

Barrett, S. (2004). The Sustainability of the Ryanair Model. *International Journal of Transport Management* 2, p. 89.

Bauman, Z. (2005). *Liquid Life*. Cambridge: Polity.

Beck, U. and Beck-Gernsheim, E. (2002). *Individualization: Institutionalized Individualism and Its Social and Political Consequences*. London: Sage.

de Boer, Y. (2015). Sind Wir noch zu retten? *Der Spiegel* 21, February.

Bray, R. and Raitz, V. (2001). *Flight to the Sun: The Story of the Holiday Revolution*. London: Continuum Publishing.

Cairns, S. and Newson, C. (2006). *Predict and Decide: Aviation, Climate Change and UK Policy*. Oxford: Environmental Change Institute, University of Oxford

Calder, S. (2008), *No Frills: The Truth Behind the Low Cost Revolution in the Skies*. Virgin Books, London.

Clifton, S.-J. (2009). Carbon Trading is Useless. *The Guardian*, 5 November.

Constant III, E. (1980). *The Origins of the Turbojet Revolution*. Baltimore: John Hopkins University Press.

Cuthbert, G. (1987). *Flying to the Sun: Quarter Century of Britannia Airways Europe's Leading Leisure Airline*. London: Hodder & Stoughton.

Department for Transport (2003). *The Future of Air Transport*, Cmd 6046. Norwich: Crown Copyright.

Ellingham, M. (2006). Eco-Holidays: Fly Less, Stay Longer. *Independent on Sunday*, 24 September.

Gerike, R. (2007). Ecological and Economical Impacts of Low Cost Airlines. In *Handbook of Low Cost Airlines: Strategies, Business Processes and Market Environment*, ed. S. Groß and A. Schröder. Berlin: Erich Schmidt Verlag, pp. 210–11.

Giddens, A. (1990). *The Consequences of Modernity*. Cambridge: Polity Press.

Gössling, S. and Peeters P. (2007). 'It Does Not Harm the Environment!': An Analysis of Industry Discourses on Tourism, Air Travel and the Environment. *Journal of Sustainable Tourism* 15(4), pp. 402–17.

Groß, S. and Schröder, A., eds (2007). *Handbook of Low Cost Airlines: Strategies, Business Processes and Market Environment*. Berlin: Erich Schmidt Verlag.

Harvey, D. (1989). *The Condition of Postmodernity*. London: Blackwell.

Hebdige, D. (2002). *Hiding in the Light*. London: Routledge.

Heppenheimer, T. (1995). *Turbulent Skies: History of Commercial Aviation*. New York: John Wiley.

Honoré, C. (2004). *In Praise of Slow: How a Worldwide Movement is Challenging the Cult of Speed*. London: Orion.

ICAO (1971). *Development of Civil Air Transport*. Montreal: ICAO

—— (1978). *Civil Aviation Statistics of the World*. Montreal: ICAO.

Johnson, V. and Cottingham, M. (2008). *Plane Truths: Do the Economic Arguments for Aviation Growth Really Fly?* London: New Economics Foundation.

Klein, N. (2014). *This Changes Everything: Capitalism versus the Climate*. New York: Simon & Schuster.

Lyotard, J.-F. (1986). *The Postmodern Condition: A Report on Knowledge*. Manchester: Manchester University Press.

Lyth, P. (2003a). Reverse Thrust: American Aerospace Dominance and the British Challenge in Jet Engines, 1941–58. In *Tackling Transport*, ed. H. Trischler and S. Zeilinger. London: Science Museum, pp. 81–98.

—— (2003b). 'Gimme a Ticket on an Aeroplane …': The Jet Engine and the Revolution in Leisure Air Travel, 1960–75. In *Construction d'une Industrie touristique aux 19e et 20e siècles. Perspectives internationales*, ed. L. Tissot. Neuchâtel: Editions Alphil, pp. 118–20.

Lyth, P. and Dierikx, M (1994). From Privilege to Popularity: The Growth of Leisure Air Travel Since 1945. *Journal of Transport History* Series 3, 15(2), pp. 97–116.

McCarthy, T. (2009). A Natural Intersection: A Survey of Historical Work on Mobility and the Environment. In *Mobility in History: The State of the Art in the History of Transport, Traffic and Mobility*, ed. G. Mom, G. Pirie and L. Tissot. Neuchâtel: Éditions Alphil, pp. 61–81.

Miliband, E. (2009). Miliband: We Will Protect Air Travel for the Masses. *The Guardian*, 14 July.

Miller, G., Rathouse, K., Scarles, C., Holmes, K. and Tribe, J. (2007). *Public Understanding of Sustainable Leisure and Tourism: A Report for the Department for Environment, Food and Rural Affairs*. London: DEFRA.

Odoni, A. (2009). The International Institutional and Regulatory Environment. In *The Global Airline Industry*, ed. P. Belobaba, A. Odoni and C. Barnhart. Chichester: John Wiley & Sons, pp. 30–32.

Office for National Statistics (ONS) (2013). *Travel Trends*. London: ONS.

Omega (2008). *Carbon Neutral and Carbon Offsetting*. Report in *The Independent*, 25 August.

O'Neill, B. (2006). I Love Cheap Flights. *The Guardian*, 19 May.

Pine II, B.J. and Gilmore, J. (1999). *The Experience Economy: Work is Theatre and Every Business a Stage*. Cambridge, MA: Harvard Business School Press.

Ryley, T. (2009). Public Reluctant to Cut Flying. *The Guardian*, 5 October.

Sewill, B. (2005). *Fly Now, Grieve Later: How to Reduce the Impact of Air Travel on Climate Change*. London: Aviation Environment Federation.

Sheller, M. and Urry, J. (2000). The City and the Car. *International Journal of Urban and Regional Research* 24, pp. 737–57.

Skapinker, M. (1997). No Frills Airlines. *Financial Times*, 20 November.

Stern, N. (2006a). *The Economics of Climate Change: Executive Summary*. London: HM Treasury.

——— (2006b). Wege aus der Treibhausfalle. *Der Spiegel*, 4 May.

Urry, J. (2000). *Sociology Beyond Societies: Mobilities for the 21st* Century. London: Routledge.

——— (2004). The 'System' of Automobility. *Theory, Culture and Society* 21(4/5), pp. 25–39.

——— (2007). *Mobilities*. Cambridge: Polity.

Watson, R. (2013). Global Carbon Dioxide in Atmosphere Passes Milestone Level. *The Guardian*, 10 May.

Williams, J. (1968). Holiday Traffic by Air. *Journal of the Institute of Transport* 32(10), p. 372.

Epilogue

Colin Divall, Julian Hine and Colin Pooley

Collectively, the chapters presented in this volume present a powerful argument for the role of a historical perspective in the development of transport policies. They have covered a wide range of transport modes, issues and time periods and we do not feel that they need further elaboration in a lengthy conclusion. However, we do offer some very brief thoughts about possible future research directions and transport-related planning issues where a historical understanding could be of value. With the exception of Chapter 1, all the contributions to this volume have been on the UK. Despite the impressive efforts of North American (Rose et al. 2006) and Dutch scholars in particular, a fuller assessment of how a range of other countries have (or have not) incorporated a historical perspective into their transport policies awaits further research, and would almost certainly require a large multi-disciplinary and international research project. This would be a very worthwhile endeavour as it could, for instance, be used to explore the extent to which different paths of transport development have led to either convergent or divergent policies today.

One factor that is implicit in several of the chapters in this volume is that of scale. This is something that often seems to be neglected when policies (as in transport) are predominantly determined by central government decisions. The issue of scale can be viewed from a variety of perspectives. At a global scale, and following from the comments above, it is clearly of value to undertake comparative cross-country analyses. Rather than emphasising the aspects of British transport histories that are perceived as distinctive, it may be of more value to identify similarities with other countries and to learn from their experiences. This could be true across all transport modes ranging, for instance, from high-speed rail to the spread of e-bikes. A similar comment applies at the meso-level of transnational groupings such as the European Union, where attempts to develop and apply a common approach to transport and mobility policies across several nation states have so far received comparatively little attention from historians. (Henrich-Franke 2010; van der Vleuten and Kaijser 2006; Jensen 2005; Dienel 2004; Merger and Polino 2004; Nijkamp et al. 1998) Factors of scale are equally important at the national level. Policies developed in Westminster, and constructed primarily with a London-centred view of the country, may not be equally appropriate in all parts of the United Kingdom. Histories are always both temporally and spatially specific, and what works in one location may not work in another. This argument can be disaggregated and advanced at many levels.

For instance, a London (and by association English) perspective on transport policy may not be perceived to be so applicable in Scotland, Wales or Northern Ireland. But, a metropolitan (and by association southern) perspective may also be viewed as equally inappropriate in northern cities such as Manchester, Liverpool, Leeds or Newcastle. Within regions the same arguments apply. Urban and rural transport demands and priorities are clearly very different, as are the needs (and constraints) affecting small and large urban settlements. Even within one urban area there is a need to be aware of the significance of scale. As is emphasised in Chapter 2, local communities develop particular characteristics and may develop their own strategies and practices for enabling daily mobility. The way this works in one community may be very different from another, even within the same urban area. We suggest that the role of differential historical experiences across Britain (and elsewhere) is a topic that would repay further investigation.

At the time of writing (May 2015) it seems that some quite significant political shifts are taking place in the UK, with potential impacts on future transport policies. The extent to which change will actually occur, of course, remains to be seen. Although many aspects of transport policy in Scotland have been devolved since 1998 (Scottish Parliament 2015), the emergence of a strong Scottish Nationalist Party, not only in Scotland but also at Westminster, means that in the future transport policies within Scotland may become increasingly differentiated from those in England. At the same time, calls for greater regional devolution within England have gathered pace, and if current plans to devolve many powers from Westminster to the large city regions come to fruition then it is likely that we shall see the development of more locally focused transport policies, designed to suit the needs of the city in which they operate. Manchester is the first English city likely to be given such powers, which include control of transport as well as public health, policing, housing and planning (Wintour 2015). Reorganisation of local government, and the shifting of responsibilities, between different layers of administrative authority, is of course not new; but it would seem that the UK is entering a new phase of administrative reorganisation with the potential for substantial devolution of powers from Westminster. We suggest that, in doing so, it is also important to be cognisant of the history of previous reorganisations, especially the impacts of unintended consequences of change. It is striking, for example, that despite Vigar's (2002) pioneering efforts to trace the tangled relationship between central-government and local-authority transport policy since the Second World War, we have no systematic history of the Whitehall department that was ostensibly a central player in such endeavours. Perhaps the very lack of an official history of the Department for Transport reflects the widely held perception that ever since its founding in 1919 as the Ministry of Transport the department has played second fiddle to other, more powerful forces within Whitehall and government. Transport is expensive (although arguably not as expensive as it ought to be given the uncosted environmental and social consequences of 'excessive' mobility) and so it is not surprising to find the guiding hand of the Treasury behind many aspects of transport policy in the UK.

In organising the workshops from which most of the chapters in this volume originate, we have been keen to also explore how transport histories can inform debates around contemporary mobility: yet it is also clear that ideas and notions of mobility practices from the past may also be useful in seeking to understand possible future travel behaviours. As policies seek to encourage less carbon intensive modes of transport, and for that matter more collective public modes of transport, it is possible that we can learn from previous generations' documented travel experiences to develop insights into patterns of provision and how these have shaped attitudes towards personal mobility, accessibility to job opportunities and goods and services. In a relatively short period of 60 years, personal mobility and lifestyle has been dramatically reshaped by increasing access to the motor car. In 1952, 59 per cent of passenger kilometres in the UK were undertaken by public transport (rail and bus/coach), while by 2013 this had declined to 14 per cent, compared to a just over a threefold increase, to 83 per cent, in passenger kilometres travelled by car over the same period (Department for Transport 2014). This has impacted on decisions about where we choose to live, shop and undertake leisure activities and also on how daily life is undertaken. Because of the car we are no longer wedded to the idea of comprehensive proximity to public networks, despite being increasingly encouraged to use public transport for the journey to work. It is not beyond us to contemplate our own future mobility in light of the growing need to reduce the amount of carbon used in transport systems and – at least in the long-term – rising fuel prices: but at the same time it also requires us to rethink how we use our own neighbourhoods and facilities given these pressures and the growing impact of ICT.

At their most basic almost all transport policies intend to facilitate the easy movement of people from one location to another. In doing so they must balance the competing demands of cost, speed, comfort, accessibility, safety, environmental impact and customer satisfaction. In this volume we have sought to cover at least some of these issues, ranging from those concerned with social and environmental justice to the marketing of different modes to the travelling public. There are many other angles that could be covered, and we hope that these chapters will help to stimulate further research and interactions between historians and policy makers.

References

Department for Transport (2014). Transport Statistics Great Britain. https://www.gov.uk/government/statistics/transport-statistics-great-britain-2014 (accessed 18 May 2015).

Dienel, H.-L., ed. (2004). *Unconnected Transport Networks: European Intermodal Traffic Junctions 1800–2000*. Frankfurt: Campus Verlag.

Henrich-Franke, C. (2010). European mobility policy: a topic to be discovered *Mobility in History: The Yearbook of the International Association for th History of Traffic, Transport and Mobility* 1, pp. 221–7.

Jensen, A. (2005). The Institutionalisation of European Transport Policy from a Mobility Perspective. In *Social Perspectives on Mobility*, ed. T.U. Thomsen L.D. Nielsen and H. Gudmundsson, pp. 127–53.

Merger, M. and Polino, M.-N. (2004). *COST340: Towards a European Intermoda Transport Network: Lessons from History: A Critical Biography*. Paris: AHICF

Nijkamp, P., Rienstra, S. and Vleugel, J. (1998). *Transportation Planning and th Future*. Chichester: John Wiley & Sons.

Rose, M., Seely. B. and Barrett, P. (2006). *The Best Transportation System in the World: Railroads, Trucks, Airlines, and American Public Policy in th Twentieth Century*. Oxford: University of Philadelphia Press.

Scottish Parliament (2015). Devolved and Reserved Matters Explained. http:/ www.scottish.parliament.uk/visitandlearn/25488.aspx (accessed 18 May 2015)

Vigar, G. (2002). *The Politics of Mobility: Transport, the Environment and Publi Policy*. London: Spon Press.

van der Vleuten, E. and Kaijser, A., eds (2006). *Networking Europe: Transnationc Infrastructures and the Shaping of Europe, 1850–2000*. Sagamore Beach Science History Publications/USA.

Wintour, P. (2015). George Osborne offers devolution route to cities with electe mayor. *The Guardian*, 14 May. http://www.theguardian.com/politics/201⁵ may/14/george-osborne-invites-cities-to-follow-manchester-route-to devolution (accessed 18 May 2015).

Appendix:
Key Historical Resources for UK Transport Planners and Policy Makers

As a well as brief guide to methodologies of the usable past and history learning, this appendix lists just a few of the many resources that might be useful to anyone wanting to gain a better understanding of how the historical development of the UK's transport system shapes and constrains the policies and practices open to us in the future. Along with academic texts, we have included a few popular histories when these provide a quick and reliable overview of a subject. The emphasis is on the period after 1945, although we have also included earlier material when it is important to understand the long-term implications of past decisions and events. While most of the resources refer directly to the UK, we have mentioned some overseas texts, both as exemplars of how a usable past might be written and for comparison with the UK's approach to transport and transport policy. Finally, while most of the sources listed here are retrospective, we have included a handful of contemporary texts that we judge to have been particularly relevant to UK transport policy since 1945.

Approaches to the Usable Past and History Learning

Divall, C. (2010). Mobilizing the history of technology. *Technology and Culture* 51(4), pp. 938–60.

——— (2011). Transport History, the Usable Past and the Future of Mobility. In *Mobilities: New Perspectives on Transport and Society*, ed. M. Grieco and J. Urry. Farnham: Ashgate, pp. 305–19.

——— (2012). Business history, global networks and the future of mobility. *Business History* 54(4), pp. 542–55.

Graham Jr, O. (1983).The uses and misuses of history in policymaking. *The Public Historian* 5(2), pp. 5–19.

Guldi, J. and Armitage, D. (2014). *The History Manifesto*. Cambridge: Cambridge University Press.

Hirsh, R. (2011). Historians of technology in the real world: reflections on the pursuit of policy-oriented history. *Technology and Culture* 52(1), pp. 6–20.

History and Policy. http://www.historyandpolicy.org/ (accessed 18 May 2015).

Liparito, K. (2000). The historian in the rose garden? *Technology and Culture* 41(3), pp. 537–48.

Michael, D. and Chen, S. (2006) *Serious Games: Games that Educate, Train, and Inform*. Boston: Thomson Course Technology PTR.

Mirvis, P., Ayas, K. and Roth, G. (2003) *To the Desert and Back: The Story of the Most Dramatic Business Transformation on Record*. San Francisco: Jossey Bass.

Neustadt, R. and May, E. (1986) *Thinking in Time: The Uses of History for Decision Makers*. New York: The Free Press.

Raadschelders, J. (1994). Administrative history: contents, meaning and usefulness. *International Review of Administrative Sciences* 60, pp. 117–29.

Roth, G. and Kleiner, A. (1996). *Field Manual for the Learning Historian*. Boston: MIT.

Stave, B. (1983). A conversation with Joel A. Tarr: urban history and policy. *Journal of Urban History* 9(2), pp. 195–232.

Stearns, P. (1982a). Applied history and social science. *Social Science History* 6(2), pp. 219–26.

——— (1982b). History and policy analysis: toward maturity. *The Public Historian* 4(3), pp. 4–29.

Thane, P. (2009). History and policy. *History Workshop Journal* 67, pp. 140–45.

Toussaint, H. (2005). History as a Powerful Learning Instrument in the Search for Innovation. In *Organizing Innovation. New Approaches to Cultural Change and Intervention in Public Sector Organizations*, ed. M. Veenswijk. Amsterdam/Washington, DC: IOS Press.

Zelizer, J.E. (2000). Clio's lost tribe: public policy history since 1978. *Journal of Policy History* 12(3), pp. 369–94.

Transport Policy and Planning

Doherty, I. and Shaw, J. (2008). *Traffic Jam: Ten Years of 'Sustainable' Transport in the UK*. Bristol: Policy Press.

Dudley, G. and Richardson, J. (2001). *Why Does Policy Change? Lessons from British Transport Policy, 1945–99*. London: Routledge.

Dyble, L. (2009). Reconstructing transportation: linking tolls and transit for place-based mobility. *Technology and Culture* 50(3), pp. 631–48.

Eddington, R. (2006). *The Eddington Transport Study: The Case for Action: Sir Rod Eddington's Advice to Government*. London: HMSO.

Flyvbjerg, B. (2009). Survival of the unfittest: why the worst infrastructure gets built – and what we can do about it. *Oxford Review of Economic Policy* 25(3), pp. 344–67.

Flyvbjerg, B., Bruzelius, N. and Rothengatter, W. (2003). *Megaprojects and Risk: An Anatomy of Ambition*. Cambridge: Cambridge University Press.

Headicar, P. (2009). *Transport Policy and Planning in Great Britain*. London: Routledge.

Hine, J. and Mitchell, F. (2003). *Transport Disadvantage and Social Exclusion: Exclusion Mechanisms in Transport in Urban Scotland*. Farnham: Ashgate.

Karner. A. (2013). Multimodal dreamin': Californian transportation planning, 1967–77. *Journal of Transport History* 34(1), pp. 39–57.

OMEGA Centre (2012). *Mega Projects: Executive Summary: Lessons for Decision-Makers: An Analysis of Selected Large-Scale Transport Infrastructure Projects*. London: OMEGA Centre, UCL. http://www.omegacentre.bartlett. ucl.ac.uk/publications/reports/mega-project-executive-summary/ (accessed 18 May 2015).

Rose, M., Seely. B. and Barrett, P. (2006). *The Best Transportation System in the World: Railroads, Trucks, Airlines, and American Public Policy in the Twentieth Century*. Oxford: University of Philadelphia Press.

Royal Commission on Environmental Pollution (1994). *Transport and the Environment: Eighteenth Report*. London: HMSO.

Sheail, J. (2002). *An Environmental History of Twentieth-Century Britain*. Houndmills: Palgrave, pp. 177–217.

Starkie, D. (1982). *The Motorway Age*. Oxford: Pergamon Press.

Vigar, G. (2002). *The Politics of Mobility: Transport, the Environment and Public Policy*. London: Spon Press.

General and Multi-Modal

Aldcroft, D. (1975). *British Transport Since 1914: An Economic History*. Newton Abbot: David & Charles.

Bagwell, P. and Lyth, P. (2002). *Transport in Britain: From Canal Lock to Gridlock*. London: Hambledon and London.

Bonavia, M. (1987). *The Nationalisation of British Transport: The Early History of the British Transport Commission, 1948–53*. London: Macmillan Press.

Divall, C. (2003). Transport, 1900–1939. In *A Companion to Early Twentieth-Century Britain*, ed. C. Wrigley. Oxford: Wiley-Blackwell, pp. 286–301.

Dyos, H. and Aldcroft, D. (1974). *British Transport: An Economic Survey from the Seventeenth Century to the Twentieth*. Harmondsworth: Pelican Books.

Filarski, R. (2004). *The Rise and Decline of Transport Systems: Changes in Historical Context*. Rotterdam: Ministry of Transport and Public Works.

Horner, C. and Greaves, J. (2011). Mobility spotting: running off the rails in the transport historiography of the United Kingdom. *Mobility in History* 2, pp. 151–8.

Letherby, G. and Reynolds, G., eds (2009). *Gendered Journeys, Mobile Emotions*. Aldershot: Ashgate.

Mom, G., Divall, C. and Lyth, P. (2010). Towards a paradigm shift? A decade of transport and mobility history. *Mobility in History* 1, pp. 13–40.

Roth, R. and Divall, C., eds (2015). *From Road to Rail and Back Again? A Century of Transport Competition and Interdependency*. Farnham: Ashgate.

Individual Modes

Aviation

Cairns, S. and Newson, C. (2006). *Predict and Decide: Aviation, Climate Change and UK Policy*. Oxford: Environmental Change Institute, University of Oxford.
Doganis, R. (1992). *The Airport Business*. London: Routledge.
Groß, S. and Schröder, A. (2007). *Handbook of Low Cost Airlines: Strategies, Business Processes and Market Environment*. Berlin: Erich Schmidt Verlag.
Heppenheimer, T. (1995). *Turbulent Skies: History of Commercial Aviation*. New York: John Wiley.
Lyth, P. (1995). The Changing Role of Government in British Civil Air Transport 1919–49. In *The Political Economy of Nationalisation in Britain, 1920–1950*, ed. R. Millward and J. Singleton. Cambridge: Cambridge University Press, pp. 65–87.
——— (1998). Chosen Instruments: The Evolution of British Airways. In *Flying the Flag: European Commercial Air Transport since 1945*, ed. H.-L. Dienel and P. Lyth. Basingstoke: Macmillan, pp. 50–86.
——— (1999). Sky Wars: Conflicting Approaches to Air Transport Regulation in Europe and the United States 1920 to 1990. In *Institutions in the Transport and Communications Industry: State and Private Actors in the Making of Institutional Patterns, 1850–1990*, ed. L. Andersson-Skog and O. Krantz. Canton, MA: Science History Publications/USA, pp. 93–111.
Simmons, C. and Caruana, V. (2001). Enterprising local government: policy, prestige and Manchester Airport, 1929–82. *Journal of Transport History* 22(2), pp. 126–46.

Coastal Shipping and Inland Waterways

Armstrong, J. (1996). Introduction: The Cinderella of the Transport World: The Historiography of the British Coastal Trade. In *Coastal and Short Sea Shipping*, ed. J. Armstrong. Aldershot: Scolar Press, pp. ix–xxiv.
——— (2009). *The Vital Spark: The British Coastal Trade, 1700–1930*. St. John's, Nfld: International Maritime Economic History Association.
Boughey, J. and Hadfield, C. (2008). *British Canals: The Standard History*. 9th edn. Stroud: The History Press.

Railways

Albalate, D. and Bel, G. (2014). *The Economics and Politics of High-Speed Rail: Lessons from Experiences Abroad*. Plymouth: Lexington Books.
Bagwell, P. (2004). The sad state of British railways: the rise and fall of Railtrack, 1992–2002. *Journal of Transport History* 25(2), pp. 111–24.

Biddle, G. and Simmons, J. (1997). *The Oxford Companion to British Railway History: From 1603 to the 1990s.* Oxford: Oxford University Press.

Casson, M. (2009). *The World's First Railway System: Enterprise, Competition and Regulation on the Railway Network in Victorian Britain.* Oxford: Oxford University Press.

Carter, I. (2001). *Railways and Culture in Britain: The Epitome of Modernity.* Manchester: Manchester University Press.

Crompton, G. (1999). Railway Nationalization in the United Kingdom. In *Institutions in the Transport and Communications Industry: State and Private Actors in the Making of Institutional Patterns, 1850–1990*, ed. L. Andersson-Skog and O. Krantz. Canton, MA: Science History Publications/USA, pp. 133–51.

Doherty, I. (1999). *Making Tracks: The Politics of Local Rail Transport.* Aldershot: Ashgate.

Glaister, S. (2006). Britain: Competition Undermined by Politics. In *Competition in the Railway Industry: An International Comparative Perspective*, ed. J. Gómez-Ibáñez and G. de Rus. Cheltenham: Edward Elgar, pp. 49–80.

Gourvish, T. (1986). *British Railways 1948–73: A Business History.* Cambridge: Cambridge University Press.

——— (1999). The Regulation of Britain's Railways: Past, Present and Future. In *Institutions in the Transport and Communications Industry: State and Private Actors in the Making of Institutional Patterns, 1850–1990*, ed. L. Andersson-Skog and O. Krantz. Canton MA: Science History Publications/USA, pp. 117–32.

——— (2002). *British Rail 1974–97: From Integration to Privatisation.* Oxford: Oxford University Press.

——— (2006). *The Official History of Britain and the Channel Tunnel.* London: Routledge.

——— (2008). *Britain's Railways 1997–2005: Labour's Strategic Experiment.* Oxford: Oxford University Press.

Letherby, G. and Reynolds, G. (2005). *Train Tracks: Work, Play and Politics on the Railways.* Oxford: Berg.

Loft, C. (2006). *Government, the Railways and the Modernization of Britain.* London: Routledge.

——— (2013). *Last Trains: Dr Beeching and the Death of Rural England.* London: Biteback Publishing.

Scott, P. (2002). British railways and the challenge from road haulage, 1919–39. *Twentieth Century British History* 13(2), pp. 101–20.

Wolmar, C. (2007). *Fire and Steam: How the Railways Transformed Britain.* London: Atlantic Books.

Roads and Mechanised Road Transport

Armstrong, J., Aldridge, J., Boyes, G., Mustoe G. and Storey, R., eds (2003). *Companion to British Road Haulage History.* London: Science Museum.

Barker, T. and Gerhold, D. (1995). *The Rise and Rise of Road Transport, 1770–1990*. Cambridge: Cambridge University Press.

Buchanan, C. (1958). *Mixed Blessing: The Motor in Britain*. London: Leonard Hill

Gibson, T. (2001). *Road Haulage by Motor in Britain: The First Forty Years* Aldershot: Ashgate.

Hibbs, J. (1975). *The Bus and Coach Industry: Its Economics and Organization* London: J.M. Dent.

Koerner, S. (2011). The rediscovery of the motorcycle in history. *Mobility in History* 2, pp. 275–81.

MacDonald-Walker, S. (2000). *Bikers: Culture, Politics and Power*. Oxford: Berg

Merriman, P. (2007). *Driving Spaces: A Cultural–Historical Geography of England's M1 Motorway*. Oxford: Blackwell.

―――― (2012). *Mobility, Space and Culture*. London: Routledge, part II.

―――― (2015). Motorways and the Modernisation of Britain's Road Network 1937–70. In *From Rail to Road and Back Again: A Century of Transport Competition and Interdepency*, ed. R. Roth and C. Divall. Farnham: Ashgate pp. 315–38.

Mom, G. (2004). *The Electric Vehicle: Technology and Expectations in the Automobile Age*. London: Johns Hopkins University Press.

Mulley, C. and Higginson, M., eds (2014). *Companion to Road Passenge Transport History*. Walsall: Roads and Road Transport History Association.

O'Connell, S. (1998). *The Car and British Society: Class, Gender and Motoring 1896–1939*. Manchester: Manchester University Press.

Plowden, W. (1973). *The Motor Car and Politics in Britain*. Harmondsworth Pelican.

Rooney, D. (2014). The political economy of congestion: road pricing and the neoliberal project, 1952–2003. *Twentieth Century British History* 25(4), pp 628–50.

Scott, P. (1998). The growth of road haulage, 1921–59: an estimate. *Journal of Transport History* 19(2), pp. 138–55.

Thoms, D., Holden, L. and Claydon, T., eds (1998). *The Motor Car and Popula Culture in the 20th Century*. Aldershot: Ashgate.

Tyme, J. (1978). *Motorways versus Democracy: Public Inquiries into Road Proposals and Their Political Significance*. London: Macmillan.

Urban, Peri-Urban and Rural Transport

Armstrong, J. (2000). From Shillibeer to Buchanan: Transport and the Urban Environment. In *The Cambridge Urban History of Britain. Volume III 1840–1950*, ed. M. Daunton. Cambridge: Cambridge University Press, pp. 229–60.

Barker, T. and Robbins, M. (1963, 1974). *A History of London Transport*. 2 vols London: Allen & Unwin.

Divall, C. and Bond, W., eds (2003). *Suburbanizing the Masses: Public Transport and Urban Development in Historical Perspective*. Aldershot: Ashgate.

Haywood, R. (2009). *Railways, Urban Development and Town Planning in Britain, 1948–2008*. Farnham: Ashgate.

Hibbs, J. (1989). *The History of British Bus Services*. 2nd edn. Newton Abbot: David & Charles.

Mulley, C. (1998). The nationalisation of the bus industry: the Transport Act, 1947: its underlying philosophy and initial progress. *Journal of Transport History* 19(2), pp. 122–36.

Pooley, C., Turnbull, J. and Adams, M. (2005). *A Mobile Century? Changes in Everyday Mobility in Britain in the Twentieth Century*. Aldershot: Ashgate.

St John Thomas, D. (1963). *The Rural Transport Problem*. London: Routledge & Kegan Paul.

Steering Group and Working Group on Urban Traffic (1963). *Traffic in Towns: A Study of the Long Term Problems of Traffic in Urban Areas* [the Buchanan Report]. London: HMSO.

Taylor, S., ed. (2001). *The Moving Metropolis: A History of London's Transport since 1800*. London: Laurence King Publishing.

Walking and Cycling

Amato, A. (2004). *On Foot: A History of Walking*. London: New York University Press.

Hillman, M. and Whalley, A. (1979). *Walking is Transport*. London: Policy Studies Institute.

Norton, P. (2010) Urban mobility without wheels: a historiographical review of pedestrianism. *Mobility in History* 1, pp. 111–15.

Oosterhuis, H. (2014). Bicycle research between bicycle policies and bicycle culture. *Mobility in History* 5, pp. 20–36.

Pooley, C. with Jones, T., Tight, M., Horton, D., Scheldeman, G., Mullen, C., Jopson, A. and Strano, E. (2013). *Promoting Walking and Cycling: New Perspectives on Sustainable Travel*. Bristol: Policy Press.

Rosen, P. (2002). *Framing Production: Technology, Culture and Change in the British Bicycle Industry*. London: MIT Press.

Solnit, R. (2000). *Wanderlust: A History of Walking*. London: Penguin.

Stoffers, M. and Ebert, A.-K. (2014). New directions in cycling research: a report on the Cycling Rountable at T^{2}M Madrid. *Mobility in History* 5, pp. 9–19.

Other Resources

Periodicals

The *Journal of Transport History* has published articles since 1953 that either directly address the relevance of the past to current policy or provide useful contextual knowledge for transport policy makers. While its geographical focus was originally the UK, it now aims to cover the entire globe, as does *Transfers: Interdisciplinary Journal of Mobility Studies*, published since 2011. Both journals are associated with the International Association for the History of Transport, Traffic and Mobility (T²M), which since 2009 has been responsible for a useful yearbook, *Mobility in History*; this is only available to members: t2m.org.The more sociologically inclined journal *Mobilities* also occasionally publishes historical articles, as does the *Journal of Transport Geography*, the *Journal of Historical Geography*, *Technology & Culture*, *Twentieth Century British History*, *Contemporary British History* and *Cultural and Social History*. This list is by no means exhaustive. As well as other history journals, some periodicals aimed at planners and policy makers such as *Transport Policy* also publish articles about the past. The periodicals of the UK's several voluntary transport societies can also be a very useful resource. Examples include the *Journal of the Railway and Canal Historical Society* and the Roads and Road Transport History Association's *Journal*.

Archives and Other Collections

The National Archives (TNA) at Kew holds the official collections relating to the Department for Transport and its predecessors, dating back to the Ministry of Transport (established in 1919) and the Board of Trade, which in the nineteenth century was responsible in particular for the regulation of railways, inland navigation and coastal shipping. Post-war civil aviation was for many years the responsibility of a separate ministry. Some of the DfT's more recent material is available on-line: for example, the National Travel Survey, https://www.gov.uk/government/collections/national-travel-survey-statistics, and DfT reports and statistics, https://www.gov.uk/government/organisations/department-for-transport.

The lack of an official or other comprehensive history of the DfT/MoT is perhaps the most regrettable of the many absences in the literature on UK transport policy and planning in the twentieth century. TNA also holds many of the business records of those transport industries nationalised in 1947: notably the railways, parts of road haulage and the bus industry, docks and harbours, inland waterways, and London's public transport. Some papers relating wholly to Scotland are held in the National Archives of Scotland, Edinburgh, while others for Northern Ireland are in PRONI, Belfast.

Prior to the First World War the development of the road network was governed almost wholly at a local level; thereafter, the Ministry of Transport took on responsibility for the inchoate national policy. Local and municipal governments were still constituted as highway authorities and, from the last decades of the nineteenth century, as overseers or providers of public transport. Many records are therefore held in local, county or regional archives. Still others are held in museums: the National Tramway Museum, Crich, Derbyshire, holds a superb, world-class collection of reports, papers, photographs and historical periodicals relating to urban transport (not just tramways) and urban planning in the UK and overseas, while the National Railway Museum, York, and the National Motor Museum, Beaulieu, Hampshire, hold, among other collections, invaluable runs of historical periodicals such as *Modern Transport* and *Commercial Motor*. The London Transport Museum is central to research on the capital, while the National Maritime Museum, Greenwich, and the National Waterways Museum, Ellesmere Port, Cheshire, hold important collections relating to coastal shipping and inland waterways. The records of small (and not-so-small) private transport operators are scattered widely and sometimes held by voluntary societies. For example, the Omnibus Society, founded in 1929, holds a little-known collection relating to bus and coach operations in the UK. Searching all these collections and for particular documents has been made easier by on-line catalogues, particularly Discovery, TNA's search engine covering over 2,500 archives in the UK as well as TNA's own collections: http://discovery.nationalarchives.gov.uk/. However not all records have been catalogued yet, and only a minority is available on-line.

Transport policy all too often overlooks the individual user, and recovering the historical experience of travel and everyday mobility is one of the most dynamic areas of current research. It is also one of the most difficult for which to locate sources. Several of the museums listed hold photographic collections relating to transport users – for instance, the National Tramway Museum's photographs of street scenes – or oral-history collections, such as the National Archive of Railway Oral History, held at the National Railway Museum. Finding other material, such as diaries and accounts of everyday travel, is often a matter of serendipity.

Index

accidents *see* railway accidents; road
    accidents
'aeromobility' 171, 177–8
agglomeration effects 103–4
Agyeman, J. 48
Ahern, Aoife ix, 8; *co-author of Chapter 4*
air travel 10, 171
    deregulation of 177–8
Albalate, Daniel 100, 103–4
alcohol consumption 118–20, 129
Alsnih, R. 65
Anderson, K. 180
appraisal of past transport investments 99
Armitage, David 4
attitudinal changes 59–60
audit as part of a marketing plan 140
Automobile Association (AA) 120–21, 125
'automobility' 58

Barnes, Alfred 88
Bauman, Zygmunt 32, 177
Beeching, Richard (and Beeching Report,
    1963) 3, 109
Bel, Germà 100, 103–4
Belgium 22, 24
benefit–cost ratio (BCR) 101, 103, 105
Berridge, Virginia 118
bicycles, use of *see* cycling
Blennerhassett, Fred (and Blennerhassett
    Report, 1976) 9, 119–24, 127
Board of Trade 81–2, 108
de Boer, Yves 172
Bohm, Steffen 127
Borkenstein, Robert 129
Bows, A. 180
Braithwaite, John 117
branding 10, 135
    definition of 138
    influence on modal choice 161–6
breathalyser tests 9, 115–18, 122, 125

Brent Cross 155
Brighton & Hove Buses 166
Britannia Airways 176–7
British Railways (BR) 88–9, 143, 148, 166
Brittan, Leon 125, 127
bus services 52–3, 58, 66–7, 146–9, 157,
    162–6
    deregulation of 146–7, 157, 164

Callaghan, James 123
Cameron, David 129
car-parking charges 157
car use
    dependence on 8, 49, 65–73
    dominant role of 2, 6, 50, 53, 58–9, 72,
        165, 175, 187
    'forced' 49
    human cost of 9
    negative consequences of 48
    restrictions on 7, 59, 157, 175
    women's access to 7, 66, 71–3
carbon dioxide (CO_2) emissions 106,
    172–4, 181
carbon offsetting 174
carbon trading 174
Castle, Barbara 9, 115–16, 125–9
Channel Tunnel rail link 98, 101
Chartered Institute of Marketing (CIM) 136
Cheap Trains Act (1883) 83
Chen, Chia-Lin 104
climate change 48–9, 106, 110, 171–4,
    180–81
    and aviation 172–4
collective skills 33–4
Collet, C.D. 83
commercial travellers 84–5, 88
community studies 33–8
community transport schemes 71–3
commuter travel 10, 83, 153, 157, 163
congestion charging 59, 157

consultative bodies of transport users 9, 88–90
consumer protection 80
consumer society 175
continuity in policy processes 19
Cook, Thomas 81, 176
co-presence while travelling 31
corporate histories 16, 20–21
cost–benefit analysis (CBA) 100–105
Cottingham, M. 180
Crossrail 158, 166
Cunco, Terence 166
Cunningham, Sally 128
customisation 136
cycle lanes 54–8
    views on 57
cycling 5, 23–4, 53–9, 110, 154, 175
    views on 57

Daily Express 125
decision-making processes
    history of 19
    at the level of the individual 6
    use of history in 18
demand management in transport 10, 153
Department of the Environment (DoE) 122–3, 126
Department for Transport (DfT) 98, 141, 186
deregulation
    of airlines 177–8
    of bus services 146–7, 157, 164
devolution 186
Divall, Colin ix, 3–4, 9, 23, 87; *author of Chapter 6, co-author of Introduction and Epilogue and co-editor*
Drew, Q.C. 129
drink driving 9, 115–22, 125–8
Duncier, M. 41
Durie, A.C. 120–21
Dutch transport system 21–3

EasyJet 178–9
economic and econometric analysis 25, 139–40, 150, 160
economic modelling 25
economic policies 6
Eddington Transport Study (2006) 97, 108, 110

Edinburgh 164
electrification schemes 160–61, 166–7
Ellingham, Mark 181
Elliot, John 159
emissions
    from aircraft 171
    from vehicles 48–9
environmental justice 8, 47–6
    definition of 48
environmentalism 173, 180–82
European Union 185
Evans, B. 48
express trains 82, 159

Feminist Archive North 35, 44
Field, Frank 4
Filarski, Ruud 22–3
financial crises 25
First Group 164–5
First World War 86
Fitzpatrick Associates 67–8
Flyvbjerg, B. 9, 98, 101, 107
focus groups, use of 68–73
Foreign and Commonwealth Office 4
Forsdike, Nicola ix, 10, 145; *author of Chapter 8*
Fowler, Norman 9, 116, 123–7
France 100–101, 104–5
freight transport 5
Friends of the Earth 174, 177

Garthwaite, Al 39
Geldof, Sir Bob 181
gendered aspects of transport 7–8, 32, 77
geographies of opportunity 44
Gerike, R. 174
Gilbert, John 121
Gladstone, W.E. 80
global warming *see* climate change
Goffman, E. 40
Google Earth 37
Gourvish, Terry 103
Grand Rapids project 129
Great Eastern Railway (GER) 158–61
Great Exhibition (1851) 81
Green, Chris 144–5
greenhouse gas (GHG) emissions 48, 106–7, 173

Grieco, M. 31–2
Groningen University 25
Guldi, Jo 4

Hague, William 4
Hailsham, Lord 118
Haji-Ioannou, Stelios 178
Hall, Sir Peter 102–4, 108
Hanmer, J. 33, 35–6
Harrogate & District buses 166
Hartley, M. 154
Harvey, David 178
Havard, John 117
Heath, Edward 116, 122, 126
Heathrow Airport 2
Heinz brand 138
Hensher, D. 65
Heseltine, Michael 122
Higginson, Martin x, 10; *author of*
        Chapter 9
Higham, Charles 87
high-speed rail (HSR) 97–110, 140, 185
Hine, Julian x, 8, 66; *co-author of*
        Introduction, Chapter 4 and
        Epilogue and co-editor
Hirsh, Richard 19
history and historians, role of 4, 15, 18, 24,
        105, 140–51, 185
History and Policy network 3–4
Hodgson, Frances x, 7; *author of Chapter 2*
Holmes, K. 180
Holyoake, George 83
Honoré, C. 178
Horan, John 121–2
Hore-Belisha, Leslie 54
Horizon Holidays 176–7
House of Commons Public Accounts
        Committee 108
House of Commons Select Committee on
        Transport 147
House of Lords Economic Affairs
        Committee 108
HS1 project 98, 101
HS2 project 3, 9, 97–110, 158
HS3 project 97

infrastructure investment 2, 59, 77, 102,
        136, 139, 158, 166–7

Ingilby, J. 154
integrated transport networks 147
Intergovernmental Panel on Climate
        Change (IPCC) 172
Inter-Mediate (charity) 4
internet resources 35, 38, 167
Ireland 65–73
Ishaque, M. 50

James Committee 121
Japan 100–101
jet engines 171, 173, 176, 178
Johnson, V. 180
Jones, G. 161–2
Joseph Rowntree Foundation 49

Kamruzzaman, M. 66
Kelvill, Paul 147
Kenyon, S. 49
Klein, Naomi 172
Kleiner, A. 17
Koskela, H. 38–9
Kotler, P. 138
KPMG (consultants) 103
Kyoto Protocol (1997) 172–3

Laker, Freddie 176–7
Langton, Ted 176
learning
        contextual and behavioural 7, 19, 22
        from other countries' experience 4,
                11, 185
        from the past 1, 5–6, 24–5, 135, 150, 187
learning histories 17–18, 25
Leeds City Libraries 35
Leeds–Settle–Carlisle railway 148
'light rail' 165–6
Lille 104
'liquid lives' 177–8, 180
Liverpool Street station 163
local government reorganisation 186
local joint committees 86–9
London and North Eastern Railway
        (LNER) 160
London and North Western Railway
        (LNWR) 85
London Passenger Transport Board
        (LPTB) 157, 164

London rail termini 158
London and South Western Railway
        (LSWR) 160–61
low-cost airlines (LCAs) 178–80
Lucas, K. 49
Luckin, Bill x, 9, 50; *author of Chapter 7*
Luton Airport 176
Lyth, Peter xi, 10; *author of Chapter 10*

McCabe, F. 68
McCarthy, Tom 171
McDonald, M. 137
Mackie, P. 102
McLuhan, Marshall 24
McNeil, Sandra 39
Manchester 51–4, 104, 158, 165–6, 186
Mander, S. 180
marketing 7, 10, 135–43, 150, 153
        definition of 136–7
        '4 Ps' framework 142–3
        historical evidence on the effectiveness
                of 141–9
        phases of 161–4
Marples, Ernest 115, 125–6
May, E.R. 18
Meadowhall, Sheffield 155, 165
mega transport projects (MTPs) 98–109
        definition of 98
        political nature of 105
Mercedes (company) 165
Mersey Tunnel 55
Metro Centre (Gateshead) 155
Metro network (West Yorkshire) 135,
        145–9, 164
Metrolink (Manchester) 165–6
Metropolitan Railway and 'Metro-land'
        158, 163, 166
Midland Railway 82
Midwinter, Eric 89
Miliband, Ed 181
Miller, G. 180
Ministry of Transport (MoT) 86, 88 ,109,
        186, 196
mobility 5, 175–6, 187
        urban 154–7
        see also 'aeromobility'; 'automobility'
modal share and modal shift in transport
        106–7, 135–6, 141, 148–50, 153–7

effect of branding on 161–6
modelling techniques 25, 139–41, 150, 160
Mulley, Fred 119
municipal branding 164

National Association of Rail Passengers
        (NARP) 89
National Association of Railway Travellers
        (NART) 87
National Consumer Council 89
National Cyclists' Union 55
National Travel Survey 6
nationalisation of railways 88
Neal, Mrs M.H. 88
need for travel 2
Needham, Duncan 3
neighbours, relationships with 42–3
Netherlands, the 21–4
Network SouthEast 135, 143–5, 163
network theory 108
Neustadt, R. 18
new product development 137
Niblett, M. 102
Noland, R. 50
North Eastern Railway (NER) 160
North Report (2010) 128–9
Northampton 163
Norway 129
'nudges', cultural 182

older people, travel problems of 8, 65,
        70–73
O'Leary, Michael 181
OMEGA Centre 98–9, 174
'optimism bias' 102
organisational culture and values 17
Orpington & District Rail Passengers
        Association 89
overcapacity 79

Page, Graham 115, 125
'parliamentary trains' 80–83, 181
passenger representation 8–9, 77–9, 90
passenger transport authorities (PTAs) 135,
        145–6, 157
passenger transport executives (PTEs) 157,
        163–4
path dependency 2, 11

pedestrianisation schemes 165
Pedestrians' Association 116–17
persistence of transport technologies 1–2
Peyton, John 122–3, 127
Philips (company) 16, 25
Pickett, Kate 4
Piketty, Thomas 4
Plane Stupid group 182
planning authorities 23
policy
    definition of 5
    as distinct from what actually happens 6
pollution 59
Pooley, Colin xi, 8; *author of Chapter 3,
    coauthor of Introduction and
    Epilogue and co-editor*
postmodernity 177–8
Powell, Enoch 124, 127
Powell, Jonathan 4
'predict and provide' policy 10, 107,
    139–40, 153, 157
Priemus, H. 107
privatisation
    of bus services 146, 164
    of rail services 123, 148
public interest 81
public opinion 125
public space 32, 44
public transport in general 66, 73, 166,
    175, 187
Pugh, Martin 128

quality management (QM) 25

Raadschelders, Jos 19
rail services
    investment in 148–9
    privatisation of 123, 148
rail travel 8, 22, 81, 105
railway accidents 80
Railway Act (1921) 86
Railway Clearing House 85
Railway Companies Association 82–3
Railway Regulation Acts (1842 and 1844)
    80–82
Raitz, Vladimir 176
Raphael, Adam 118, 121
Rathouse, K. 180

'Reclaim the Night' organisation and
    marches 35, 39, 44
reference-class forecasting 102
Reid, Robert 143
Research Excellence Framework (REF) 4
rhetorical use of history 100
Rijkswaterstaat, the 7, 15–24
    history programme of 15–21, 24
road accidents 9, 48, 50, 54–5, 60, 115,
    121, 123, 128–9
road pricing 59
Road Safety Act (1967) 9
road safety measures 56, 116–28
Rodgers, Bill 122–3, 127
Ross, Laurence 118
Roth, G. 17
Royal Automobile Club (RAC) 121
Royal Society for the Prevention of
    Accidents (RoSPA) 117, 126
rural areas, travel in 8, 65–7, 70–73
Rural Transport Programme (RTP) in the
    Republic of Ireland 67
Ryanair 178–9, 181
Ryley, T. 181

Salford 52
Sandoz disaster (1986) 18
Saunders, S. 33, 35–6
Scarles, C. 180
Schein, E.R. 17
school travel 154–5
Scotland 186
season-ticket holders 84
seat-belt legislation 123–7
Second World War 88, 175
segmented marketing 162
senior citizens 67; *see also* older people
Severnside Line, Bristol 164
Shackley, S. 180
Sharp, Richard 135
Sheerman, Barry 124
Shell (company) 16
Shiefelbusch, Martin 77
Shin, Hiroki xi, 8; *author of Chapter 5*
shopping trips 155
short breaks 180–81
signage 159–60
simulation games 18, 24

skill development 34
Skytrain 177
smartcards, use of 149–50
Smith, Rod 102
social capital 44–5
social exclusion 66–7, 73
    definition of 49
social justice 8, 47–60
social media 150, 167
social networks 40–43
Sonning rail disaster (1841) 80
Southern Electric 163–4, 166
Southern Railway (SR) 159–64
Southwest Airlines 178
Spain 100
Stampp, Kenneth M. 3
Stanley, J. 49
Stern, Sir Nicholas (and Stern Report,
    2006) 171–2, 180
Stone, Deborah 128
storytelling about the past 17
strategic thinking 141
subsidised services 146, 157
sustainable travel 11, 23, 60, 67–8, 107
Sutcliffe, Peter 36–7, 39
Switzerland 22

taxation and tax exemptions 81–4, 174,
    181
'technological fixes' 107
Tedlow, R. 154
TGV network 105
Thane, Pat 116, 128
Thatcher, Margaret 165
Thompson, Roy 177
Tomaney, John 104
tourism 10, 176–80
Toussaint, Bert xi–xii, 4, 7; *author of
    Chapter 1*
trams and tramways 51–4, 58–9, 157, 162,
    165, 167
Transport Act (1968) 145
Transport Act (1981) 9
Transport Act (1985) 146–7
Transport Focus 77–8
transport planning 139–40
TravelWatch organisations 77

Treasury influence on transport policy 186
Tribe, J. 180
trolley buses 52–3
Tyndall Report (2005) 180

understanding of the past 3–4, 8, 10, 50,
    135, 139, 141, 151, 153, 185
United Kingdom Commercial Travellers
    Association (UKCTA) 85
United States 22, 50
urban transport 153–67
Urry, John 106, 127, 175
user-generated content 44–5

van Wee, B. 107
Vella-Brodrick, D. 49
Vickerman, R. 99, 102
Vigar, G. 186
'vigilance' skills 35–8

Walker, G. 48
Walker, Sir Herbert 159
Walker, Peter 122
walking 5, 7–8, 31–45, 110, 154–5
Watkin, Edward 83
Watson, Bob 172
Waymark, P. 121–3
Web 2.0 technology 44–5
Weir, L. 68
West Yorkshire PTE 135, 145–9
Western Avenue, Middlesex 54
Widgery, Lord 121
Wilkinson, Richard 4
Williams, A. 154
Williams, J.E.D. 176–7
Willis, P. 31
Wilson, Harold 126
women's experience of walking 7–8,
    31–45
workmen's tickets and workmen's trains
    83–4, 163
Wright, Orville and Wilbur 171

'Yorkshire Ripper', the 36; *see also*
    Sutcliffe, Peter

Zelizer, Julian 19

For Product Safety Concerns and Information please contact our EU
representative GPSR@taylorandfrancis.com
Taylor & Francis Verlag GmbH, Kaufingerstraße 24, 80331 München, Germany